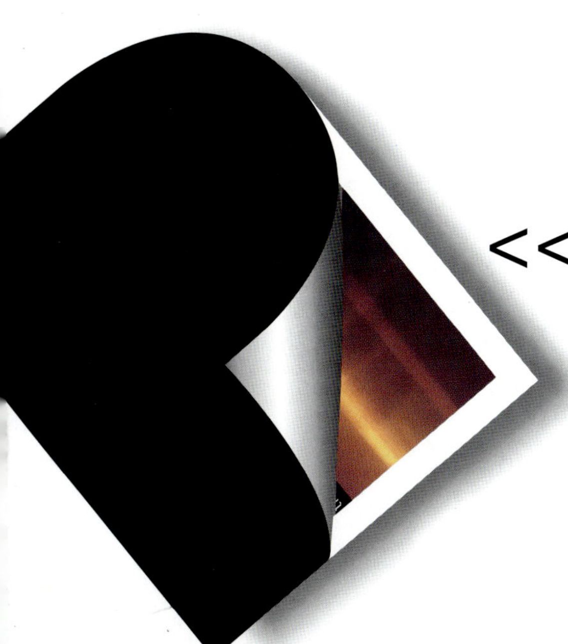

<<< peel back to expose

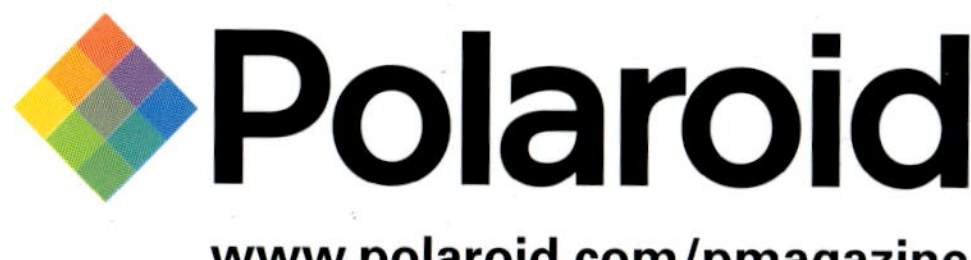

No. 169 / Winter 2002 Aperture

50th Anniversary, Part II

WORK IN PARTS I AND II BY

Ansel Adams, Robert Adams, Diane Arbus, Richard Avedon, Harry Callahan, Cornell Capa, Robert Capa, Paul Caponigro, Henri Cartier-Bresson, Walter Chappell, Chuck Close, Lois Connor, Gregory Crewdson, Bruce Davidson, Lynn Davis, Mitch Epstein, Barbara Ess, Donna Ferrato, Martine Franck, Masahisa Fukase, Adam Fuss, Gianni Berengo Gardin, Mario Giacomelli, Ralph Gibson, Allen Ginsberg, David Goldblatt, Nan Goldin, Philip Jones Griffiths, Jan Groover, David Hockney, Eikoh Hosoe, Peter Hujar, Graciela Iturbide, Mimmo Jodice, Nicholas K. Kahn and Richard S. Selesnick, Robert Glenn Ketchum, Josef Koudelka, Barbara Kruger, Dorothea Lange, Clarence John Laughlin, Annie Leibovitz, Danny Lyon, Sally Mann, Robert Mapplethorpe, Mary Ellen Mark, Don McCullin, David McDermott and Peter McGough, Ralph Eugene Meatyard, Susan Meiselas, Ray K. Metzker, Duane Michals, Lee Miller, Richard Misrach, Tina Modotti, Inge Morath, Barbara Morgan, Ugo Mulas, Michael Nichols, Nam June Paik, John Pfahl, Pierre et Gilles, Sylvia Plachy, Sigmar Polke, Raghu Rai, Robert Rauschenberg, Eugene Richards, Gerhard Richter, Miguel Rio Branco, Sebastião Salgado, Lise Sarfati, Ferdinando Scianna, Charles Sheeler, Cindy Sherman, Stephen Shore, Raghubir Singh, Clarissa Sligh, W. Eugene Smith, Frederick Sommer, Doug and Mike Starn, Maggie Steber, Chris Steele-Perkins, Joel Sternfeld, Paul Strand, Thomas Struth, Shomei Tomatsu, Larry Towell, Javier Vallhonrat, Nick Waplington, Alex Webb, Brian Weil, Minor White, Garry Winogrand, Joel-Peter Witkin, David Wojnarowicz, Franco Zecchin, and more . . .

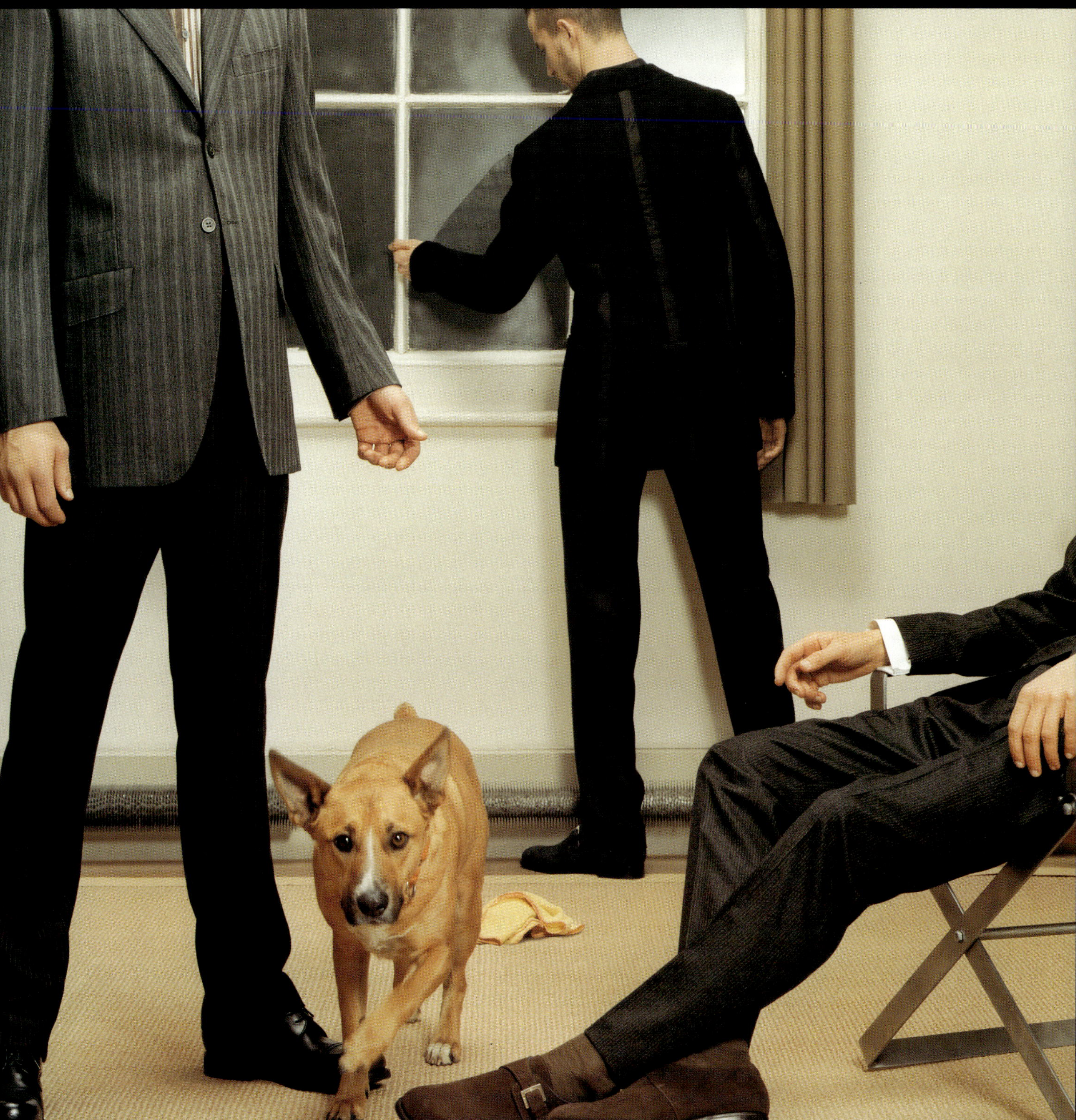

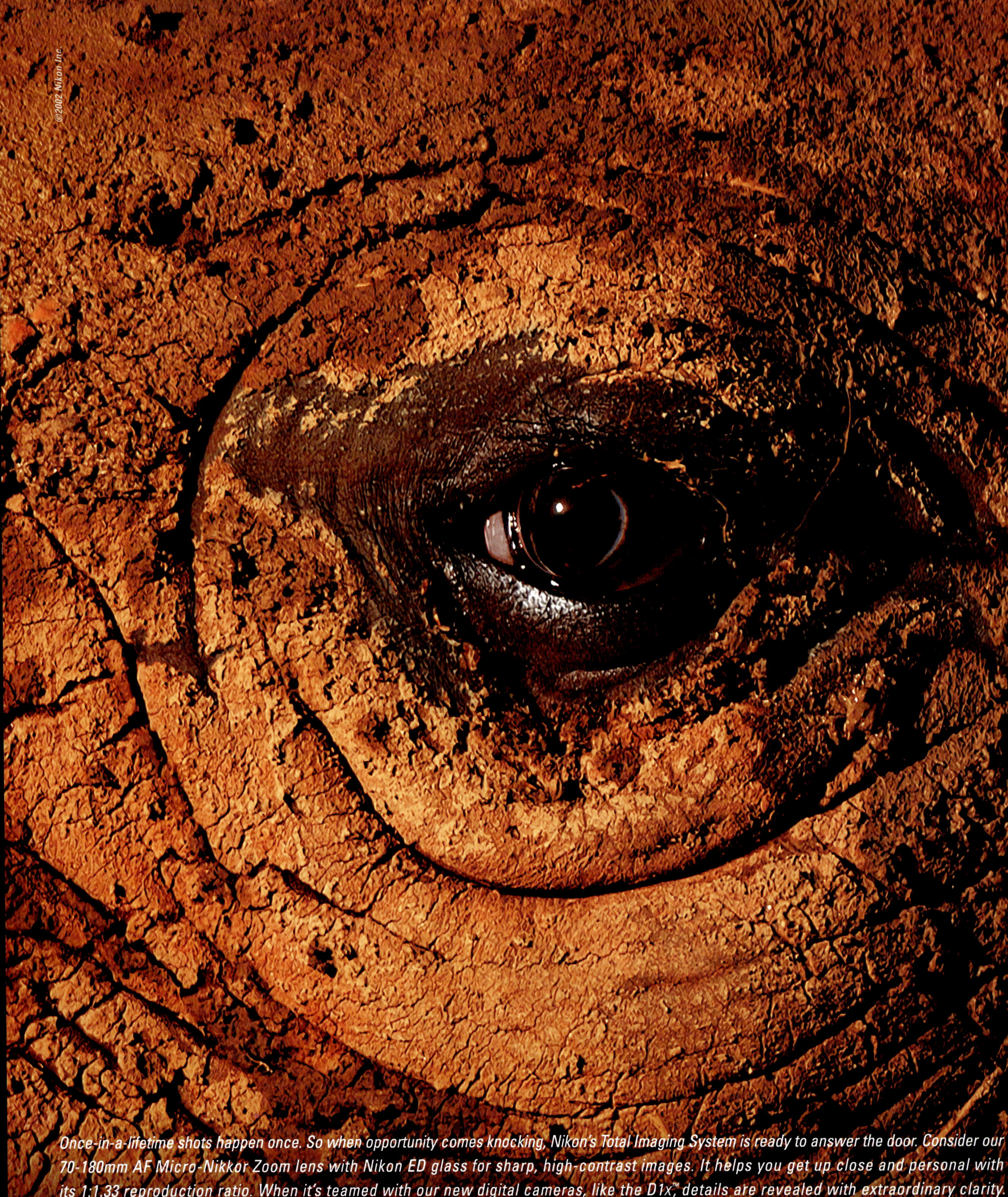
©2002 Nikon Inc.
Once-in-a-lifetime shots happen once. So when opportunity comes knocking, Nikon's Total Imaging System is ready to answer the door. Consider our 70-180mm AF Micro-Nikkor Zoom lens with Nikon ED glass for sharp, high-contrast images. It helps you get up close and personal with its 1:1.33 reproduction ratio. When it's teamed with our new digital cameras, like the D1x™, details are revealed with extraordinary clarity.

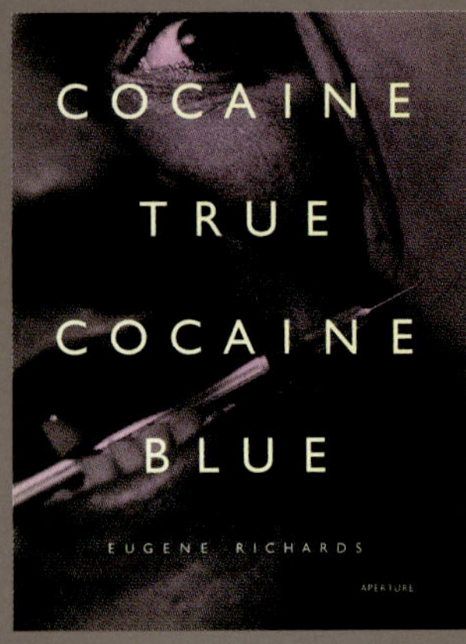

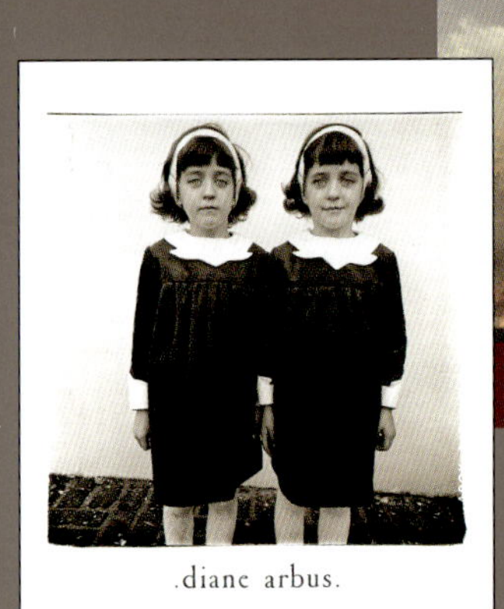

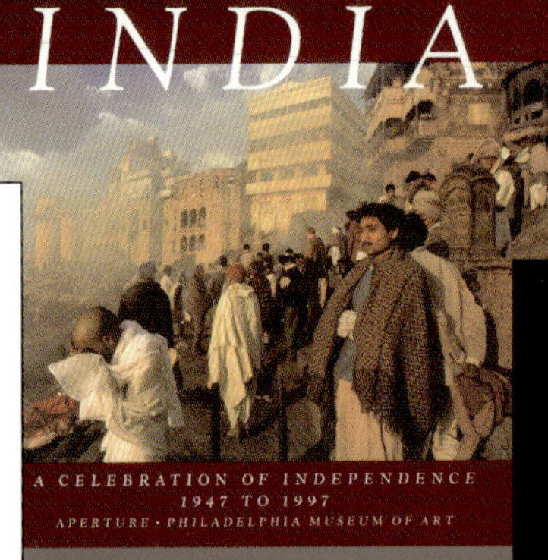

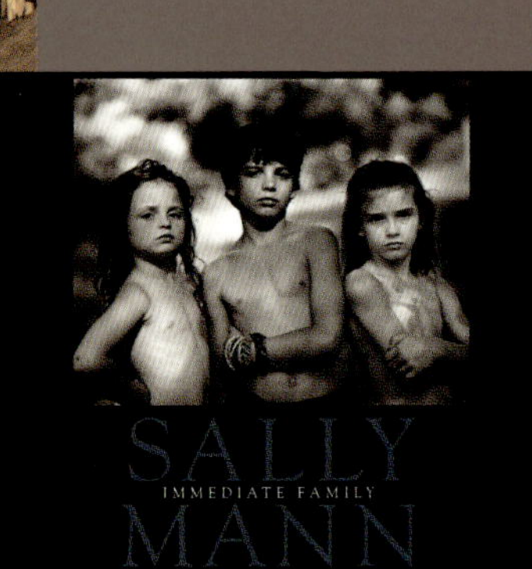

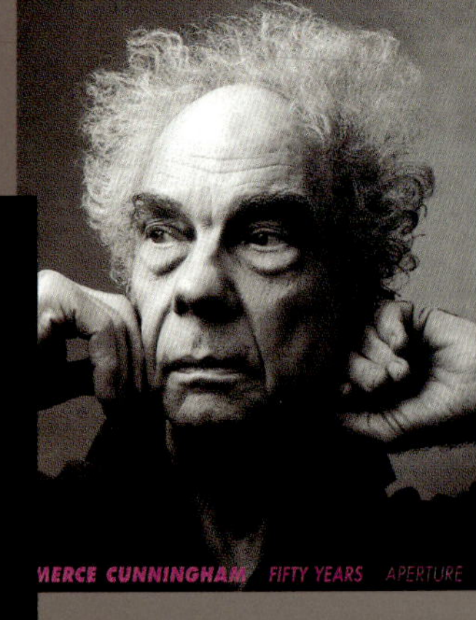

THE SYNCHRONIES OF NATURE, such as the way a bestiary of clouds will seem to stream overhead like a narrative across the expanse of the sky, while a rock face almost bubbles on a mountainside in compressed geologic time, are all around us if we choose to make the mental leap. And it will be a better one if we don't bend what we see to our preconceptions: as, for example, the clouds to a specifically zoological bestiary. But the Great Bear and Big Dipper in the firmament have anchored tribal peoples for longer than we'll know, and the linkage of a bestiary with the ontogeny of our dreams may have a power that abstract expressionism lacks. Shamans presumably knew both, and perceived the grim ballet in the twists that old, much-punished trees have undergone in order to accommodate the wind or heal after a lightning strike, somewhat in the way *we* do, even before ballet could serve them as a metaphor. Out-of-doors, geometry, like intuition, is always curved.

And with landscapes, the intensity of our response to the nuances of beauty and drama argues for a grace that is more than mathematical or anthropological. That is, we grew up as a species climbing trees and on the veldt; yet we respond quite as intrinsically to surf. And flowers court insects, but also move *us*—as can clouds wreathing a massif by happenstance, or long, sheeny grass growing as tightly as sun and soil permit, when it undulates with the wind: though we don't eat flowers or wild grasses or snow peaks or clouds in the wind, or mate with them. They don't warm our bodies or save our lives. Nor do songbirds, rainbows, or a rippling, glistering lake. There is a slow-fuse, out-of-body ecstasy at the doorstep, if we have the eyes and ears for it.

—EDWARD HOAGLAND, from "Ansel Adams at 100," *Aperture*, no. 166, 2002

SOJOURN IN THE REALM OF DREAMS

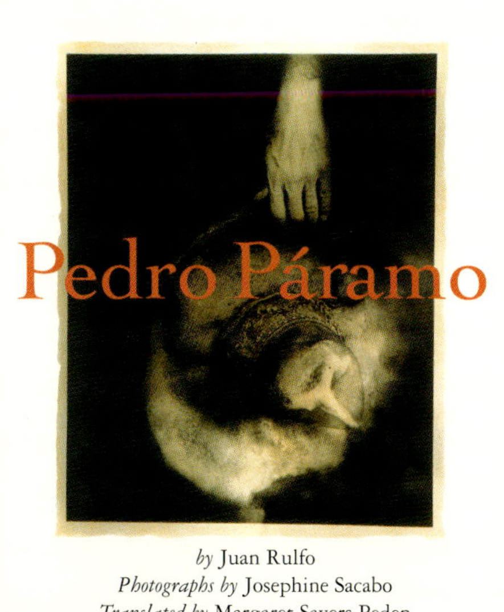

PEDRO PÁRAMO

BY JUAN RULFO
PHOTOGRAPHS BY JOSEPHINE SACABO
TRANSLATED BY MARGARET SAYERS PEDEN

Deserted villages of rural Mexico, where images and memories of the past linger like unquiet ghosts, haunted the imaginations of two artists—writer Juan Rulfo and photographer Josephine Sacabo. This volume brings together Rulfo's dream-like novel *Pedro Páramo* and Sacabo's photographic series "The Unreachable World of Susana San Juan: Homage to Juan Rulfo" to offer a dual artistic vision of the same unforgettable story.

Wittliff Gallery of Southwestern and Mexican Photography Series
Bill Wittliff, Editor
49 color photos, $35.00 cloth

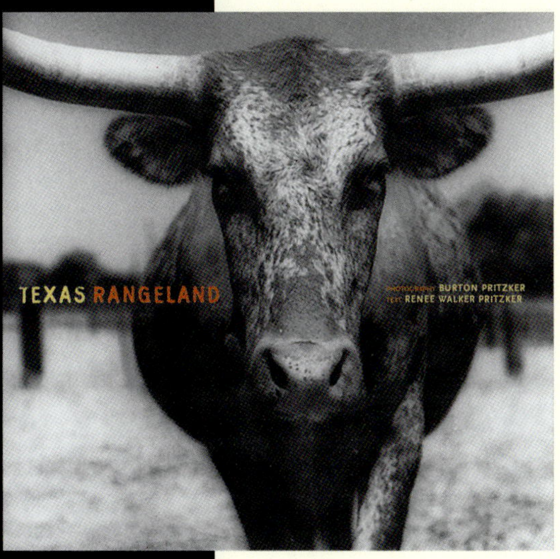

TEXAS RANGELAND

PHOTOGRAPHS BY BURTON PRITZKER
TEXT BY RENÉE WALKER PRITZKER
FOREWORD BY ROY FLUKINGER

Burton Pritzker has sojourned in the Texas of dreams and brought it all back in these evocative photographs. In making pictures of those most Texan of icons—cows, bulls, and steers—Pritzker captures whole moments in time and place with all their play of forms, textures, and light. In his cattle, you'll find sweetness, fragility, bravado, strength, and monumentality—the underlying essence of Texas itself.

60 duotone photos, $39.95 cloth

Browse our complete photography catalog online at www.utexas.edu/utpress/subjects/art.html

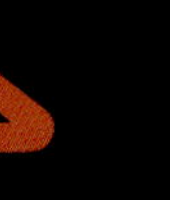

UNIVERSITY OF TEXAS PRESS
800-252-3206 WWW.UTEXAS.EDU/UTPRESS

the EOS EF lens system You're ready to explore. And with the widest selection of over 50 autofocus lenses, ranging from 15mm to 1200mm, there are virtually no boundaries. From our Ultrasonic Motor technology that enables you to focus quickly and quietly. To our Image Stabilizer lenses that keep images completely steady. Cutting-edge technologies created with renowned Canon optics. Great photographs are all around you. The question isn't where you'll find them, but where will they find you?

EXPLORE
ONE'S
Surroundings

-Eric Meola

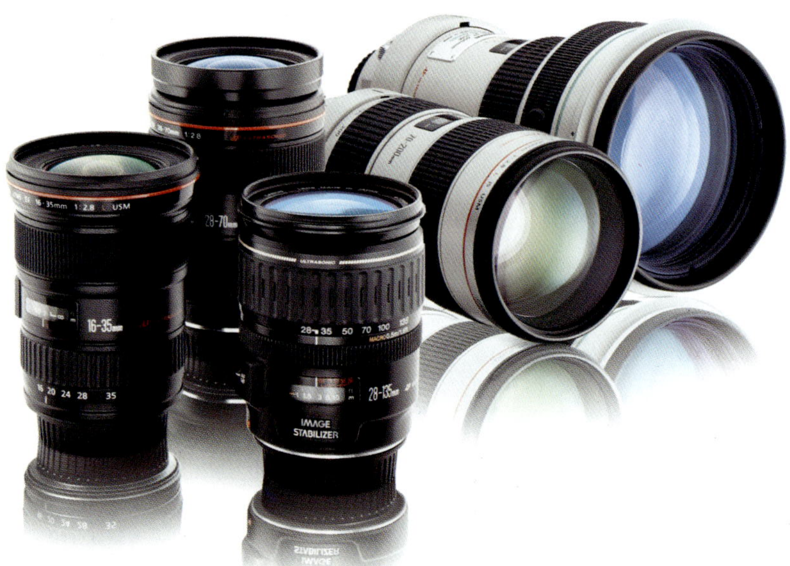

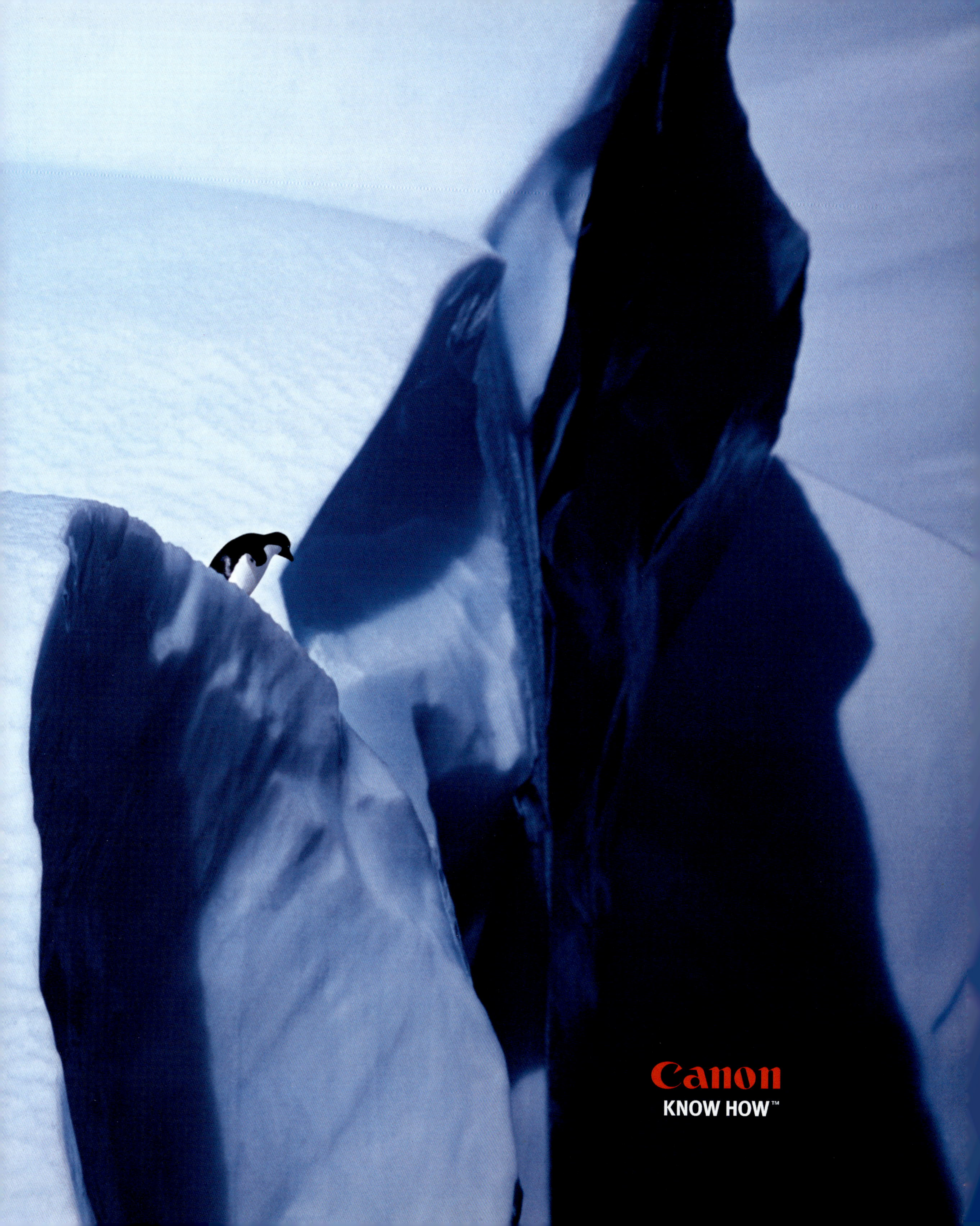
Canon
KNOW HOW™

APERTURE FOUNDATION PROGRAMS

Aperture Books For more than thirty years, Aperture's books have set the standard for photography publications of uncompromising quality. Aperture has published more than 400 titles and its books are distributed worldwide. Aperture Book Center: 20 East 23rd Street, New York, NY 10010. Phone: (212) 505-5555, ext. 300. Fax: (212) 979-7759. Aperture Millerton Book Center: Route 22 North, Millerton, New York, 12546. Phone: (518) 789-9003. Books can be purchased from our website, www.aperture.org, or from bookstores everywhere.

Traveling Exhibitions and Aperture's Burden Gallery Aperture provides international audiences with a wealth of exceptional photography through its Traveling Exhibitions program and the Burden Gallery in New York City. For a catalog or information on Aperture's traveling exhibitions, and on events at the Burden Gallery, call: (212) 505-5555 ext. 300. Fax: (212) 979-7759. E-mail: info@aperture.org. Aperture's Burden Gallery is located at 20 East 23rd Street, New York, New York 10010.

The Paul Strand Archive The Paul Strand Archive, located in Millerton, New York, is an invaluable resource for the study of photographic modernism and its origins. It contains the life's work of this master photographer, as well as the work of other important photographers. For further information, call: (518) 789-9003.

Limited-Edition Prints and Portfolios Aperture offers exhibition-quality prints to collectors of fine photography. These treasures include works by pioneers of the medium as well as images by contemporary masters. For a catalog or further information, call: (212) 505-5555, ext. 300.

Aperture's Work-Scholar Program Aperture's Work-Scholar Program offers comprehensive internships for young scholars: hands-on experience in publishing, exhibition programming, and the Foundation's business operations. For further information, call: (212) 505-5555, ext. 336, or e-mail: mdescey@aperture.org.

Website Aperture's website, www.aperture.org, offers convenient worldwide online access to information about Aperture's publications, exhibition programs, special events, exclusive offers, and more. The site is updated regularly.

With ordinary printers, you see a Goddess with a pierced ear.

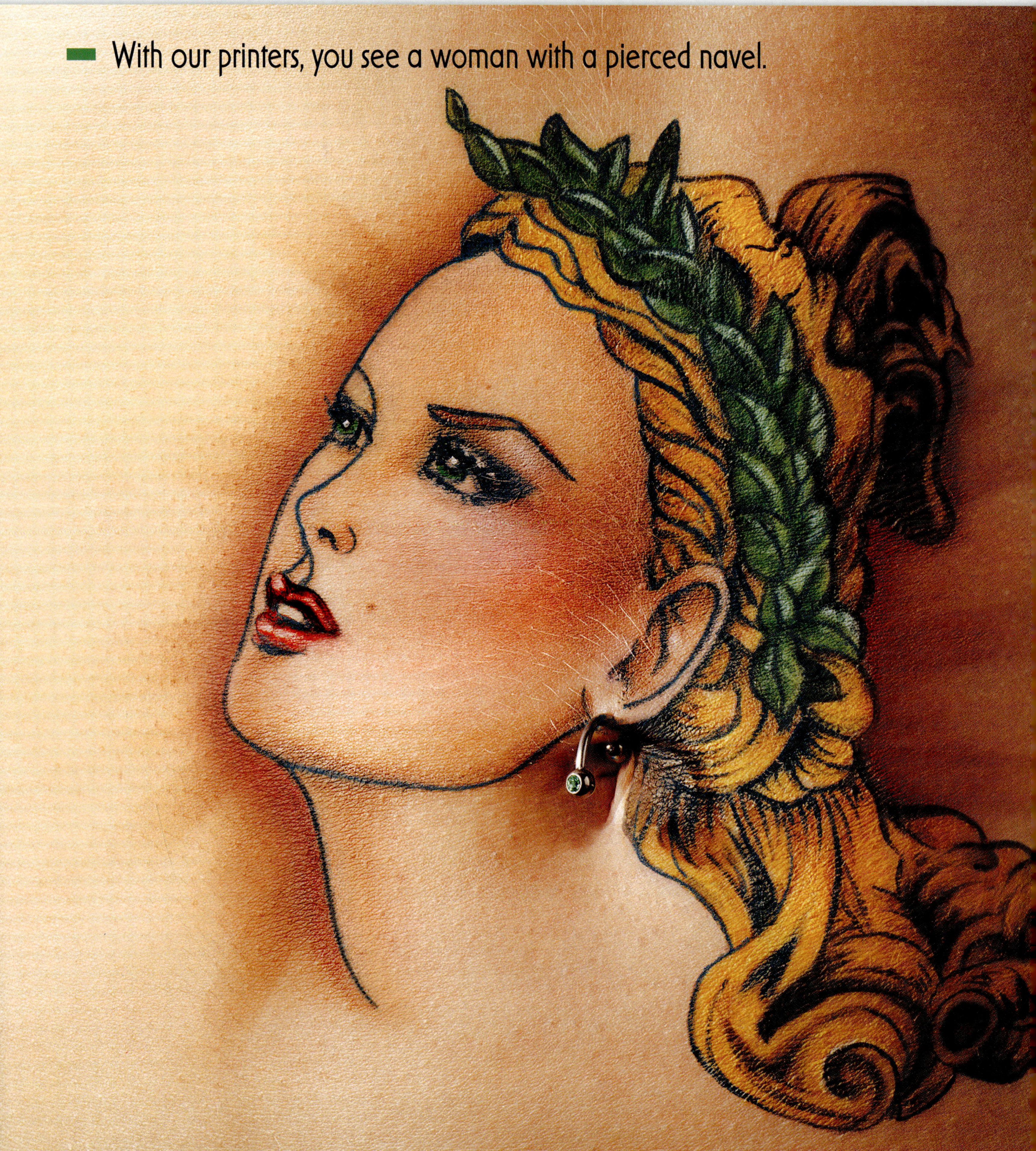

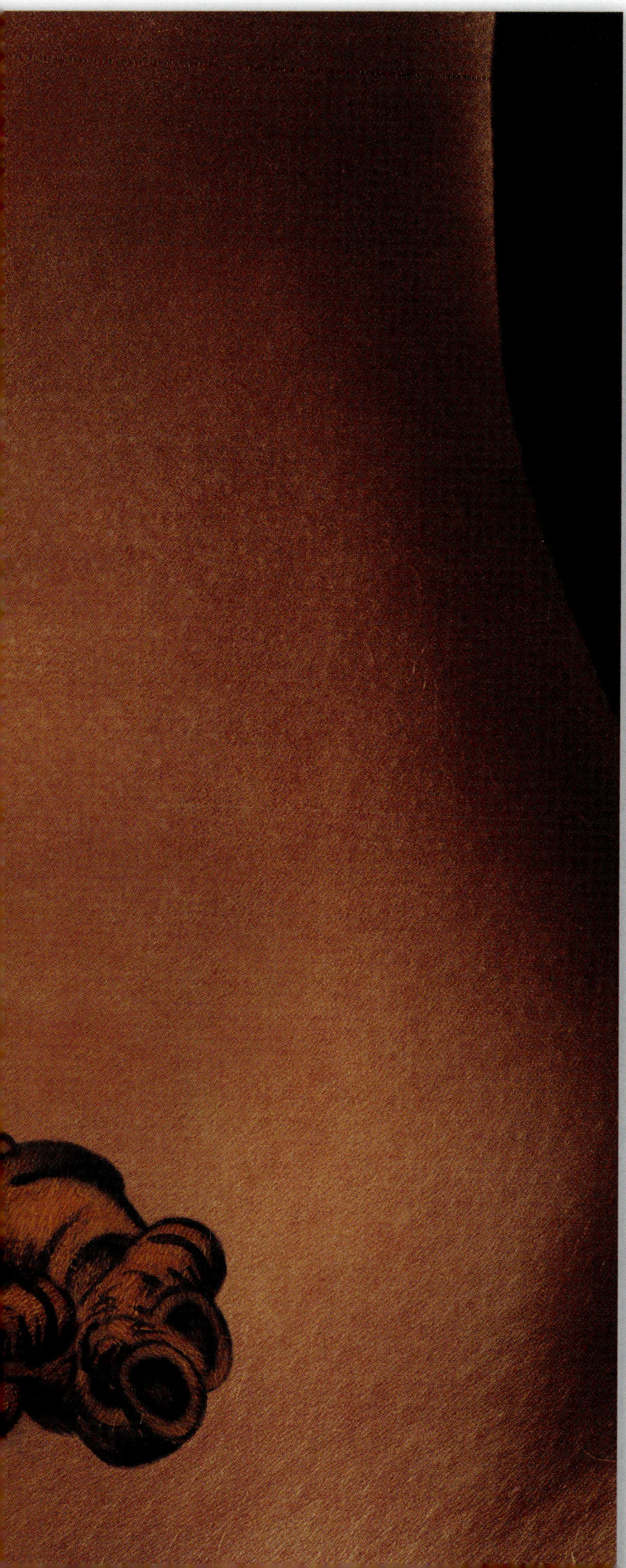

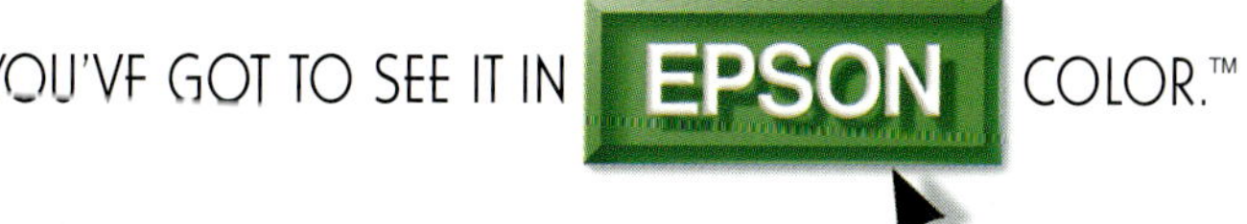

No doubt that's one incredible tattoo. Rendered perfectly enough to turn a belly button into an earlobe. But perhaps the most stunning examples of color and detail aren't the ones created by the artist, but those revealed by an Epson. Just look at the gradation of skin tones and clarity of those fine stomach hairs. Why, it's enough to give any photographer goose bumps. And as you can see here, you wouldn't be the only one. For a free print sample or more info call 1-800-GO EPSON or visit epson.com.

Epson Stylus Photo 2200 (13"x44") Revolutionary new 7-color UltraChrome™ pigment inks for the highest color gamut available in archival printing • Interchangeable Photo and Matte Black inks to optimize density and produce the deepest, darkest blacks • New Light Black ink for a smoother, more neutral grayscale.

Epson Stylus Photo 1280 (13"x44") 6-color dye inks • The professional standard for printing color photography.

Epson Stylus Photo 960 (8½"x44") 6-color dye inks with the smallest droplet for flawless gradations • Individual ink cartridges • Roll paper holder and automatic cutter.

Epson Stylus Photo 1280 $399
(after a $100 mail-in rebate)

Epson Stylus Photo 960 $349

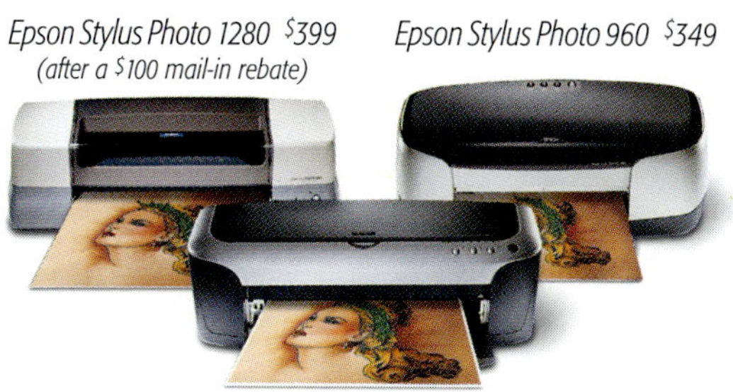

Epson Stylus Photo 2200 $699

MARY ELLEN MARK

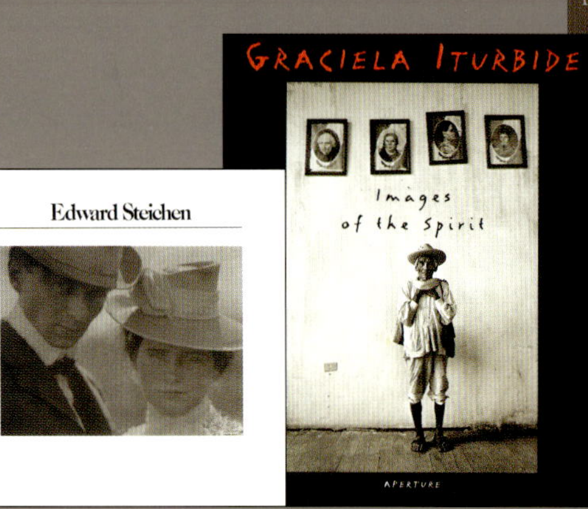

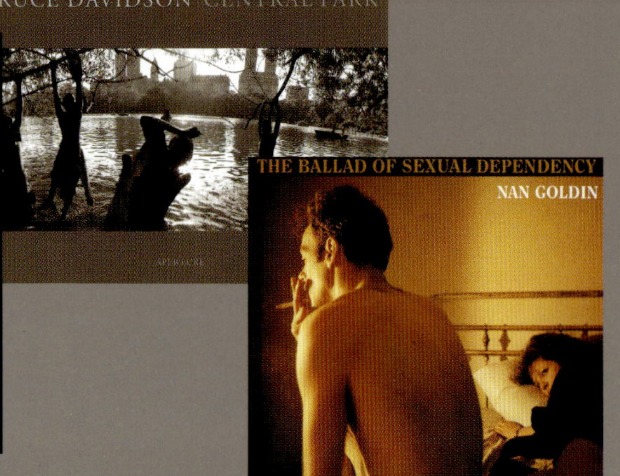

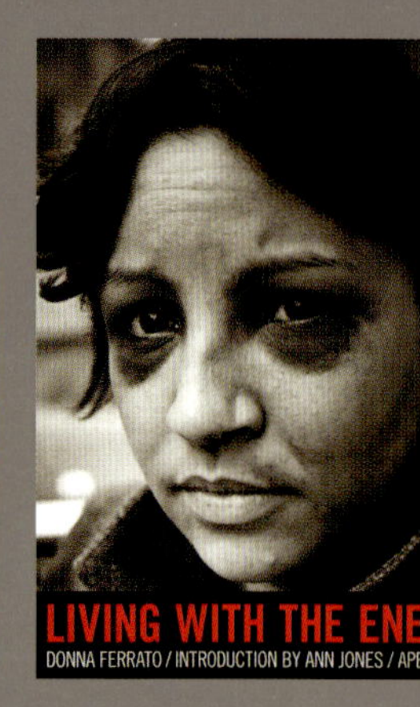

SO WHAT IS FAMILIAR TO ONE of us may very likely be familiar to another. Sweat in the eyes, sun on the back, cold in the heart—these things we all know. More important, we all know something of what they mean. Hard work, warm weather, pain, we all have enough in common to make most of our many worlds companion to each other. We eating, we sleeping, we mourning and rejoicing, we hating, we loving—it is the same with these. These we know; so knowing, these we see; and it is in these that a great photograph speaks, not of eating and sleeping, but of ourselves. Whether of a board fence, an eggshell, a mountain peak or a broken sharecropper, the great photograph first asks, then answers, two questions. "Is that my world? What, if not, has that world to do with mine?"

—Dorothea Lange and Daniel Dixon,
from "Photographing the Familiar,"
Aperture vol. 1, no. 2, 1952

Visions & Voices

A CELEBRATION OF GENIUS IN PHOTOGRAPHY

By R. H. CRAVENS

PARTS III AND IV, CONCLUSION
(Parts I and II of this essay appeared in *Aperture* 168)

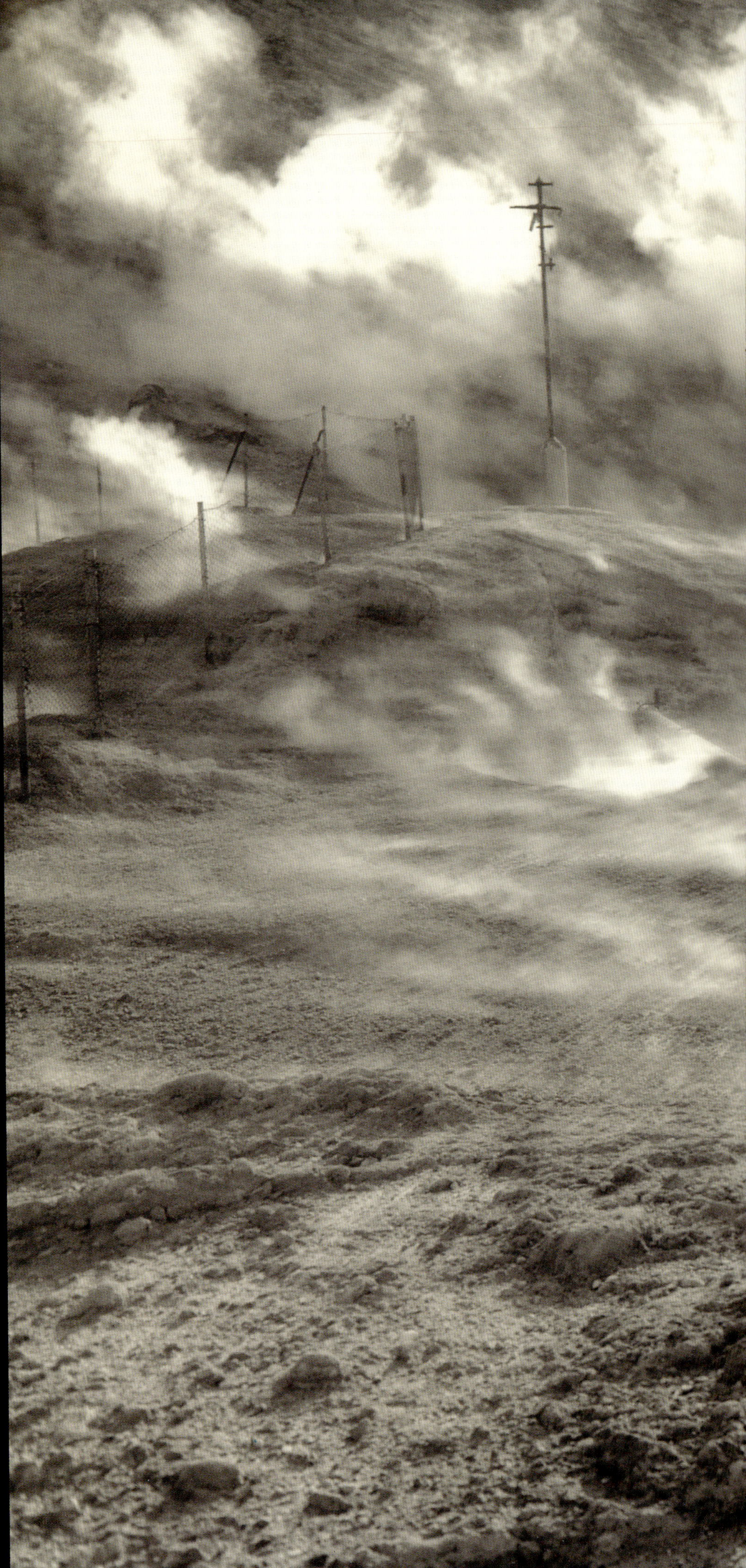

Mimmo Jodice, *Solfatara Volcano*, Pozzuoli, Naples, Italy, 1990–1995; from *Mediterranean* (Aperture, 1995).

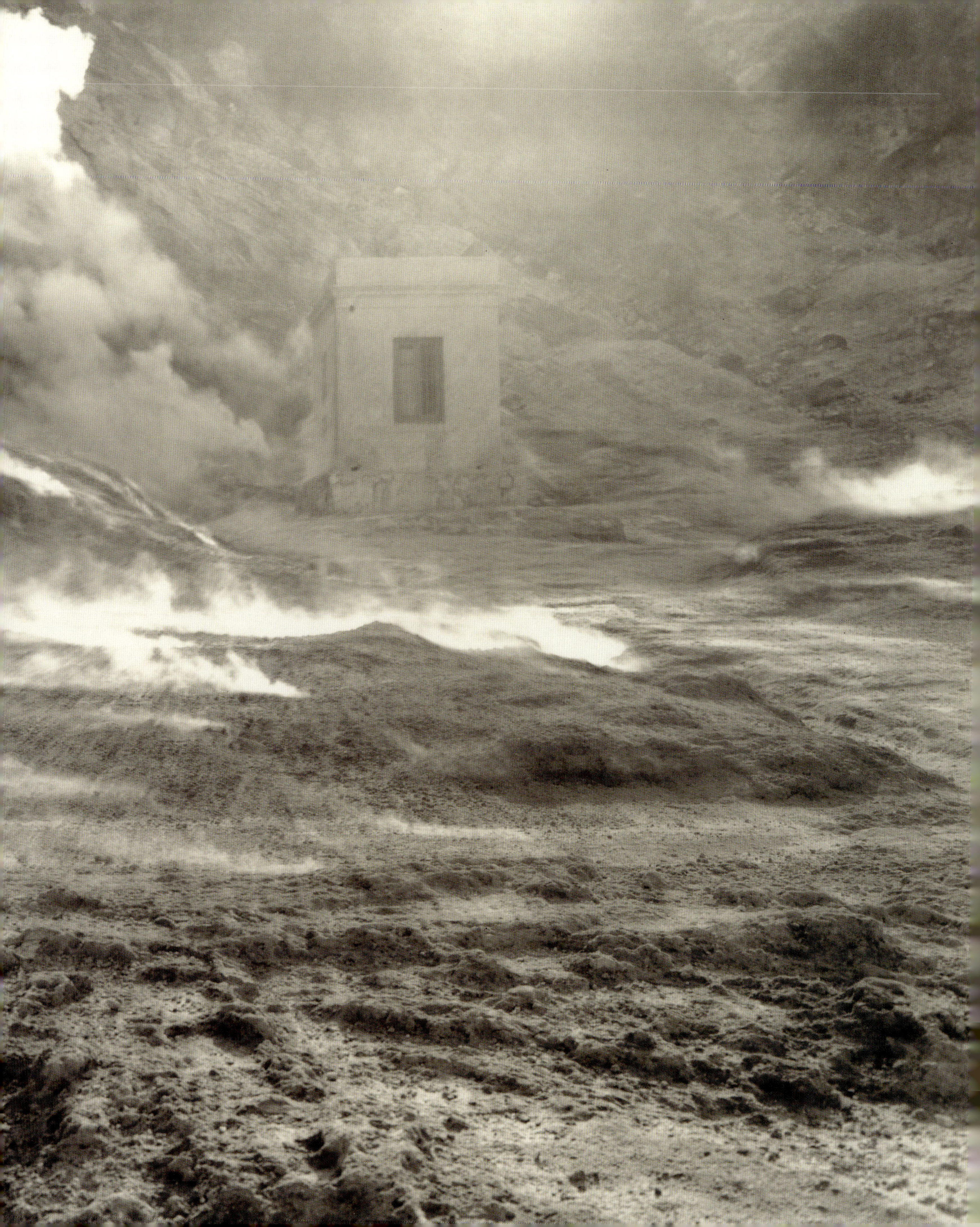

PART III

The Indispensable Art: Survival

Director:
For art may need long years of true devotion
To bring perfection to the light of day.
The brilliant passes, like the dew at morn;
The true endures, for ages yet unborn.
—Johann Wolfgang Goethe, *Faust*, Part One, Prelude

The old man lumbered down the stairs in a weathered bathrobe at eleven A.M., an unusually late hour for a photographer. But at age eighty-one, Paul Strand could rise at any hour he damned well pleased. What awaited him at the bottom of the stairs gave him a shock and sent him back up toward his bedroom in a very bad mood. He had seen a goodly portion of his life's work, hundreds of photographs including the very best of his one-of-a-kind masterpieces, spread out and covering nearly every square foot of the main room of his provincial French farmhouse. The early riser, twenty-eight-year-old Michael Hoffman, had been up since dawn placing, rearranging, and sequencing them.

"I had no choice," Michael recalled years later.

> We were trying to get ready for the first major Strand retrospective in a quarter century. We'd gone through more than a thousand prints and were trying to get it down to around four hundred and fifty. But every time I'd suggest removing one, Paul would say, "What's wrong with that one? What don't you like about it?" And back it would go in the pile. I was getting desperate. But when Paul saw the ones I'd chosen all over his floor, he was very unhappy—at least, at first. Then, after a while, he came back down the stairs and stared and said, "I've never looked at them this way before. I've never seen the way they look in these kinds of relationships." And then he got more and more excited, and we made the final selection within the next day or so.

Only a few years in time, but an enormous passage of growth—of insight, experience, and breadth of ambition—had been traveled by Michael since his first encounter with Strand in 1966. Then, reluctantly, Strand and his wife Hazel had gone to Michael's and Misty's Brooklyn apartment for lunch. "Almost the first question I asked," Michael said, "was what did he think of Stieglitz's concept of 'Equivalents.' And Paul growled, 'Rubbish! Pure rubbish!' It wasn't an easy meeting, but Hazel and Misty—who had far more social graces than either Paul or I—got on famously. Besides, I had something to offer." What Michael proposed was nothing short of revolutionary from Strand's perspective: republication of his critically acclaimed but seldom seen *Mexican Portfolio*. Strand didn't believe it could be done: an edition of fifty portfolios of twenty prints each. But Michael had come prepared with more than an idea. He set out, just as he had with Minor, to prove himself indispensable, and his timing was impeccable. Strand was concerned about his legacy and what would become of his oeuvre, encompassing a span from 1915 to Michael's Orgeval visit in 1971. His life's work could only be described as epic. And it had been peculiarly neglected.

NOTE TO READERS: ***Aperture*****'s system of numbering issues underwent a change in 1975, when** ***Aperture*** **vol. 19, no. 4 was followed by** ***Aperture*** **77; all subsequent issues are numbered consecutively.**

The only child of hard-working, often financially pressed parents—his father sold French bric-a-brac, his mother taught kindergarten—Strand was born on Manhattan's Upper West Side in 1890. His parents sacrificed to send him to the progressive Ethical Culture School a few blocks away from their home; there he came under the influence of Lewis Hine, the great social documentarian who taught photography classes after school to a select group. Hine also took his young protégés to Stieglitz's 291 Gallery, where Strand first encountered the works of Steichen, Gertrude Käsebier, Clarence White, and the master himself. By age twelve, Strand had already decided that he wanted to be "an artist in photography." Ten years later, he had set up as a commercial photographer.

From the outset, Strand was an obsessive devotee of craftsmanship, and a continuous explorer. His early efforts imitated the soft-focus Pictorialist and Photo-Secession imagery, and abstractions and Cubist studies inspired by Picasso, Braque, and other artists whose work he had seen in Stieglitz's gallery and publications. Then, beginning in 1916, Strand made a few images, notably *Blind Woman*, *White Fence*, and *Wall Street*, which signaled the awakening of a vision that was purely his own. Stieglitz and Steichen were both enthusiastic about the new work. Stieglitz arranged for the emerging photographs to be exhibited and also published in *Camera Work*—even dedicating the last two issues of the journal to Strand's work.

For a livelihood, which his photography did not provide, Strand began working as a freelance filmmaker in 1920 and made a succession of documentaries, culminating in 1935 with *The Plow That Broke the Plains*, a film about the ecological disaster of the Dust Bowl during the Depression. He continued his own photography throughout, and the *Mexican Portfolio* was made during his two-year stay in the country from 1932 to 1934. Strand finally gave up filmmaking in 1942, largely due to the generosity of his father, Jacob. He had been a lifelong supporter of his son's art and, finally achieving prosperity late in life, Jacob Strand helped make Paul frugally but comfortably independent.

Strand's reputation began entering Olympian realms with his 1945 retrospective at the Museum of Modern Art, curated by Nancy Newhall. At her suggestion, they collaborated on a major project, *Time in New England*, drawing upon the words of its most eloquent writers and images that Strand found in farmlands, villages, and along the sea. Strand's name also became attached to what political conservatives considered rabid Leftism (he was in fact a staunch Roosevelt New Dealer). He was appalled at the destructive McCarthyism that had overwhelmed his country. In 1950, he and Hazel Kingsbury, for several years assistant to fashion photographer Louise Dahl-Wolfe, moved to Europe. Hazel became Strand's third wife. They settled in France as permanent expatriates, and in the following years he undertook two more landmark collaborations, *La France de Profil*, with author Claude Roy, and *Un Paese: Portrait of an Italian Village*, with screenwriter Cesare Zavattini. Years later, Aperture would publish these books, along with other major Strand works, to still unmatched standards of photographic reproduction. Strand's travels expanded to Egypt, Morocco, and Ghana, but some of his greatest images were created in his own garden at Orgeval, a village twenty-three kilometers west of Paris, where he and Hazel had purchased a farmhouse in the early 1950s. Paul and Hazel periodically returned to the United States, and it was on one of these visits that Michael raised the possibility of rereleasing the *Mexican Portfolio*.

Michael had discovered in a small Brooklyn loft a nearly impoverished, eighty-four-year-old lithographer with an almost equally ancient press. Moreover, he had found another elderly man who created lacquers for religious objects, using the most authentic methods and materials. Strand was intrigued by the idea of these two anachronistic artisans and agreed to meet with them. Gradually, the prospect of reproducing the portfolio took hold. Handmade papers were ordered from Europe, then rejected because of miniscule flaws in the washing process, and remade. The portfolio—containing Strand's indelible portraits of villagers and village life—emerged over the course of the next two years. "It really was crazy," Michael said. "We were running all over Brooklyn, from printer to lacquer-maker, and Paul working one sheet at a time. Each print had to be perfect—one thousand of them! But it worked. The portfolio was finally released by Aperture and Da Capo Press in 1968."

During the two-year span of the Strand project, Michael was also engaged in frenzied, multidirectional sprints to keep *Aperture* alive. Patient, ever supportive, Shirley Burden continued picking up the basic bills for printing and mailing—whatever was not covered by subscriptions and the occasional advertisement. Michael received no salary, but he had his small army pension, his father helped out with the rent, and Misty worked for a nonprofit foundation. *Aperture*'s survival, Michael knew, depended upon repositioning it as a business—but a business fashioned uniquely in terms of its fundamental values and his own temperament and abilities.

The journal's values had been articulated by the Founders, finding expression in Minor White's editorship. First and foremost,

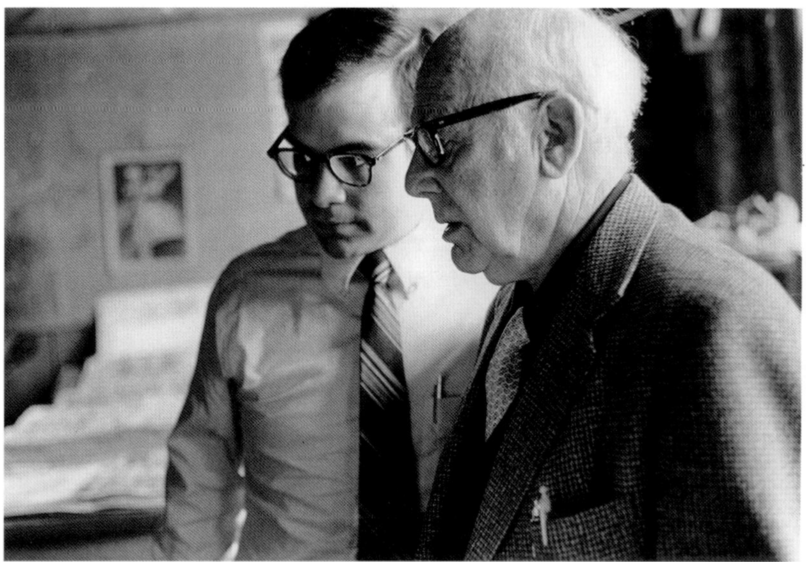

Michael E. Hoffman and Paul Strand working on the *Mexican Portfolio*, 1965. Photograph by Alen MacWeeney.

the journal existed for the benefit of the artist, to serve his or her intent. This meant that the publication was inherently antimercantilist—the profit motive must never dictate content. This freed the work from pressure upon selection of images and design, and further implied a challenge to all forms of censorship—challenges that would be met head-on in the ensuing years. Yet, even though the terms seem banal within the context, survival meant all the basics of business practice: product, supply, distribution, market, skilled labor, and infusions of capital. Such a mix of idealism and practicality was a tough sell.

Like many children of the well-to-do in the 1960s, Michael had an almost visceral resistance to working solely for money, or for pursuing any profession that his parents might regard as "normal." At the same time, he possessed—and delighted in—a prodigious skill for making a deal. This was in sharp contrast to Minor's way of working. Michael once tried to finagle a supply

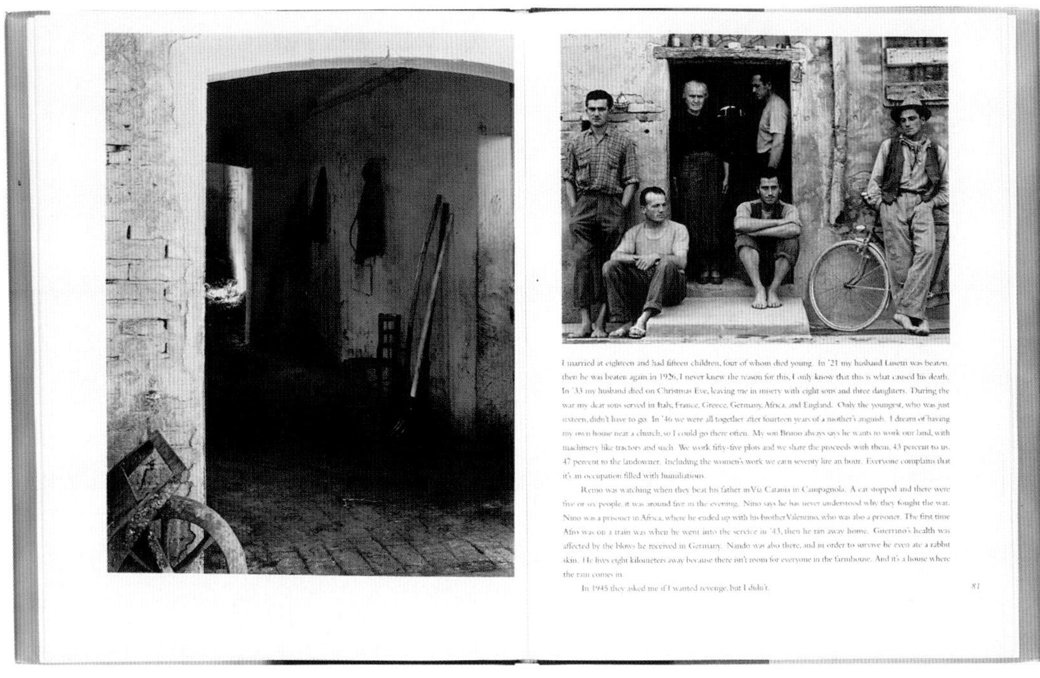

I married at eighteen and had fifteen children, four of whom died young. In '21 my husband Lasetti was beaten, then he was beaten again in 1926, I never knew the reason for this, I only know that this is what caused his death. In '33 my husband died on Christmas Eve, leaving me in misery with eight sons and three daughters. During the war my dear sons served in Italy, France, Greece, Germany, Africa, and England. Only the youngest, who was just sixteen, didn't have to go. In '46 we were all together after fourteen years of a mother's anguish. I dream of having my own house near a church, so I could go there often. My son Bruno always says he wants to work our land, with machinery like tractors and such. We work fifty-five plots and we share the proceeds with them, 43 percent to us, 47 percent to the landowner. Including the women's work we earn seventy lire an hour. Everyone complains that it's an occupation filled with humiliations.

Remo was watching when they beat his father in Via Catania in Campagnola. A car stopped and there were five or six people, it was around five in the evening. Nino says he has never understood why they fought the war. Nino was a prisoner in Africa, where he ended up with his brother Valentino, who was also a prisoner. The first time Afro was on a train was when he went into the service in '43, then he ran away home. Guerrino's health was affected by the blows he received in Germany. Nando was also there, and in order to survive he even ate a rabbit skin. He lives eight kilometers away because there isn't room for everyone in the farmhouse. And it's a house where the rain comes in.

In 1945 they asked me if I wanted revenge, but I didn't.

81

Paul Strand's
Un Paese: Portrait of an Italian Village
(Aperture, 1997), pages 80–81.

The cornerstone of Michael's plan for Aperture was the publication of photography books to a standard either lost or never before attempted. . . . [He] needed higher-quality printing at less cost. He needed designers. He needed quality control. He needed the imagery of the very best practitioners, past and present. . . .

of high-quality paper from a supplier and suggested to Minor, "Maybe we can make a deal." Minor looked at him blankly: "What's a deal?"

Michael, on the other hand, was unabashed about asking for money wherever he thought he might find it. And in wooing artists he felt should appear in *Aperture*. And in seeking out free expert advice and services, legal and otherwise. He anxiously spent what seemed an extravagant amount of money for an electric typewriter. Working late into the night, he then wrote countless fund-raising, deal-making letters, placing false initials in the lower left-hand corner of each to give the impression that Aperture had a secretary.

An office was set up in a walk-up on East 91st Street, staffed primarily by Michael and a young man with what was then an utterly useless university degree in linguistics, Charles Simic. He hadn't been able to find a job anywhere else. Simic's first volume of verse was published while he was working at Aperture, and he would later be recognized as a major American poet. In the late 1960s, he was Aperture's man-of-all-work. "I was paid a miserable salary and did everything—answered telephones, handled mail, swept floors, cleaned the bathroom, proofread, ran errands, picked up people at the airport or train or bus station, My eventual title was 'business manager,'" Simic reminisced years later, adding, "The worst was when Michael set up a distribution company with a group of other small publishers."

The Book Organization, as it was called, was a sensible idea. Small presses, indispensable to the unmarketable underpinnings of cultural life, then as now found it difficult to get their poets, short-story writers, critics, artists, and others into bookstores. They offered little profit to the big mass-market publishers, nor could they afford sales representatives or glossy, eye-catching catalogs. In 1968, one of Michael's chief collaborators in forming a distribution cooperative of such presses was Jonathan Williams, whose Jargon Society had been founded in 1950 in North Carolina. Always pressed for (or simply without) cash, Williams nevertheless had succeeded in publishing the Appalachian photographs of Doris Ulmann, *Patagoni* by Paul Metcalf, and the work of an amazing array of poets, including himself, Charles Olson, Thomas Meyer, and James Broughton, to mention only a very few. Along with the Jargon Society and Aperture, the distribution group involved such presses as Corinth Books, Eakins Press, and Glide Publications. For the bookkeeping and accounting tasks, Michael volunteered Simic.

"It was horrible," Simic recalled. "These books would sell a copy here, two or three there, and each one had to be accounted for—the money and numbers and these tiny checks sent out, and picked over, and the copies and inventories controlled, accounts kept scrupulously." The small presses could fold as spontaneously as they had sprung up, even as the details delegated to Simic reached overwhelming proportions. (Of the original group, only

Aperture, Jargon, and Eakins continue to be active under their original rubrics.) Perhaps the Book Organization's most significant achievement was the beginning of a lifelong friendship between Michael and Williams; the poet/publisher would become one of Aperture's most original contributors.

The cornerstone of Michael's plan for Aperture was the publication of photography books to a standard either lost or never before attempted. This, he hoped, would provide growing revenues over a period of time—as opposed to the short shelf life of the journal. Its subscription base grew with aching slowness; receipts never kept pace with expenses. For his plan to succeed, Michael needed higher-quality printing at less cost. He needed designers. He needed quality control. He needed the imagery of the very best practitioners, past and present, who had ever worked in the medium. He needed writers with a critical sensitivity to the photographers and their creations. He needed cash. He needed help. And then came a series of desperately needed breakthroughs.

The first of these arrived in the person of Stevan Baron, an alumnus of Minor's workshops. Baron had gone to work at Random House in book production, and began volunteering his time to help get Aperture's quarterly and later the books out—a task he performed for years without pay until Michael managed to scrounge up a small, irregular salary. Together, Michael and Baron discovered a custom printer in lower Manhattan, Sidney Rapoport. He believed that both the periodical and the books could continue to be printed by letterpress, but with a less costly method. Doubtful at first, Michael and Baron worked with Rapoport to develop an improved process of two-color, duotone printing—running pages twice through the press with different densities of inking—to achieve heightened range and tone of black-and-white photographs. Though still costly, the process was cheaper than the previous one, and the quality improved.

Another development of incalculable importance came with the help of Dorothy Norman, Nancy Newhall, and Paul Strand. Norman had been negotiating with the Philadelphia Museum of Art to donate her private collection toward the creation of a new department of photography. It was an act of astonishing generosity: five hundred vintage and study prints by Stieglitz and other artists; Stieglitz memorabilia; and two complete sets of *Camera Work*, in themselves a Holy Grail for some collectors. Having worked with Michael on her evolving project *An American Seer*, Norman joined Nancy and Strand in promoting Michael as the first curator of the museum's new department. And so in 1968, at age twenty-six, Michael was heading a floundering publishing house, though he insisted that Minor always be listed as editor; and he was the first curator of the Alfred Stieglitz Center of Photography at one of America's most prestigious museums.

Soon after, there came another windfall, from a powerful influence in American photography who, according to Michael, "didn't like Aperture particularly." With Baron and Rapoport, the Weston *Flame of Recognition*—so disastrously printed in its first incarnation—was being redone, and Michael took the layout to Bruce Downs, editor of *Popular Photography*, a magazine with the medium's largest worldwide readership. As Michael remembered, "Downs said, 'I've never agreed with anything Minor White either did or said.' I thought I was dead in the water, until he added, 'But you know, when Weston died I did nothing, and the only publication that did anything was *Aperture*. That's been on my conscience.'"

"And then," Michael continued, "Downs did the most amazing thing. He personally did the most beautiful layouts on the Weston monograph, and wrote a lovely essay. He also put in a little squib about how people could subscribe to *Aperture*. That brought in two thousand new subscribers—more than the magazine had ever had. And that brought in money so we could pay the bills."

The year 1968 heralded an uncanny process of synergy for Aperture. Michael said, "The Philadelphia Museum association was extremely important because we could now attract new artists with the prospect of major exhibitions—artists who might not have wanted to take the time and trouble of publishing in a non-paying, small-circulation journal." Aperture augmented the museum's publishing capacity, as well as attracting its own participating artists, and with them came contributions to the museum collection. It was an enlarging capacity that reached out to other institutions, notably at first the Massachusetts Institute of Technology, where Minor had been installed as professor of pho-

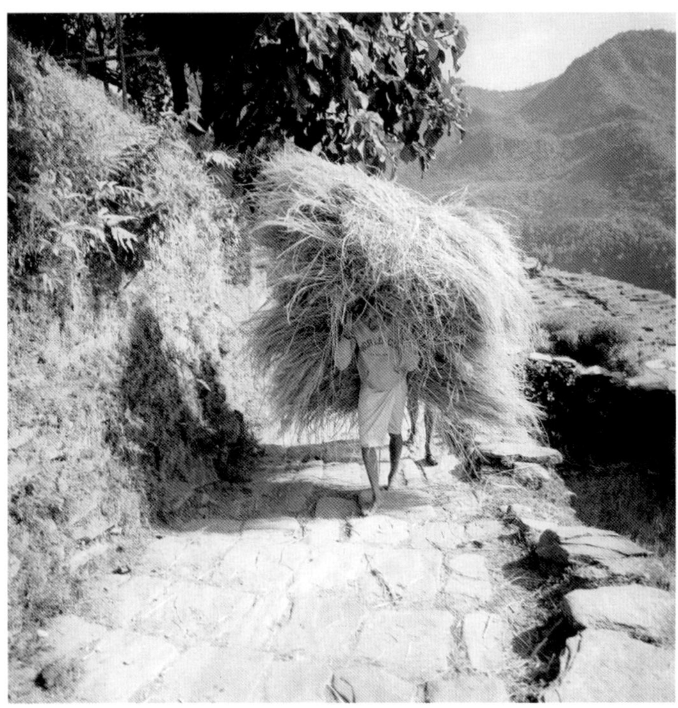

Stevan A. Baron, *Nepal*, 1987.

tography. And *Aperture*, the journal, even if it could not maintain a quarterly schedule, provided the mechanism to create issues that served simultaneously as periodical, as museum catalog, and as hardcover monograph.

It was in the same year, at a Museum of Modern Art show, that a retired, fragile Edward Steichen came up to Michael and asked, "Could you do for me what you've done for Strand?" Steichen explained that most of his early negatives and glass plates had been lost during World War I, but he had a few left. He wanted them reproduced, like the *Mexican Portfolio*, in an edition of hand-pulled gravures. According to Michael, "Steichen said the most curious, unforgettable thing. He said, 'If I had it to do over I would do it Stieglitz's way.'" In spite of all of his great success, Steichen knew it was his early work that would survive. Aware that his aged lithographer would not be up to the task, Michael agreed to try, and launched a project that years later created Aperture's Photogravure Workshop. Steichen's masterpieces reemerged, though after the photographer's death, as the Workshop's first portfolio.

Also during 1968, Michael drew upon Norman's gift for his inaugural exhibition at Philadelphia, followed by "Light 7," the first of four innovative and controversial shows Minor had originally created at MIT's Hayden Gallery. Both were deemed successful, but Michael already had laid plans for two groundbreaking events: one offering well-deserved attention to a contemporary innovator, the other designed to throw light upon photography's early history.

The innovator was Robert Frank, a Swiss-born photographer and filmmaker who had accompanied Steichen as interpreter during his European forays in search of photographs for "The Family of Man." In the 1950s Frank traveled most of the lower forty-eight states on a Guggenheim grant. He retrieved indelible, penetrating moments in the lives of *The Americans*, as the monograph of his classic photographs would be named, with a perfectly timed text by Jack Kerouac writing at his best. Frank's monograph had been published in France, and in the United States by Grove Press, and was then quickly remaindered. He had a small group of admirers, Michael prominent among them. "I had traveled where he had been. I knew he had got it exactly right," Michael said. "And I thought his was one of the most powerful, original voices in photography in the past seventy years."

Michael determined upon a major Frank exhibition at Philadelphia, with Aperture republishing *The Americans*. Frank's only instruction to Michael about the photographs was: "Don't make them look too good." Michael responded by pasting the prints, unframed and unprotected by glass, to plain paper backdrops. "I had the sense to have two complete sets of prints made," Michael said, "so Philadelphia acquired a wonderful Frank addition for the collection."

Traveling on a shoestring, Michael and Misty made their first trip together to France. They visited the Strands at Orgeval, and Michael had his first of what would be many lively encounters with Henri Cartier-Bresson. The primary purpose of the trip, however, was Michael's hopes of securing the cooperation of André Jammes, a connoisseur, collector, and historian of early photography—known to his peers as "the impeccable eye." Jammes drew upon his own collection and loans from the French Photography Society, among other institutions, to assemble images spanning from 1850 to 1865. Jammes named the show "French Primitive Photography"; "primitive," he emphasized, in the sense of *primary*, a period of discovery, pioneering, and flowering at the dawn of the medium.

Back in Philadelphia with the prized images, Michael soon became desperate as to how they could be organized into a coherent exhibition. Here were pictures as diverse as Hippolyte Bayard's earliest still life, dated 1840, of replicas of classic statuary; boulevard and war-camp views of Second Empire luminaries; scenes from a lunatic asylum—it was a bewildering assortment. Michael called on Minor for help, and after some hesitation the mentor traveled to Philadelphia. Viewing the collection, laid out erratically on the floor in handsome frames, almost his first words were: "I don't see how you're going to do this." Michael replied, "Well something has to happen because in three days hundreds of people are going to walk through those doors to see what it's all about."

Suddenly, Michael recalled, "something took over. It was like magic." Minor started moving through the images, more than two hundred of them, shuffling, grouping them in squares and lines, and an entirely new dimension emerged. Minor later described the sequencing as putting the pictures "in the present because of all that time has done to them since." Minor also directed that the walls of the galleries be painted lime green. "It just seemed totally outrageous," Michael said. Meanwhile, Michael ruffled some curatorial feathers by demanding that pieces of Rodin sculpture from the Philadelphia Museum's collection be arranged around the exhibition space. "It was right for the period," Michael said, "and helped in the flow of visitors' movements and perceptions. The statues refreshed the eye."

"French Primitive Photography" was a resounding success. Aperture's accompanying catalog, published as a double issue of the periodical and as a monograph, received lavish critical acclaim. As for Michael, the experience of working with Minor on mounting the show was an illumination unto itself. "I understood it as something totally creative, something removed from the intellectual, linear approaches of curatorial convention. It was a completely new way of looking at pictures and offering them to the public."

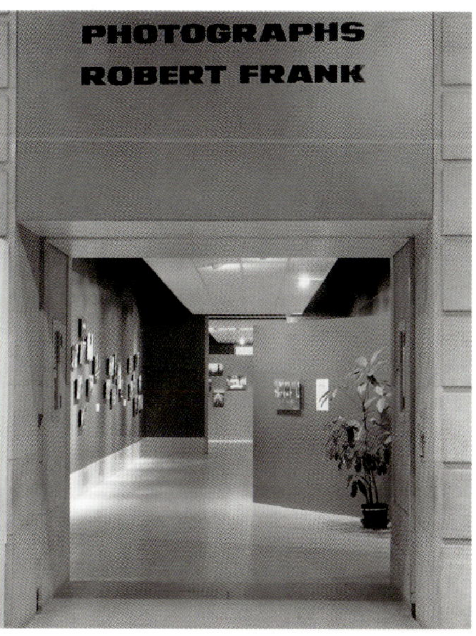

Entry to the Robert Frank exhibition, Philadelphia Museum of Art, 1969.

"The Philadelphia Museum association was extremely important because we could now attract new artists with the prospect of major exhibitions—artists who might not have wanted to take the time and trouble of publishing in a nonpaying, small-circulation journal."

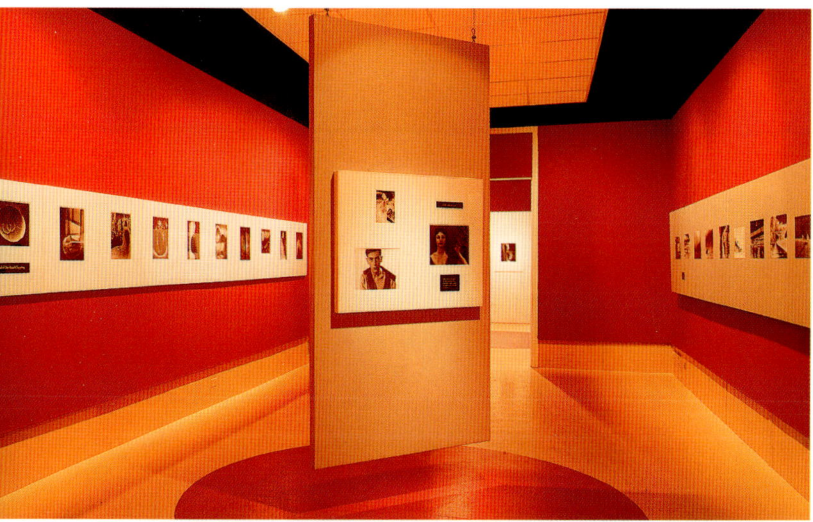

Installation view of "The Circle, Square, and Triangle" exhibition of Minor White's work, Philadelphia Museum of Art, 1969. The show was designed by White.

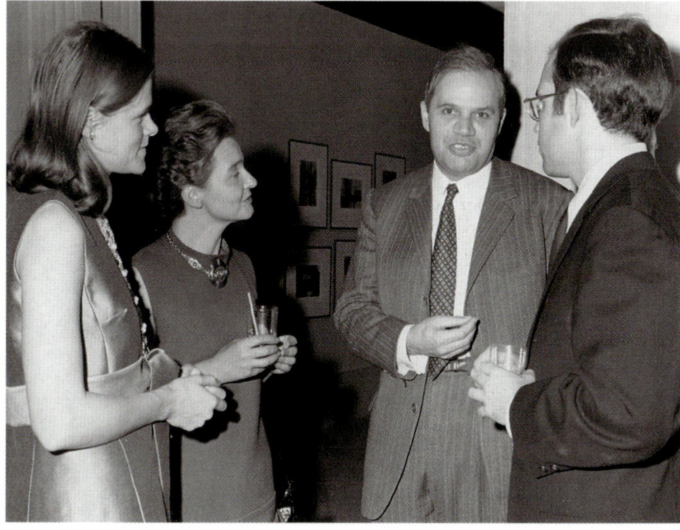

Katharine Carter Hoffman, Marie-Thérèse Jammes, André Jammes, and Michael E. Hoffman at the opening of "French Primitive Photography," Philadelphia Museum of Art, 1969.

These were halcyon days, passages from the late 1960s into the early 1970s. Michael seldom seemed to sleep, even when his schedule permitted. He and Misty were young and would often stay up through the night. Asked years later what sustained them, Michael always reverted to the same source: a sense of belonging and contributing to "a community of interest." It is a concept nearly impossible to identify with precision.

At the time, of course, the broadest popular sense of community was shaped by the anti–Vietnam War movement; by civil-rights protests; by gatherings of the young, with the inevitable associations of sex, drugs, and rock 'n' roll. These are the clichés now ensconced in mainstream memory. Yet within this generalized massing there were vital communities, constantly forming, subdividing, intersecting, and inspiring their various members—enough communities to baffle a herd of sociologists.

One source of these brachiating groupings was North Carolina's Black Mountain College. Opened in 1933, this pioneering experiment attracted select students and faculty over the course of its twenty-four-year life—including R. Buckminster Fuller, Willem de Kooning, Walter Gropius, John Cage, and Merce Cunningham (later the subject of a major Aperture monograph). Beaumont and Nancy Newhall joined the teaching staff for a few summers in the late 1940s. Black Mountain alumni were proponents and associates of the most crucial creative movements of the mid-twentieth century, from Fluxus to jazz to groundbreaking poetry to multimedia performance.

From Michael's perspective, the primary and enduring community had centered around Minor, and involved the core of Founders, gradually enlarging to the artists and audience Aperture engaged. Yet Minor's interests embraced an eclectic assortment, especially those he found of spiritual interest. Minor, a friend observed, could comfortably attend an early Catholic mass, move on to a Zen Buddhist meditation group in the afternoon, and round out the evening in a session with Gurdjieffians.

This last involvement was particularly important, because the teachings of the Greek-Armenian mystic George Ivanovitch Gurdjieff exerted a strong pull among artists, writers, and intellectuals. Michael and Misty became deeply involved, as did Steve Baron, Charles Simic, and a number of closely associated photographers, including Walter Chappell, Nathan Lyons, and Syl Labrot.

Despite a voluminous literature devoted to the life and work of Gurdjieff, who died in 1949, his influence is all but inaccessible to anyone not directly involved in the study-work groups of his successors. There are underlying precepts: that all of creation is filled with emanating energy; that this energy vibrates at differing, specified levels, broadly divided into what are called "octaves"; that an individual is a "psychophysical entity," affected by and affecting these octaves; and that each act of creation, such as an artist's, reshapes the all-inclusive experience of life. The artist's task is to be "awake," to work toward attunement with all dimensions of reality, as opposed to the great masses of mankind who, in Gurdjieff's view, are "asleep."

There are intimations, admittedly tentative, of Gurdjieffian influence to be found among Aperture contributors—from Max Waldman's dynamic and chilling images of Peter Weiss's *The Persecution and Assassination of Jean-Paul Marat as Performed by the Inmates of the Asylum of Charenton Under the Direction of the Marquis de Sade*, as directed by Gurdjieff exponent Peter Brook, to Walter Chappell's extraordinary "Metaflora" series, in which, as the photographer described it, "avalanching electrons leap into light forms, precisely exposing the energy emanations occurring spontaneously . . . on negative film."

Other groups and their catalytic protagonists further attracted Michael. Julian Beck's Living Theater embodied the spirit of communal energy in the creation of works of art. Michael befriended Lincoln Kirstein, another sometime student of Gurdjieff's, whose influence redirected the course of dance history. Kirstein was also a brilliant writer and critic, whose essay on W. Eugene Smith for a 1969 Aperture monograph survives as one of the most incisive critical appreciations of the photographer. Within the vibrancy of the Pop Art movement, Michael found a valuable ally in Henry Geldzahler, then curator of Modern art at the Metropolitan Museum of Art.

Michael determined upon one of the most ambitious publishing ventures of Aperture's history: a massive volume, measuring one foot by one foot, of nearly two hundred Minor White images accompanied by the photographer's writings over a thirty-year period. Michael trundled the giant maquette of the book to every conceivable sponsor and copublisher, meeting generally with remarks such as "You're out of your mind," and "This will bankrupt you." Michael's will to publish remained undaunted, and ultimately it was Geldzahler who found the needed funds from the National Endowment of the Arts to publish in 1969 White's *Mirrors, Messages, Manifestations*.

One irony of Michael's involvement in the cultural flurry of innovation in the arts was that his stewardship of Aperture gained the reputation of being decidedly classical, even old-fashioned. While, for example, Julian Beck, Kenneth Anger, and others were breaking the boundaries of experimental theater and filmmaking, Michael was known for exhibiting Stieglitz, Strand, nineteenth-century Frenchmen, and Edward S. Curtis's historic photographs of North American Indians. There were new imagists appearing in the periodical, particularly the darkroom magician Jerry Uelsmann, keenly examined in essays by William Parker and Peter Bunnell. But by and large, during a period when the prevailing creed was that

First and foremost, the journal existed for the benefit of the artist, to serve his or her intent. This meant that the publication was inherently antimercantilist—the profit motive must never dictate content. This freed the work from pressure upon selection of images and design, and further implied a challenge to all forms of censorship—challenges that would be met head-on in the ensuing years.

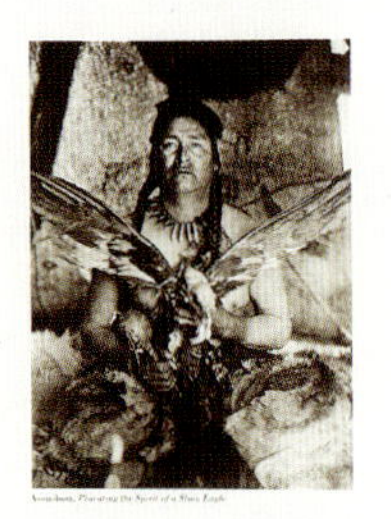

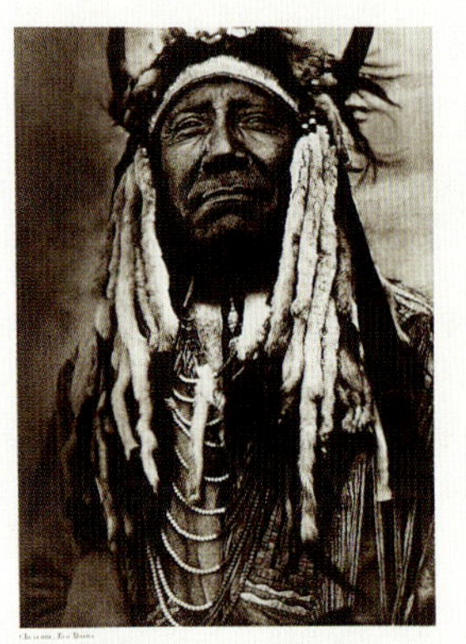

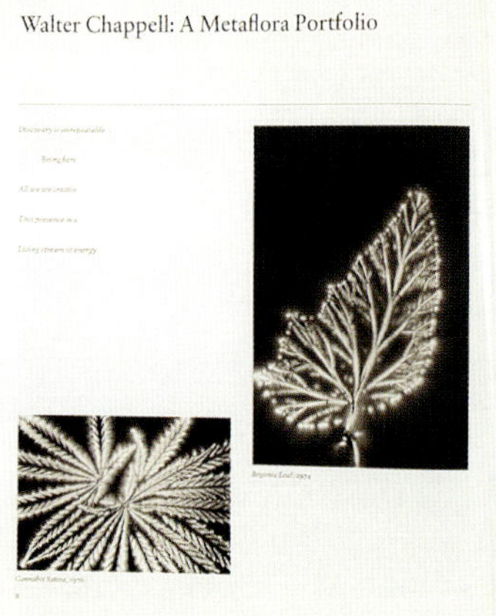
Walter Chappell: A Metaflora Portfolio

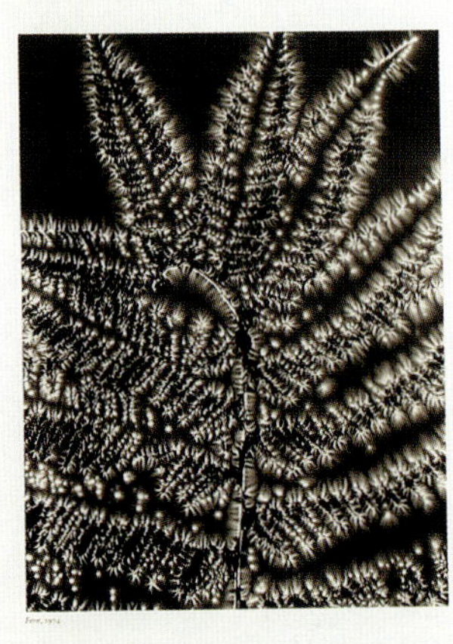

TOP: *Aperture* 81, 1978, pages 52–53: photographs by Eudora Welty.
MIDDLE: *Aperture* vol.16, no. 4, 1972, pages 34–35: photographs by Edward S. Curtis.
BOTTOM: *Aperture* 82, 1979, pages 8–9: photographs by Walter Chappell.

nobody over thirty should be trusted, Michael, it was said, seldom published anyone under forty. The justification was unassailable. There was little point in purveying the avant-garde of a medium whose most significant *garde* had been so long neglected, unseen by a larger public. In a sense, the "community of interest" Michael served was still in its infant stage. And yet one of his most profound collaborations of the period involved an artist whose unique vision would be a defining influence in both photographic and art history.

Diane Arbus began to take photographs in the early 1940s, studied with Alexei Brodovitch and Lisette Model in the mid 1950s, and published her first photographs in 1960 in *Esquire*. John Szarkowski, who took over Steichen's position at the Museum of Modern Art in 1962, included her work on "American Rites, Manners, and Customs" in his 1967 exhibition "New Documents," along with the work of Lee Friedlander and Garry Winogrand. Viewers recognized Arbus's photographs as revolutionary. In 1971, she committed suicide. The following year, Szarkowski decided to mount a major Arbus exhibition.

Although photography books and exhibition catalogs were not nearly so common then as they are today, designer Marvin Israel and Arbus's daughter Doon had already designed and edited a publication to accompany the show. But six months before the exhibition was scheduled to open, there was still no publisher willing to take it on. The Museum of Modern Art was unable to publish the book, so in July, Szarkowski approached Michael and asked if he'd look at the project. Michael looked, and without a moment's hesitation said, "We're doing it."

Michael, Szarkowski, Israel, Doon Arbus, and Sidney Rapoport worked furiously and in less than four months—in time for the opening—the monograph was ready. "We printed 2,500 copies and expected to sell maybe 500," Michael said. The exhibition attracted a quarter-million people in New York before going on a North American tour. Still in print, sales of the Arbus monograph now approach 200,000.

"It was one of those times," Michael said later, "when the public was far ahead of the rest of us, far ahead of our expectations. It was another instance of the unpredictable boundaries of a 'community of interest.'" Of Michael's role, Szarkowski later said, "No one was a villain, but Michael was a hero."

Although financial problems persisted, Michael had also managed by the end of the year to put in place vital elements of Aperture's operations. Baron was proving to be a master of production of the most difficult books under the most difficult conditions. The nagging problem of design—the source of endless complaints from Minor—began to be resolved when a young artist named Peter Bradford went to work on monographs and issues. He was assisted by Wendy Byrne, who would from then on be involved with so many Aperture publications, up to the volume now in the reader's hands. "There are many great designers," Michael acknowledged, "but very few who work with photographs well." Michael also managed to attract the pro bono services of a distinguished, highly cultivated Manhattan lawyer, Arthur Bullowa. Donating countless hours, Bullowa managed to bring clarity and businesslike order to Aperture's increasingly intricate affairs. He also introduced a much-needed temperate tone to Michael's often mercurial negotiations with artists, writers, designers, printers, potential contributors . . . with just about everyone at one time or another. Not long after, another highly regarded attorney, Robert Anthoine, would augment, then assume the role of legal advisor, friend, and confidant. Both men would serve long tenures as heads of Aperture's Board of Trustees: Bullowa from 1966 to 1986; Anthoine from 1989 to 2001.

By 1972, at thirty years of age, Michael had provided Aperture with all but the financial means for survival and growth. He was acquiring an international reputation in his role as curator at the Philadelphia Museum of Art, and he was creating his own niche in the complex, vital relationships that are the living web of cultural life. He and Misty had also started a family: their son Matthew born in 1971, and daughter Sarah born in 1973. And they had found a weekend refuge away from the city, a four-hundred-acre farm at Shekomeko in the hills of Dutchess County, about a three-hour drive from New York. Here, in the study of his old farmhouse, Michael could catch up on paperwork. And in the nearby village of Millerton he established Aperture's warehouse, distribution, and archival operations.

Michael and Misty entertained artists, friends, and family at the farm. Michael found a passion for landscaping and organic gardening, and the house was soon bounded by rows of berry bushes, vegetable fields, and through the warm months a constant flowering. It was a good, creative, challenging life. But before Michael was thirty-one, a series of losses would begin—the first was the hardest, the most indelible.

Michael had left the city early on Thursday, June 7, 1973. Misty was to follow. Late that afternoon a state trooper pulled up the drive. There had been a traffic accident. Misty, at age twenty-nine, had died.

Michael's and Misty's families provided crucial support. Michael was glad, he admitted, that some of his closest colleagues weren't around him at the time—Norman, the Newhalls, a few others. A turning point came when he consulted a Freudian psychoanalyst. During the fifth session, Michael asked, "What are you trying to accomplish with me?" The analyst responded, "I want to help you live a normal life." "But I don't want a normal life," Michael said and, terminating his own analysis, he walked out and went back to work.

A bizarre accident claimed Nancy Newhall's life the following summer. Her later years had been unkind to Nancy. Always a hard drinker she had, even in the eyes of those who most admired her, slipped over the edge and become literally a falling-down drunk. Then she decided to solve her own problems, went off by herself traveling in the West, and appeared to have beaten the alcoholism. She was sober, healthy, livelier than she had been in years, and looking forward to Beaumont's new appointment as professor of photography at the University of New Mexico in Albuquerque. They were white-water rafting on the Snake River in Grand Teton Park, Wyoming, when a large tree uprooted from the riverbank and struck Nancy, fracturing her skull. She died a week later.

In 1976, two years after Nancy's death, White and Strand died within months of each other. White's last years had been troubled by heart disease, which first became manifest in 1966 and led to a cardiac episode two years later. He undertook an intense period of new studies and meditation. As a tenured professor at MIT, he created four amazing exhibitions that found continued existence as Aperture issues/monographs—"Light 7," "Be-ing Without Clothes," "Octave of Prayer," and "Celebrations." Drawing upon photographers both famed and unknown, these projects embodied Minor's continuing sense of pure wonder, of innocence revisited and nourished and unafraid of exposure to the severity of critical intellect. In Michael's view, Minor's illness also cost him the strength and energy to resist those who would enshroud him with the guru mantle. His photography, including new works in color, continued. A deliberate clownish element entered his teaching, and his persona. Emaciated, grinning, and nude, he posed for a student, Abe Frajndlich, in a series of enacted roles called "Lives I've never lived"—as guru, gardener, philosopher, dancer, dying man, and others. But he also seriously worked with his final biographer, James Baker Hall, almost up to the moment of his death on June 24, 1976 at Massachusetts General Hospital.

Strand, whose death had occurred three months earlier, also worked up to the end in what had become the closest artistic collaboration of Michael's life. After the enormous success of his one-man show at Philadelphia in 1972 and the accompanying two-volume monograph, Strand had granted Michael his unreserved trust and loyalty. He had even insisted that Michael become his agent for the sale of his photographs, with the proviso: "If Ansel gets a thousand dollars a print, I want ten thousand." As it turned out, the marketplace was ready.

The oddly neglected aspect of Strand's career was that almost no one had ever actually seen a Strand print—prints of great richness, dimension, and transfixing vision. The exceptions were those on view at the 1945 Museum of Modern Art and 1972 Philadelphia retrospectives, and a very few others. Otherwise, Strand didn't trust what he viewed as the likely barbarous handling of his rare prints by postal and museum staff. To meet requests from exhibitors and publishers, Strand tore pages from earlier rotogravure publications of his photographs, mounted, signed, and sent them off without comment. Once knowledgeable collectors actually viewed the originals, Strand prints easily went for his asking price and more. Within a few years of beginning to show and sell them, he was a millionaire.

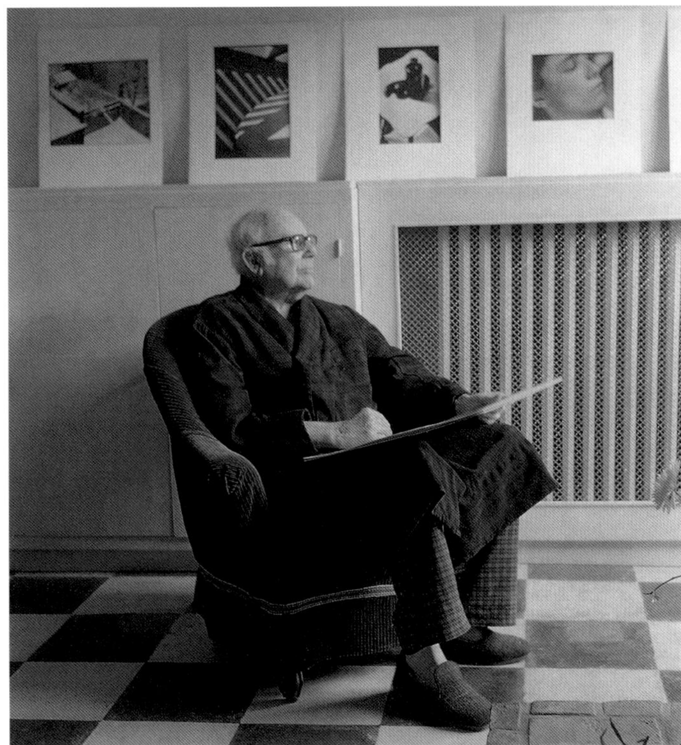

Richard Benson, Paul Strand, Orgeval, ca. 1975.

Strand in his mid-eighties devoted himself to a book on his garden photographs in collaboration with writer Catherine Duncan. Even as the work progressed, Michael proposed the unthinkable: Strand, no longer able to work in the darkroom, should allow his prints to be made, and four portfolios created, with the assistance of a talented young craftsman, Richard Benson. Hazel's response was to the point; "Over my dead body!" Michael persisted; Paul and Hazel, reluctant, allowed Benson a trial, which took place during a Strand visit to New York.

Benson was a young man who already had a reputation for conjuring pristine images from negatives, glass plates, and other media nearly lost to time and wear. With another craftsman, Jon

Goodman, he had helped recreate the press, the inks, and the copper plates of hand-pulled gravure processes lost generations ago. The two were now able to realize photographic images of great texture, depth, and sensitivity at Aperture's newly established Photogravure Workshop.

Benson's gift was (and is) his technical transmutations faithful to spirit of the artist's original vision. In New York, Strand chose a negative for Benson to print—offering no instructions—and approved the results. Benson later said that he had not been able to make an exact duplicate of the Strand print. "But then, as Paul would readily admit, he couldn't make an exact duplicate of a Strand print either!" The Strands agreed to Benson's working under Strand's direction.

In the spartan darkroom setup, Benson discovered that Strand approached each print by increments, print by print closing in on his realization of the artwork. The equipment was almost rudimentary. "I had been used to the most advanced technical instruments; with the photograph once made, it was *made*," Benson told a gathering years later. "Strand crept upon on his images until they were exactly what he wanted." Back and forth Benson would go with each print, finally to Strand's bedroom in his last weeks for the master's approval. Strand signed each print until no longer able due to the bone cancer draining his life. Benson simply sat with him in the last few days, offering comfort.

After Strand's death, Michael and Benson discovered nearly four hundred Strand prints stored at his house: not even Hazel knew they existed. Hazel returned to New York and devoted the rest of her life to Aperture and the Strand Archive located in Millerton, where she bought a small house. Hazel's timely intervention helped save Aperture from extinction.

Aperture was in fact bankrupt in 1977. Michael—with his deeply felt losses of wife, friends, and mentors—had worked indefatigably to keep the enterprise afloat. But even in the best of economies it would have been difficult. In the late 1970s atmosphere of high inflation, high interest rates, and slow growth, it was impossible. Production costs had skyrocketed; the periodical and books were too expensive for a depressed market. Michael's primary article of faith was that there be no compromise in quality. To compromise would be an unredeemable betrayal of the Founders' intentions. Better that Aperture should cease.

At his home in Beverly Hills, Shirley Burden heard the news of Aperture's impending demise and immediately caught a plane to New York. Burden was far more than a conventional scion of inherited wealth: he was an artist of some accomplishment in his own right, and deeply admired the integrity of Aperture's vision. For Aperture, his wealth had been something of a problematic blessing. He had been involved with Minor from the beginning and everyone assumed, Michael said, that this Vanderbilt heir financed everything. In fact, his contributions up to that point were very modest—"rather nickel and dime,"as another respectfully unnamed friend of Burden's put it. With Aperture's survival in doubt, Burden's role magnified.

After reviewing the balance sheets with Michael, Burden gathered Hazel into his limousine and the two agreed to guarantee funds from a matching NEA grant. Their administrators were sympathetic. At the eleventh hour, a total of $80,000 salvaged Aperture from a bankruptcy, which for a nonprofit foundation would have been terminal.

Aperture's silver anniversary passed unnoticed. Three times in its brief history, it had been brought back, phoenix-like, from the ashes. And like the phoenix, whose motto is "I am reborn," Michael was already envisioning new directions, even evolutionary changes in the Aperture commitment to an "ideal in photography."

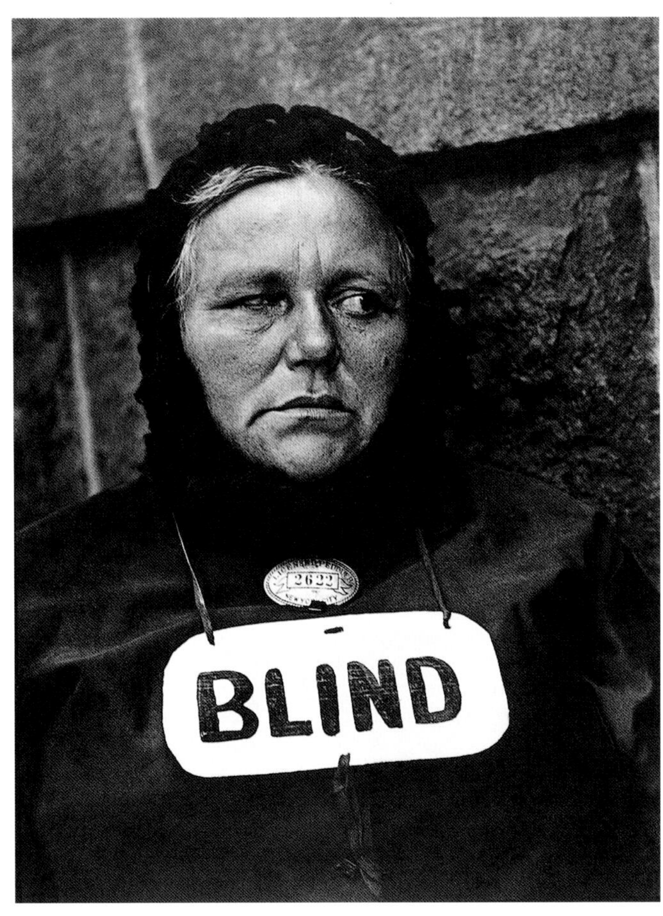

Paul Strand, *Blind Woman*, New York, 1916; from *Paul Strand: An American Vision* (Aperture, 1990).

The persistent problem in photography is how to look at it. In 1916, at the age of twenty-six, Paul Strand went to Alfred Stieglitz, whom he had visited many times before, with a splendid new series of photographs that included a number of portraits of ordinary people. They had been taken by stealth on the streets of New York with a fake brass-bound lens attached to his reflex. They remain among the very greatest American photographs. But do we see them properly?

There is no doubt of Strand's social conscience; after all, he was a pupil of Lewis Hine's. But in this youthful series, he went beyond the assignments of Jacob Riis and Hine and penetrated to a deeper level. His work that year rivals even Rembrandt in its fearless insight. The *Blind Woman* is the most celebrated. . . . The woman, with a cast in one eye, is unique, powerful within herself, with a face as marked and enduring as a boulder facing the sea. "I like," said Strand, "to photograph people who have strength and dignity in their faces. Whatever life has done to them, it hasn't destroyed them."

But do we see this woman as Strand saw her? We are deceived because she wears a sign around her neck: BLIND, and we give her the automatic, easy pity that such a title—for that's what it really is—provokes. Tears rise agreeably to our eyes, and we respond with the clouded vision of our sentimentality. The fact is, she's not a beggar: she's a licensed newspaper vendor on Lexington Avenue at 34th Street. If we change that sign to a Chinese character or, better yet, put our hand over it, the woman changes, too. We see more directly into her spirit; she is obdurate and enduring, patient, and a bit unpleasant.

—Ben Maddow, from "Tears and Misunderstanding," *Aperture* 92, 1983

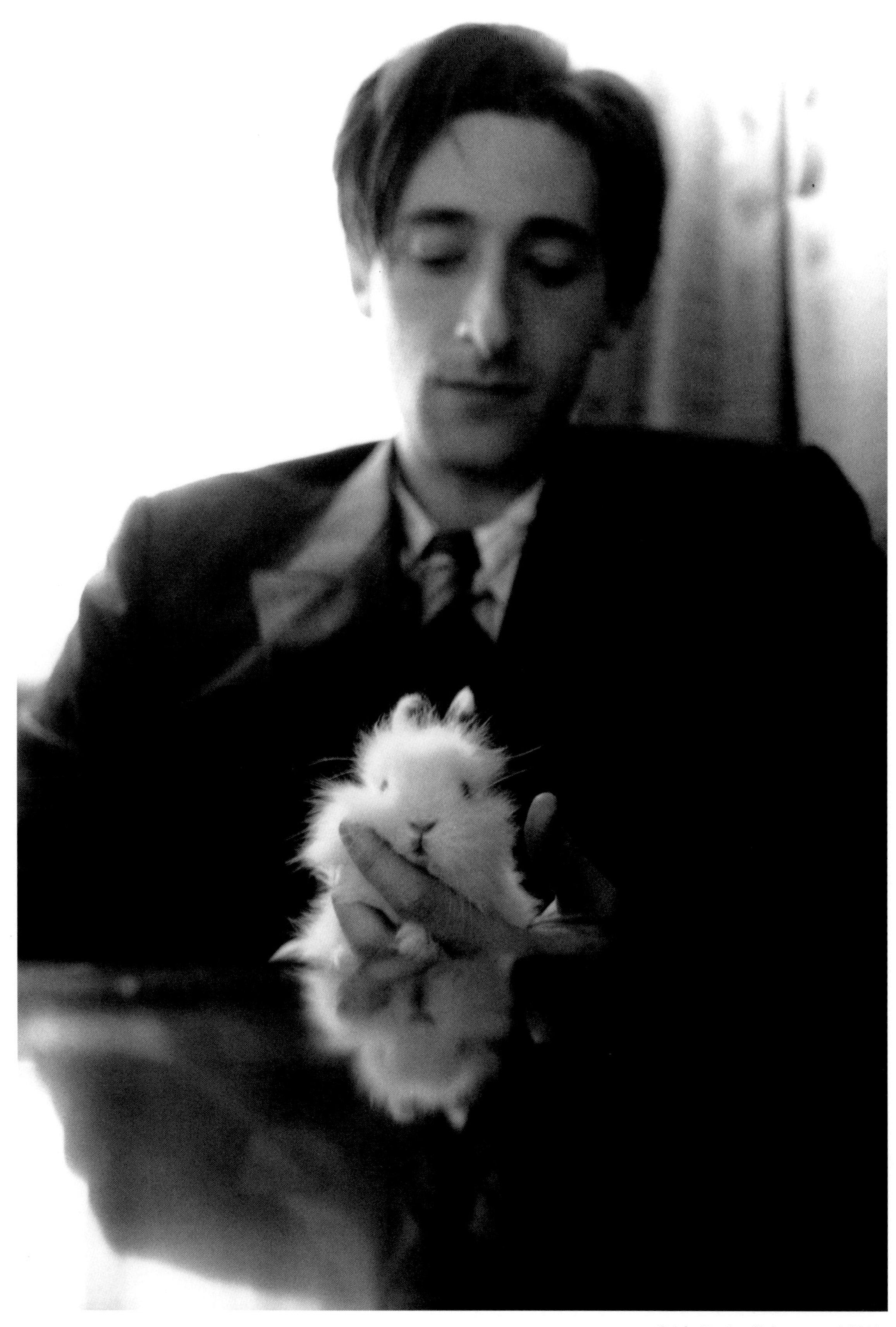

Sylvia Plachy, *Christmas card*, 2001.

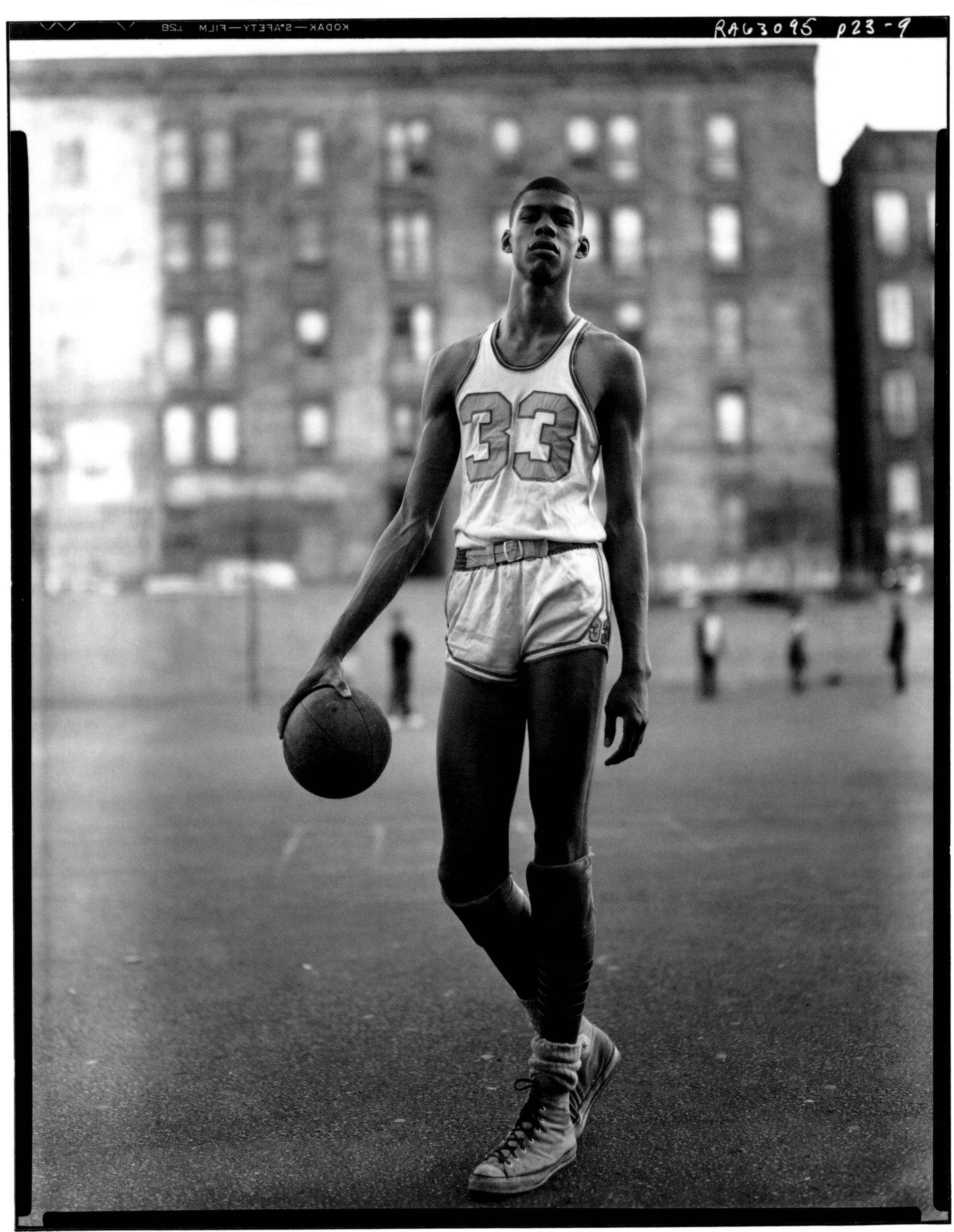
RA63095 p23-9
33

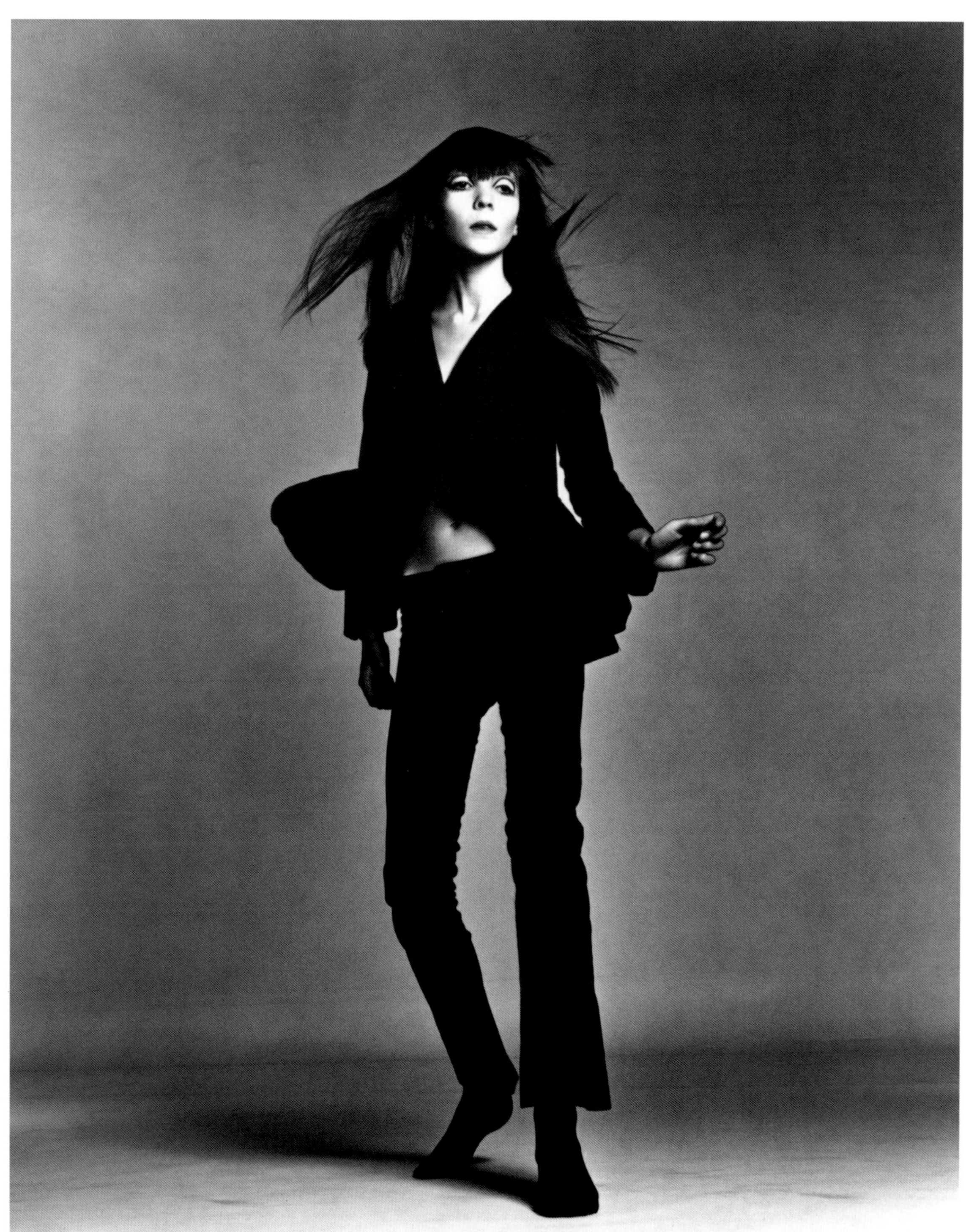

THESE PAGES: photographs by Richard Avedon.
OPPOSITE: *Lew Alcindor, 61st Street and Amsterdam Avenue*, New York City, May 2, 1963; from *Aperture* 156, 1999.
ABOVE: *Penelope Tree*, New York studio, June 1967; from *Aperture* 122, 1991.

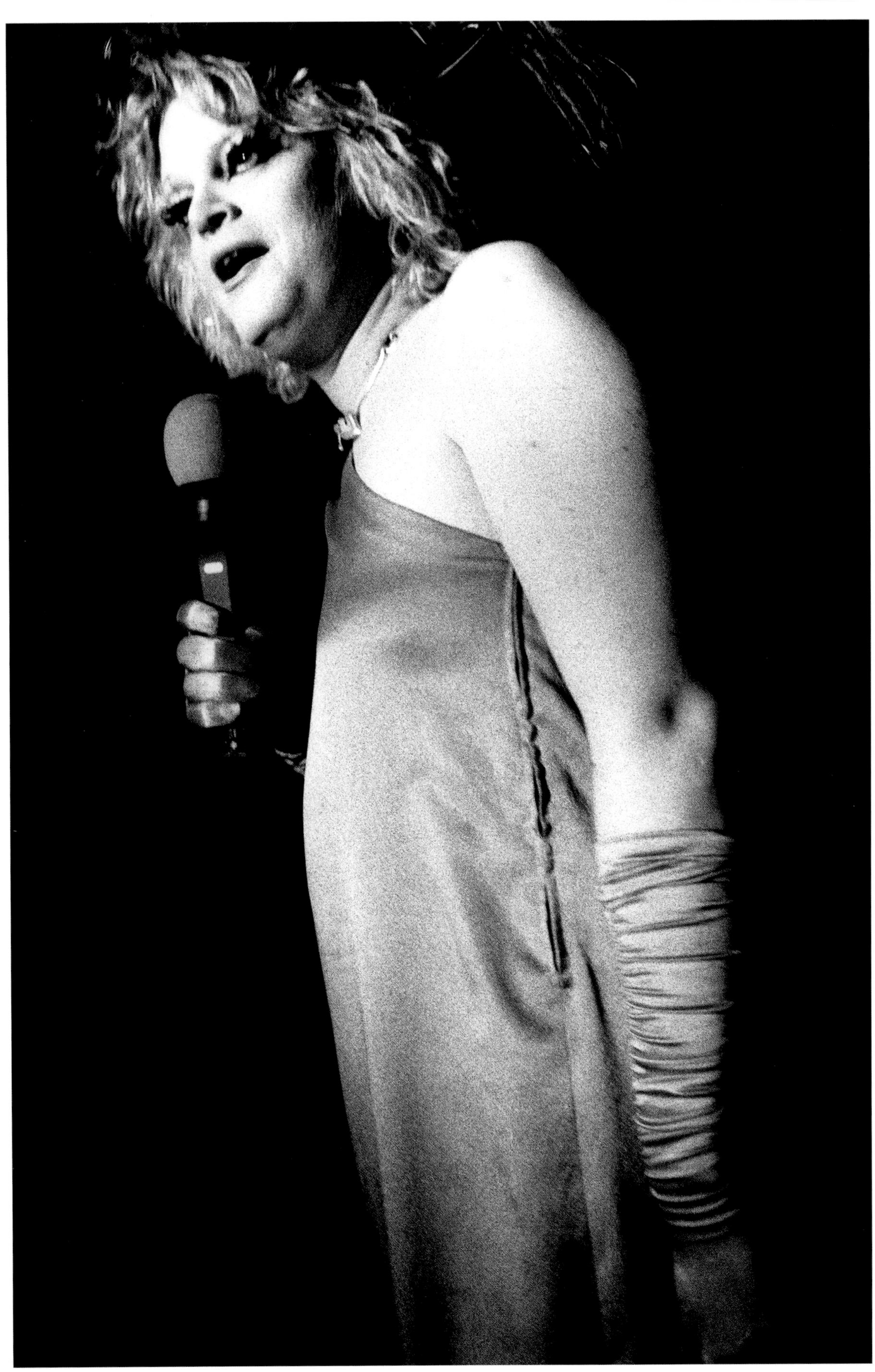

Ralph Gibson, *Drag Queen*, 2000.

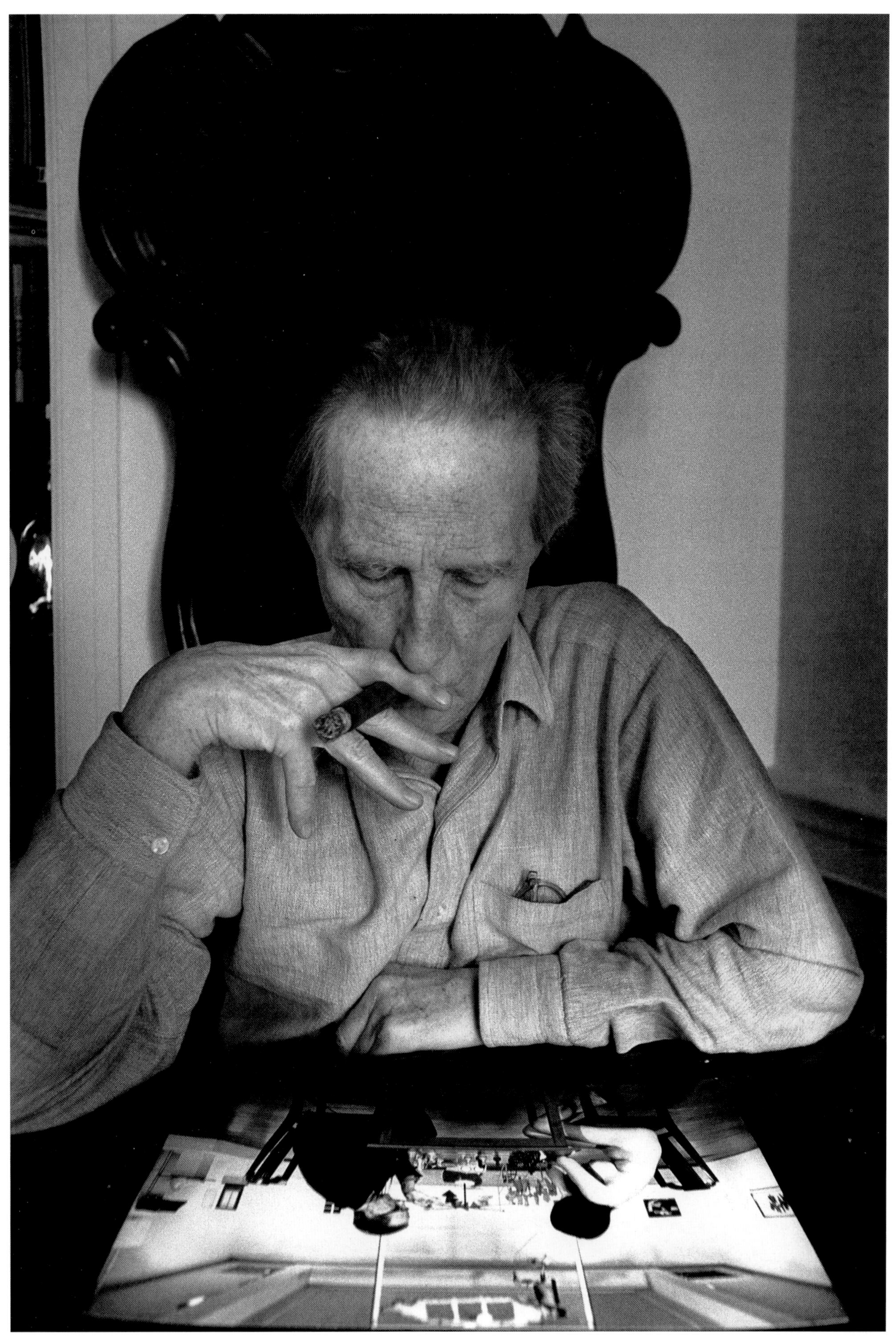

Ugo Mulas, *Marcel Duchamp*, New York, 1965;
from *Aperture* 132, 1993.

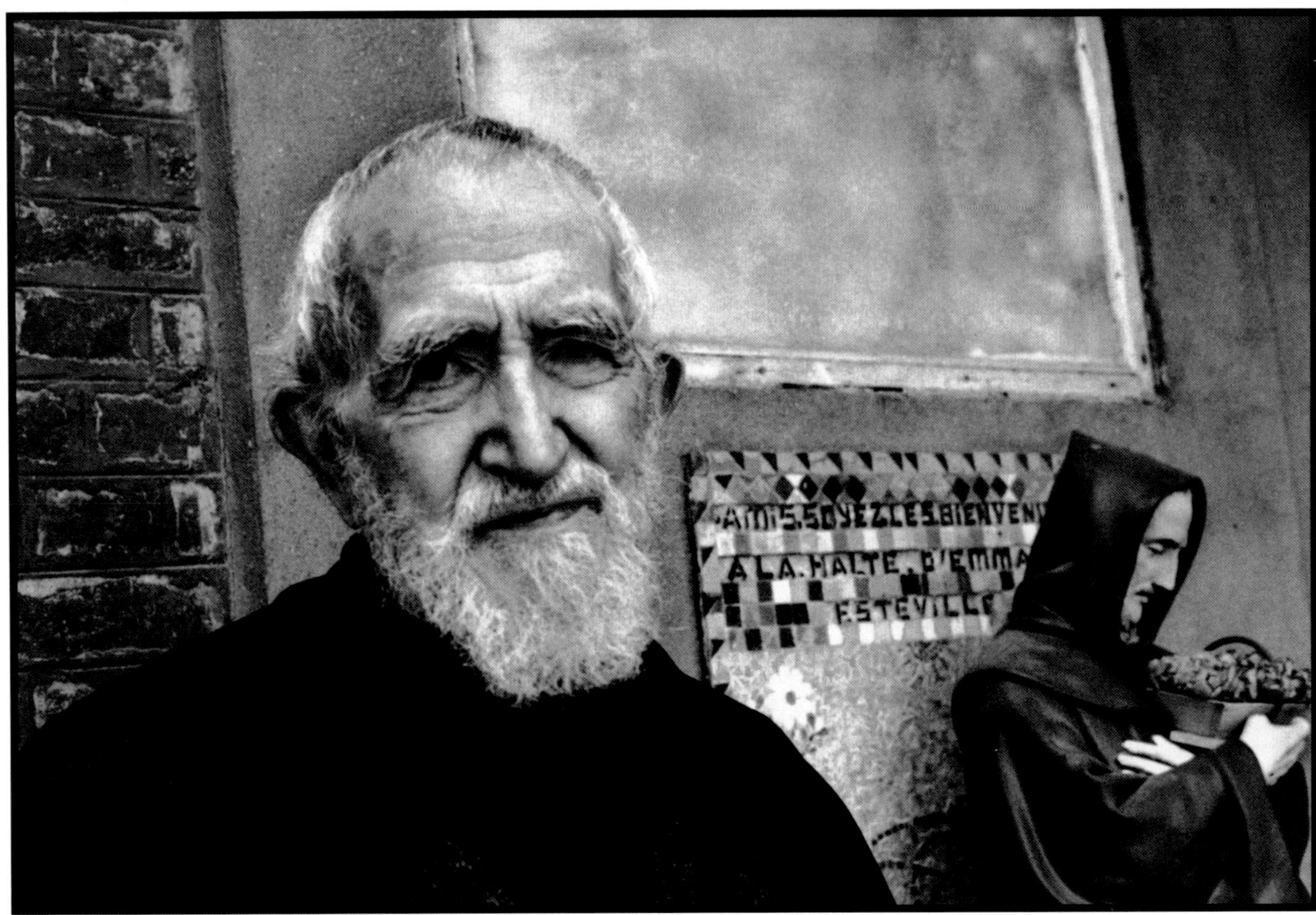

Henri Cartier-Bresson, *L'Abbé Pierre*, 1994; from *Aperture* 138, 1995.

The only thing about photography which interests me, he says, **is the aim, the taking aim.**

Like a marksman?

Do you know the Zen Buddhist treatise on archery? Georges Braque gave it to me in '43.

I'm afraid not.

It's a state of being, a question of openness, of forgetting yourself.

You don't aim blind?

No, there's the geometry. Change your position by a millimeter and the geometry changes.

What you call geometry is aesthetics?

Not at all. It's like what mathematicians and physicists call elegance, when they're discussing a theory. If an approach is elegant it may be getting near to what's true.

. . . What counts in a photo is its plenitude and its simplicity. . . .

—John Berger, from "Henri Cartier-Bresson," *Aperture* 138, 1995

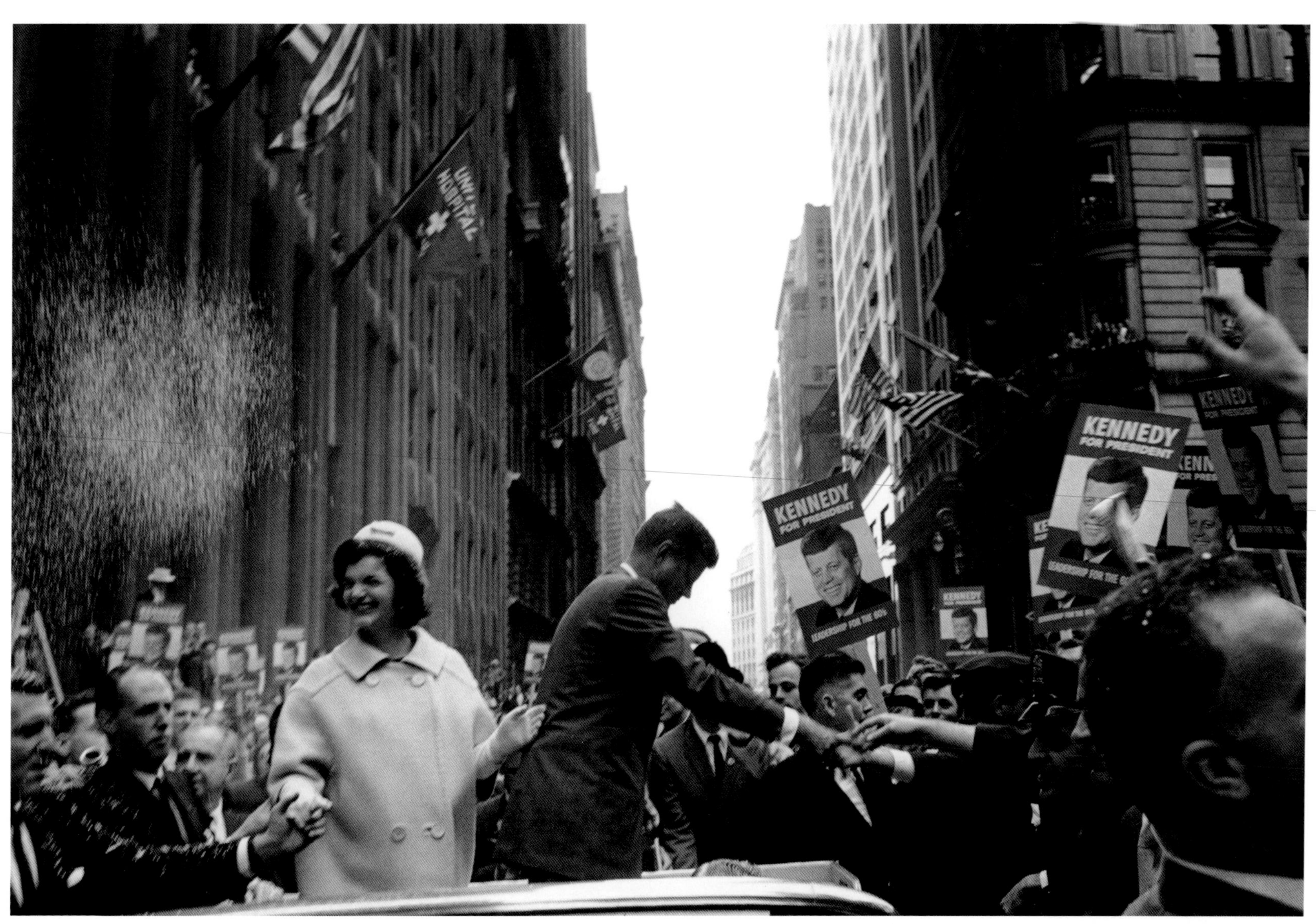

Cornell Capa, *JFK and Jackie*, New York, 1960.

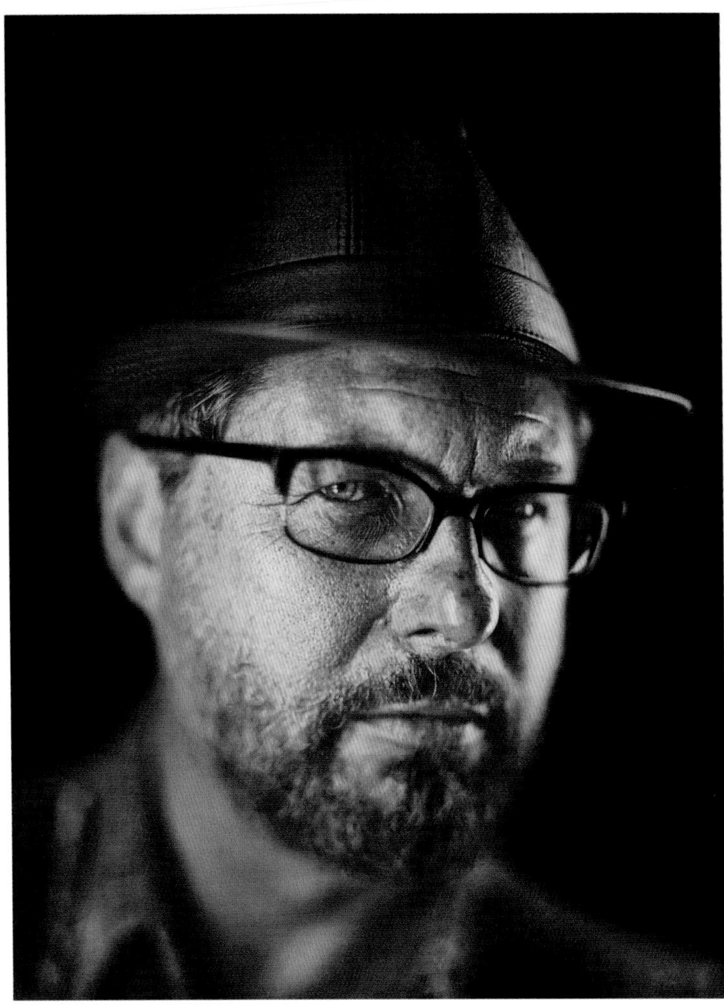

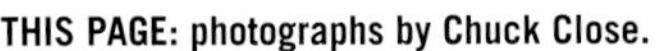

THIS PAGE: photographs by Chuck Close. *Bob*, 2000.

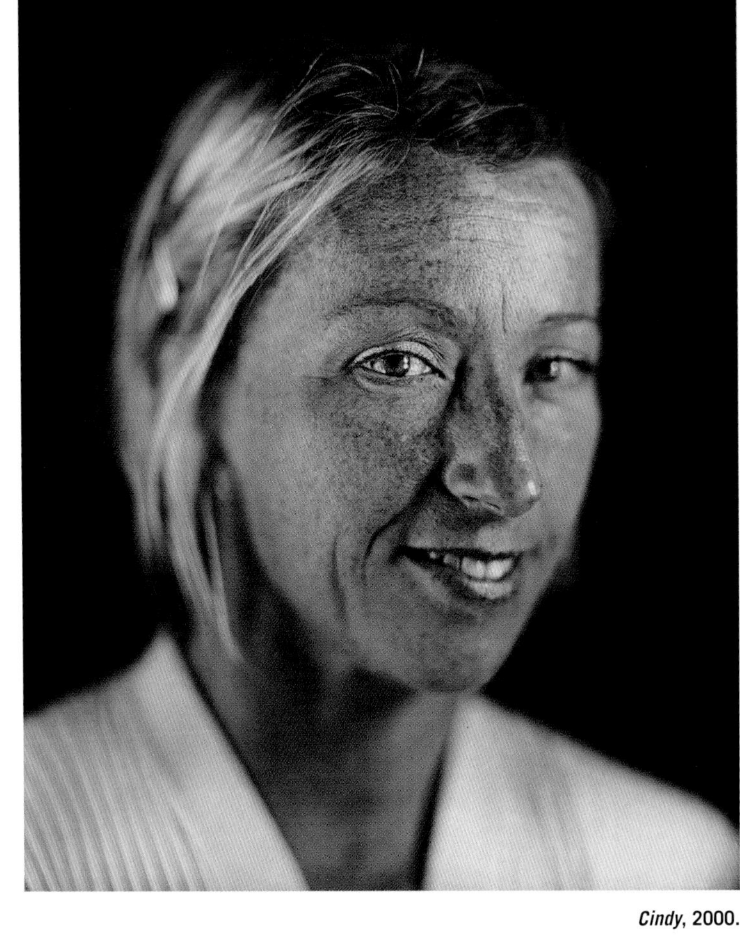

Cindy, 2000.

Jack Kerouac wrote about his friends in *The Dharma Bums* as a novel, an epic of his own. Anything that resulted in the media is fall-out from his own original creation. The ordinary magazine myth would not exist without the high artistic creation, without a mutual collaborative artistic creation between friends, that involved mythmaking; which means companions were involved in seeing each other as mythical or sacred in a sacred world primarily; or not so much *mythical* as seeing each other as *real* in a really sacred world. So my motive for taking those snapshots was to make celestial snapshots in a sacred world, recording certain moments in an eternity with a sense of sacramental presence. The sacramental quality comes from an awareness of the transitory nature of the world, an awareness that it's a mortal world, where our brief time together is limited and it's the one and only occasion when we'll be together. This is what makes it sacred, the awareness of the mortality, which comes from a Romantic conception (Keats's) as well as Buddhist understanding (as in the "Shambhala" teachings of Chogyam Trungpa, Rinpoche). They are not contradictory origins; and Buddhism was part of the cultural awareness and later practice I shared with Jack Kerouac, Gary Snyder, and Philip Whalen. . . . The poignancy of the photograph comes from looking back to a fleeting moment in a floating world. The transitoriness is what creates the sense of the sacred.

—Allen Ginsberg, from "Allen Ginsberg's Sacramental Snapshots," *Aperture* 101, 1985

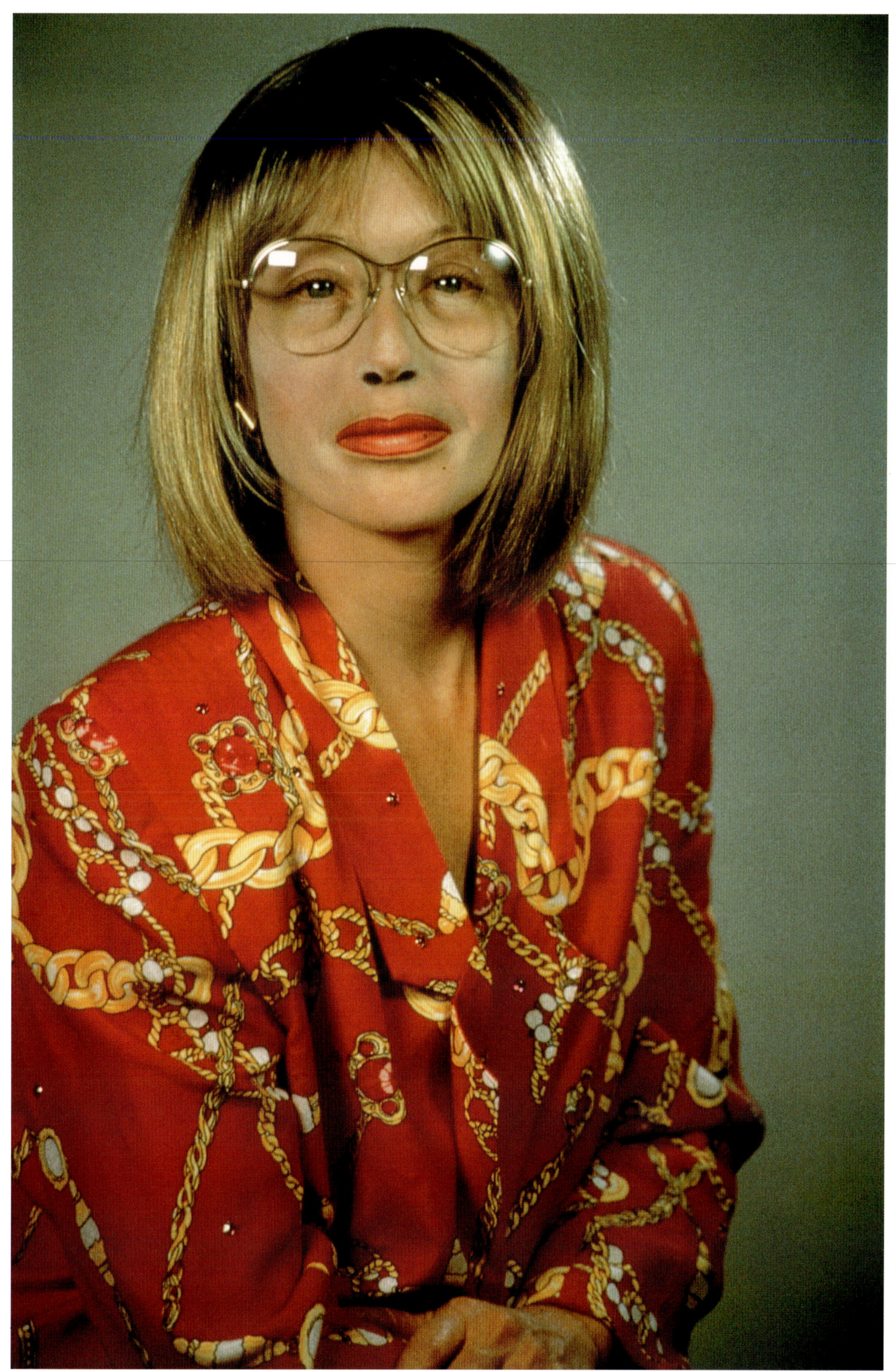

Cindy Sherman, *Untitled*, 2000.

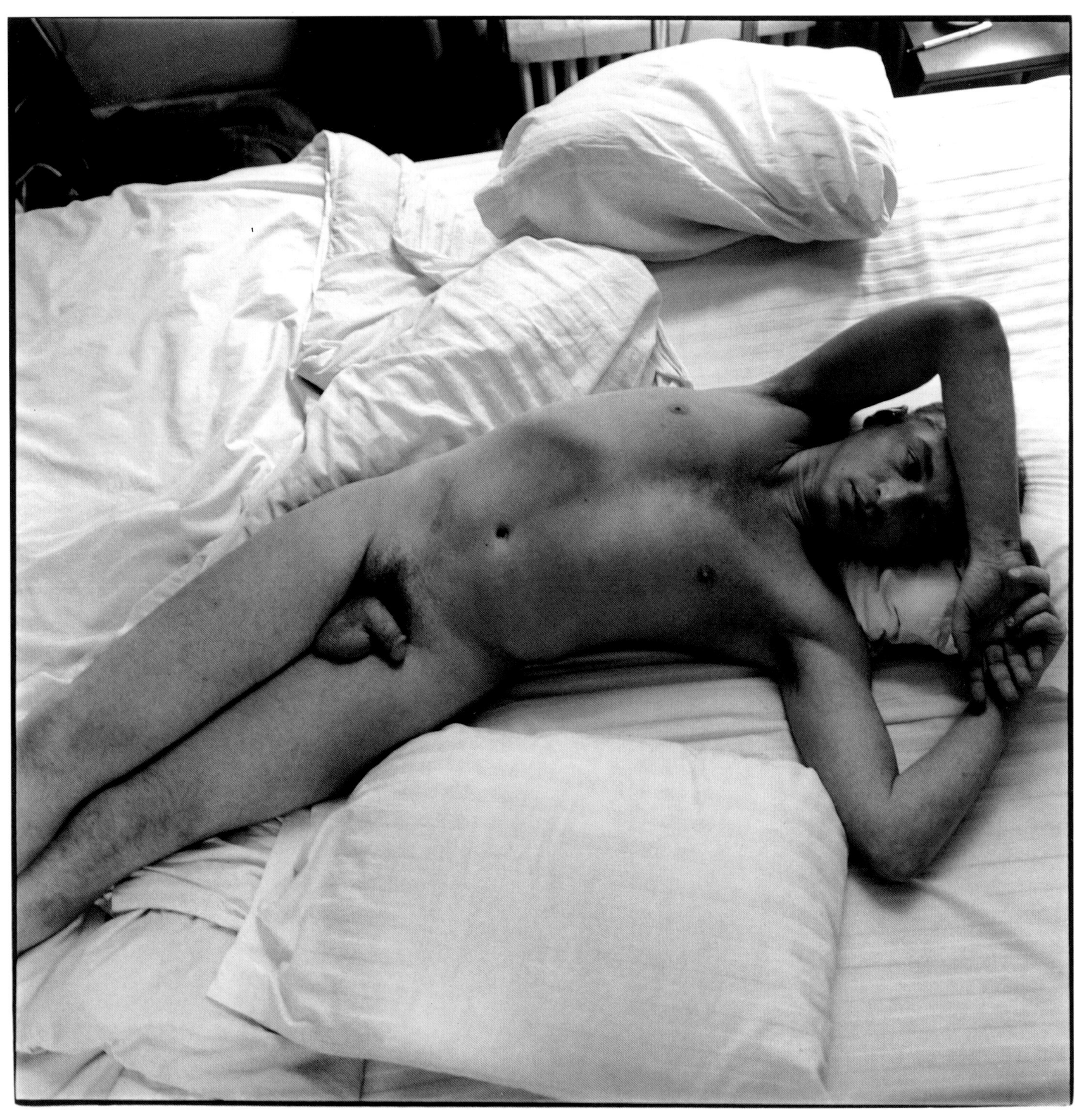

Annie Leibovitz, *Ron Vawter*, New York City, 1993; from *Aperture* 133, 1993.

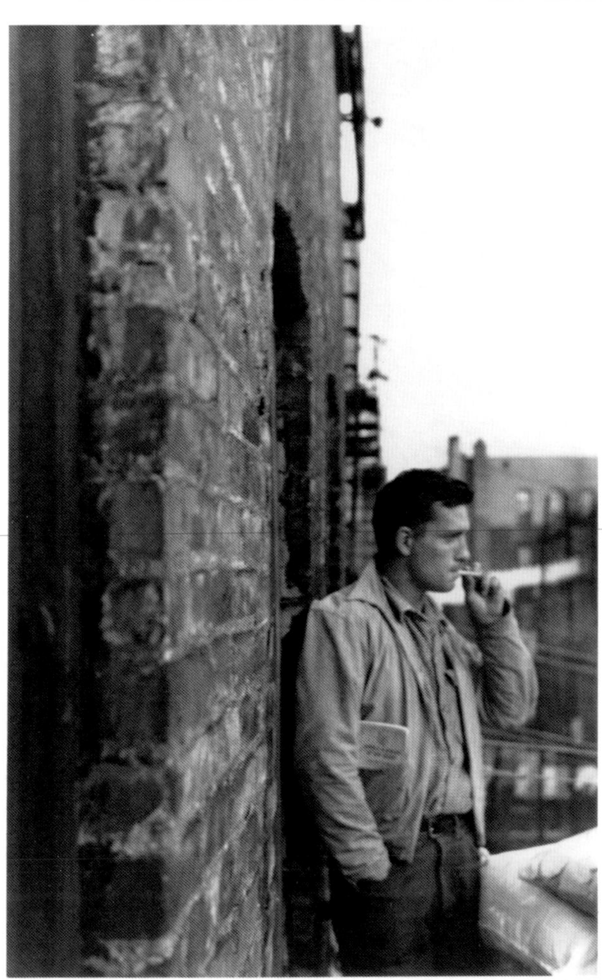

Jack Kerouac, railroad brakeman's rule-book in his pocket, couch pillows airing on fire-escape three flights up overlooking backyard clotheslines south, my apartment 206 E 7th Street between Avenues B & C, Lower East Side Manhattan. Burroughs then in residence, Corso visited often, probably September 1953. Allen Ginsberg

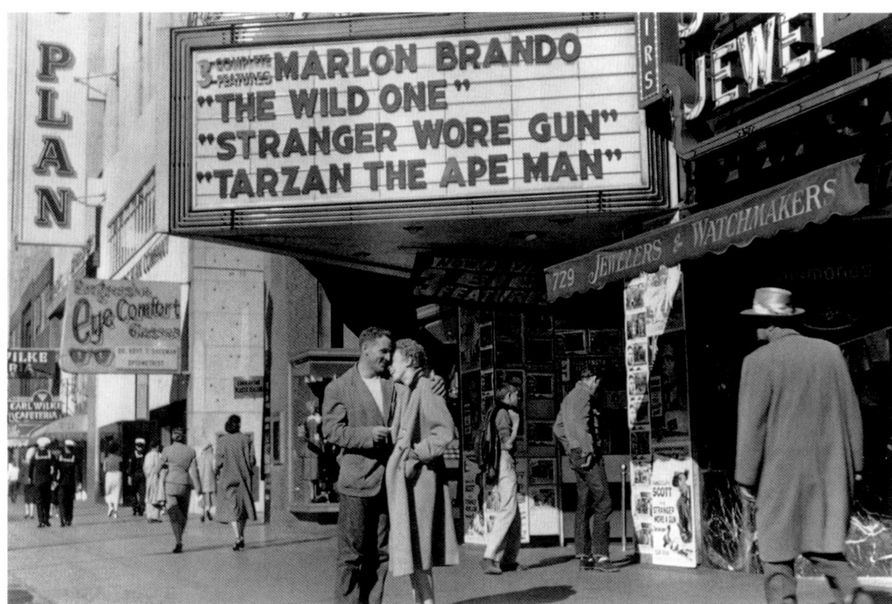

Neal Cassady and his love of that year Natalie Jackson conscious of their rôle in Eternity: Cassady had been prototype for Jack Kerouac's 1950 On The Road saga hero Dean Moriarty, as later in 1960's he'd taken the driver's wheel of Ken Kesey's psychedelic era Merry Prankster crosscountry bus "Further." Neal's illuminated American automobile energy, eager friendships & erotic enthusiasm had already written his name in bright-lit signs in our literary imaginations before movies were made imitating his charm. That's why we stopped under the Market Street marquee to fix the passing hand on the watch, San Francisco around March '55. Allen Ginsberg

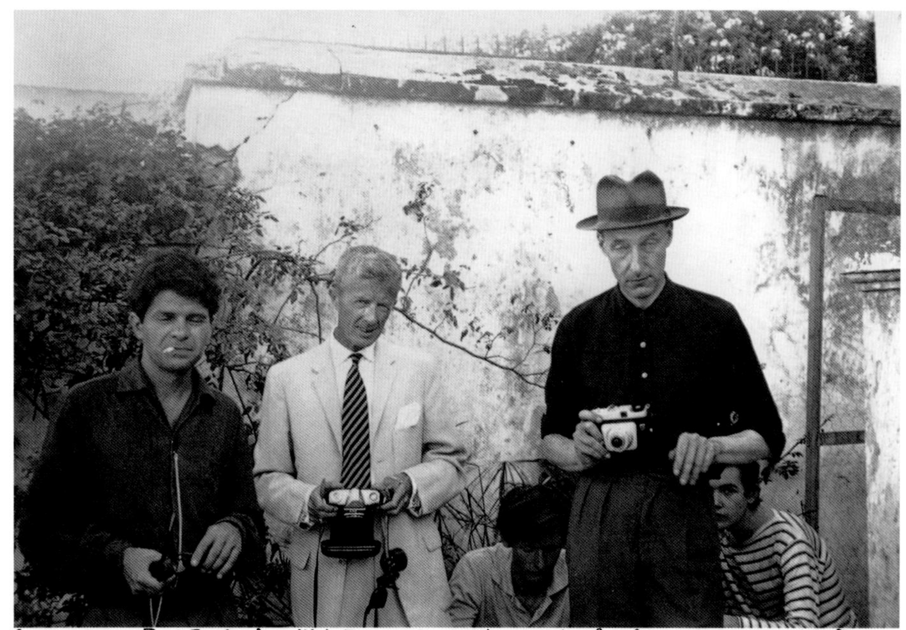

Gregory Corso, Paul Bowles & William Burroughs, behind him two dead boys, shades of the late Ian Sommerville & Michael Portman deceased crouching before garden wall, we all took our cameras out under blue sky, brilliant summer day, Villa Muneria Tanger 1961. Allen Ginsberg

THIS PAGE: photographs by Allen Ginsberg; from *Aperture* 101, 1985.

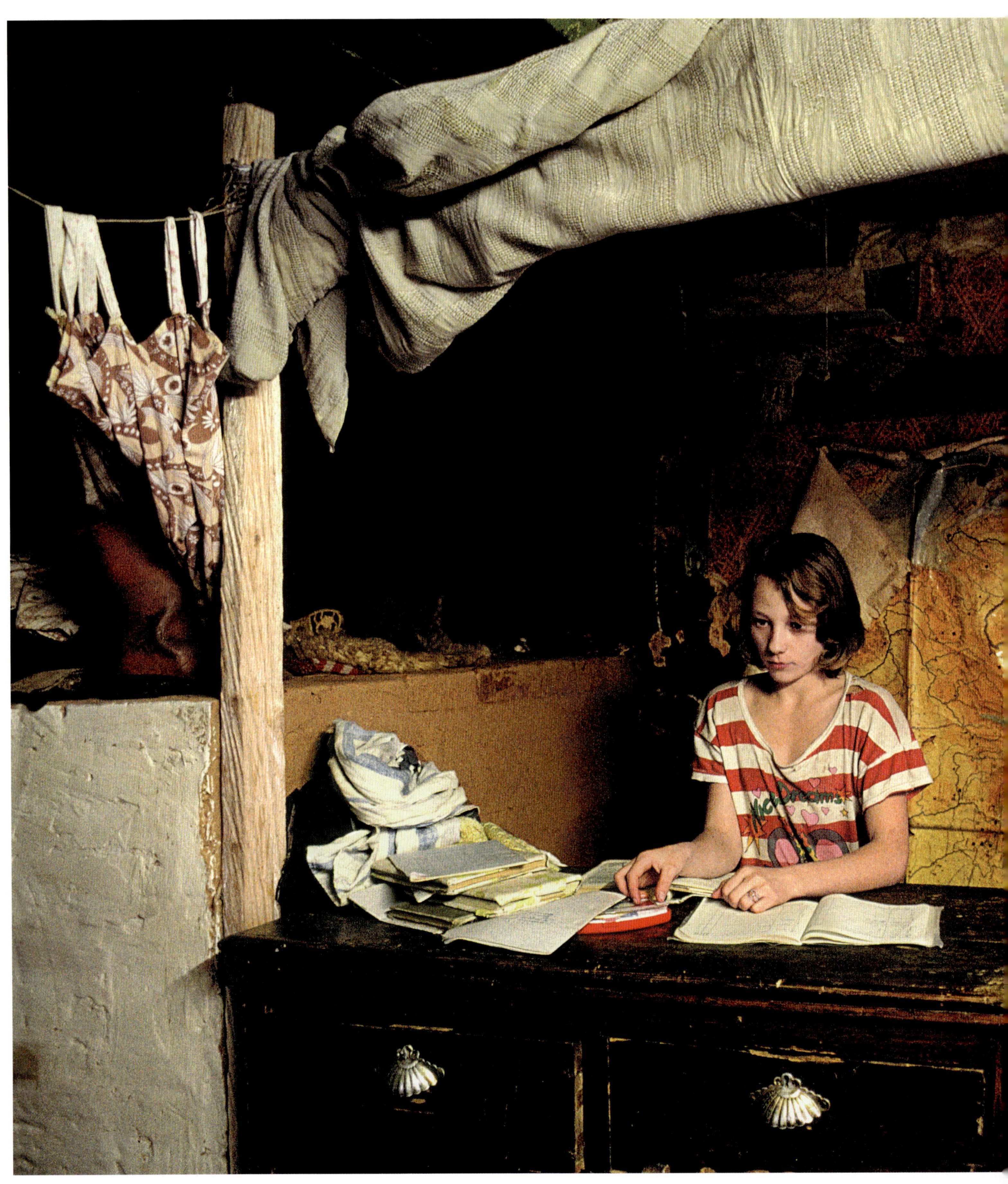

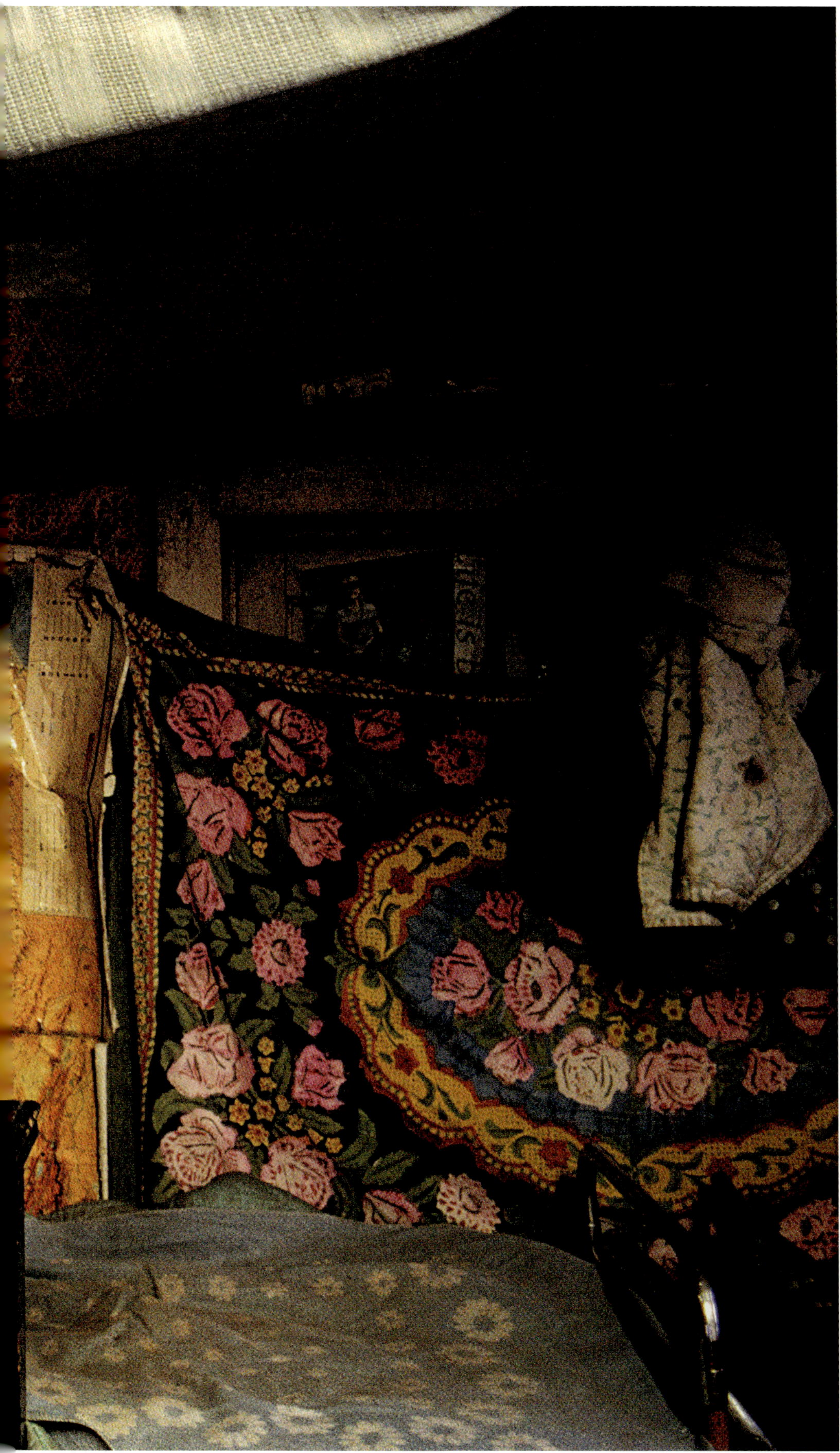

Lise Sarfati, *Tieriekhino I*, 2000.

Though not a poet, nor a painter, nor a composer, he is yet an artist, and as an artist undertakes not only risks but responsibility. And it is with responsibility that both the photographer and his machine are brought to their ultimate tests. His machine must prove that it can be endowed with the passion and the humanity of the photographer; the photographer must prove that he has the passion and the humanity with which to endow the machine.

—Dorothea Lange and Daniel Dixon, from "Photographing the Familiar," *Aperture* vol. 1, no. 2, 1952

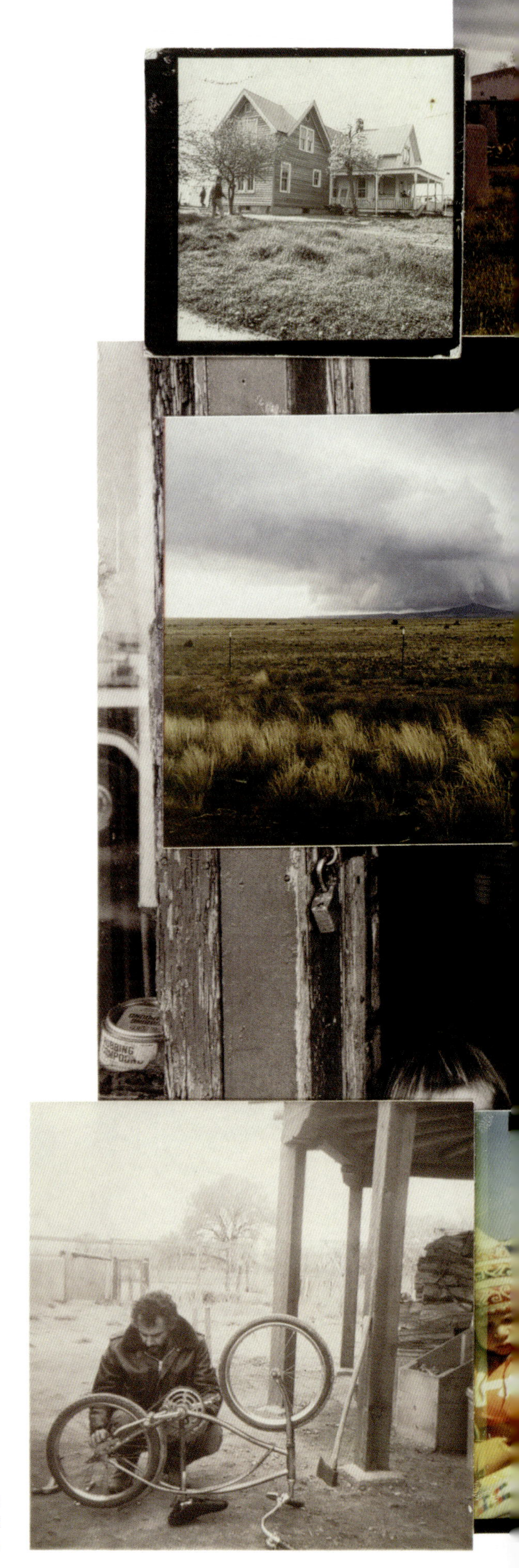

Danny Lyon, *Nancy*, 1981;
from his book
Knave of Hearts, 1999.

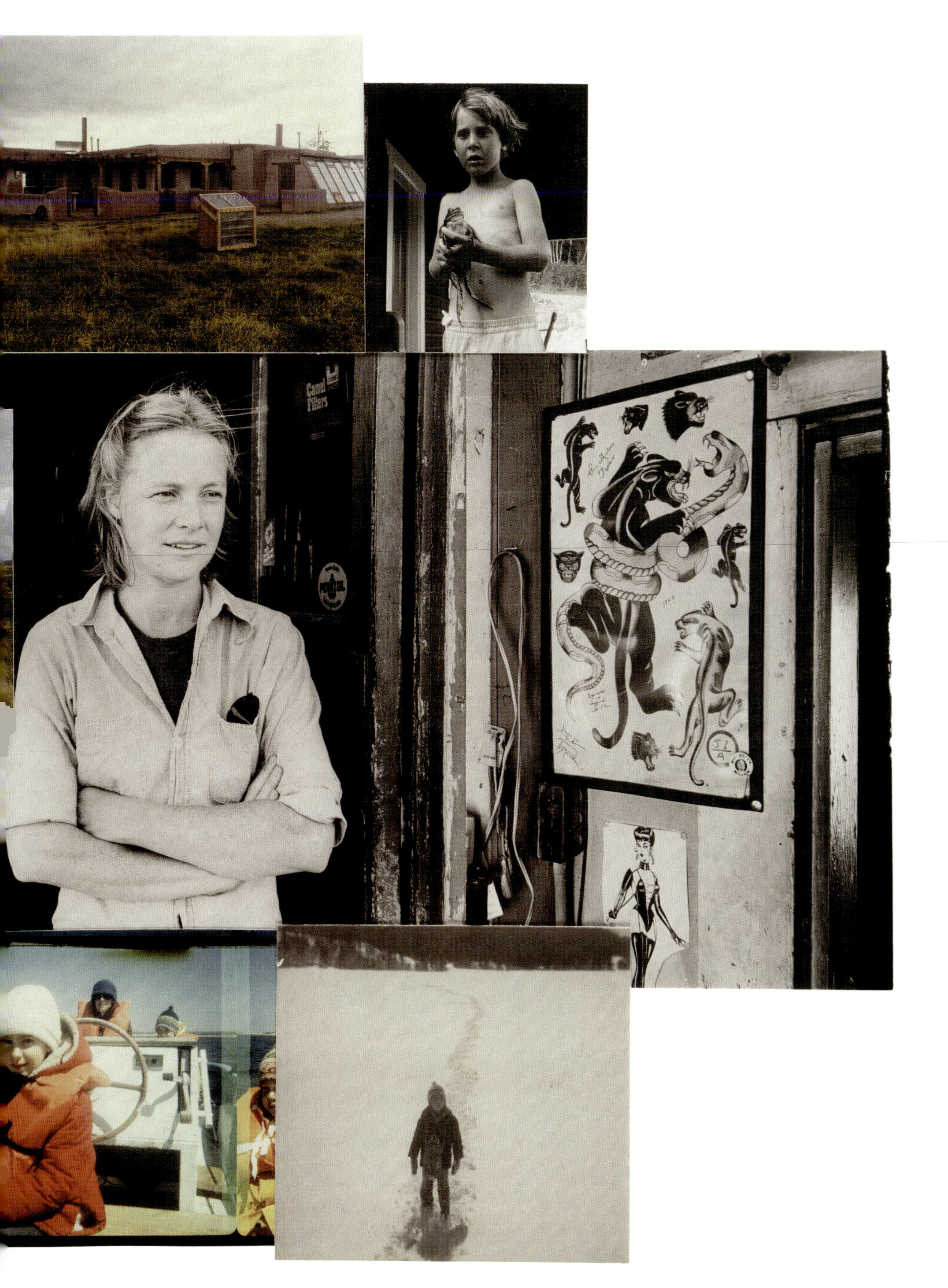
Camel
Filters
51
A

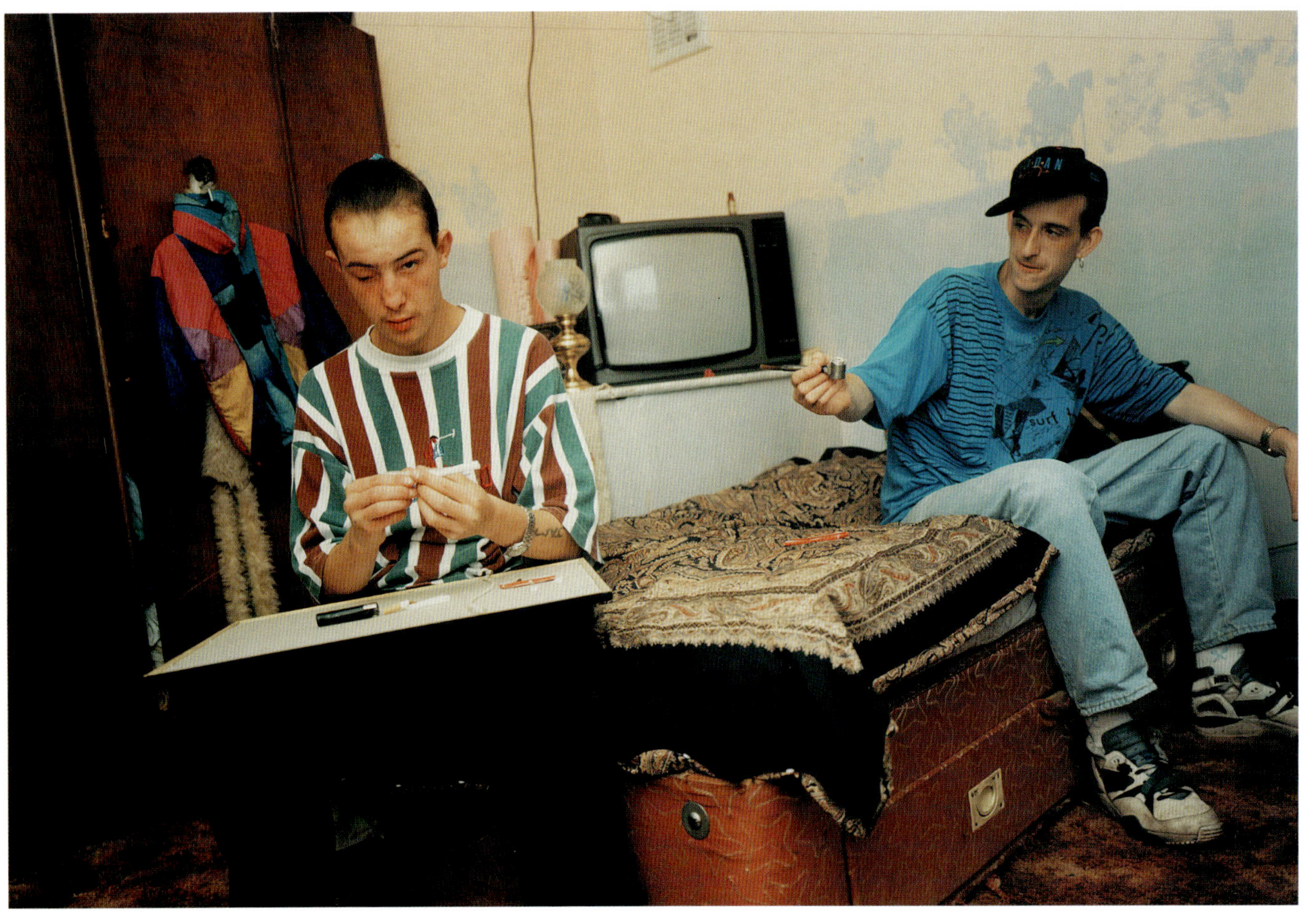

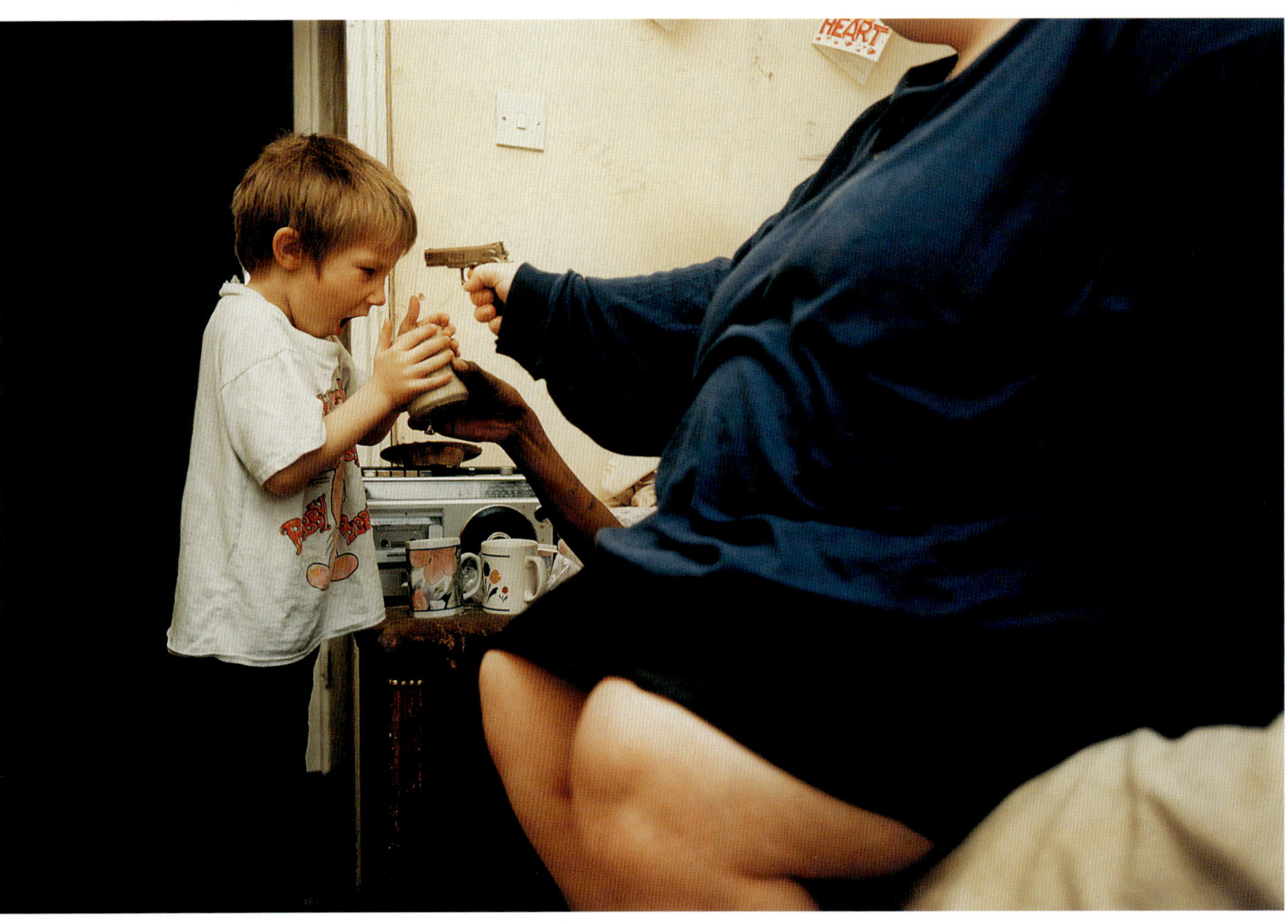

THIS PAGE: photographs by Nick Waplington, from the series "Living Room," 1996–97.

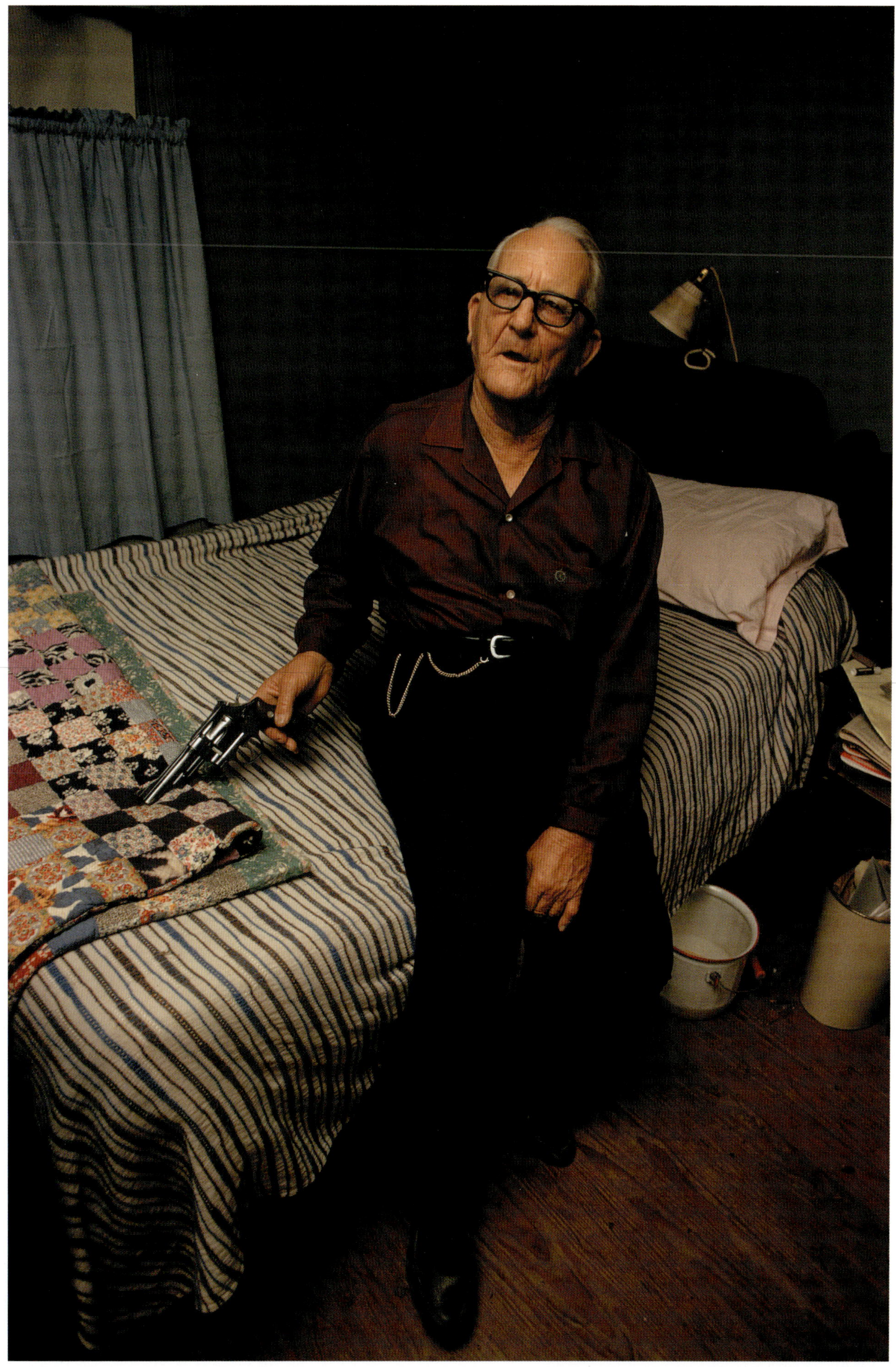

William Eggleston, *Untitled (Morton, Mississippi)*, 1969–70.

The combination of sexual content and photography makes for a particularly explosive mix, and not just for members of fundamentalist groups. The reasons for their disapproval are clear; images that depict sexuality outside of marriage and procreation encourage immorality (or so we are to believe), and thereby subvert the traditional social arrangements conservatives would like to reinstate. But for the average citizen, sexual imagery can be difficult and disturbing too. Heirs to a Victorian cultural tradition that regarded sexual pleasure with profound suspicion, we greet explicit images of sexuality with anxiety and an underdeveloped history of looking. Distinctions that viewers are accustomed to making—between fantasy and behavior, image and reality—become curiously evanescent when it comes to sex. Our unease often increases if the sexual acts depicted are unfamiliar or unconventional. . . .

—Carole S. Vance, from "Photography, Pornography and Sexual Politics," *Aperture* 121, 1990

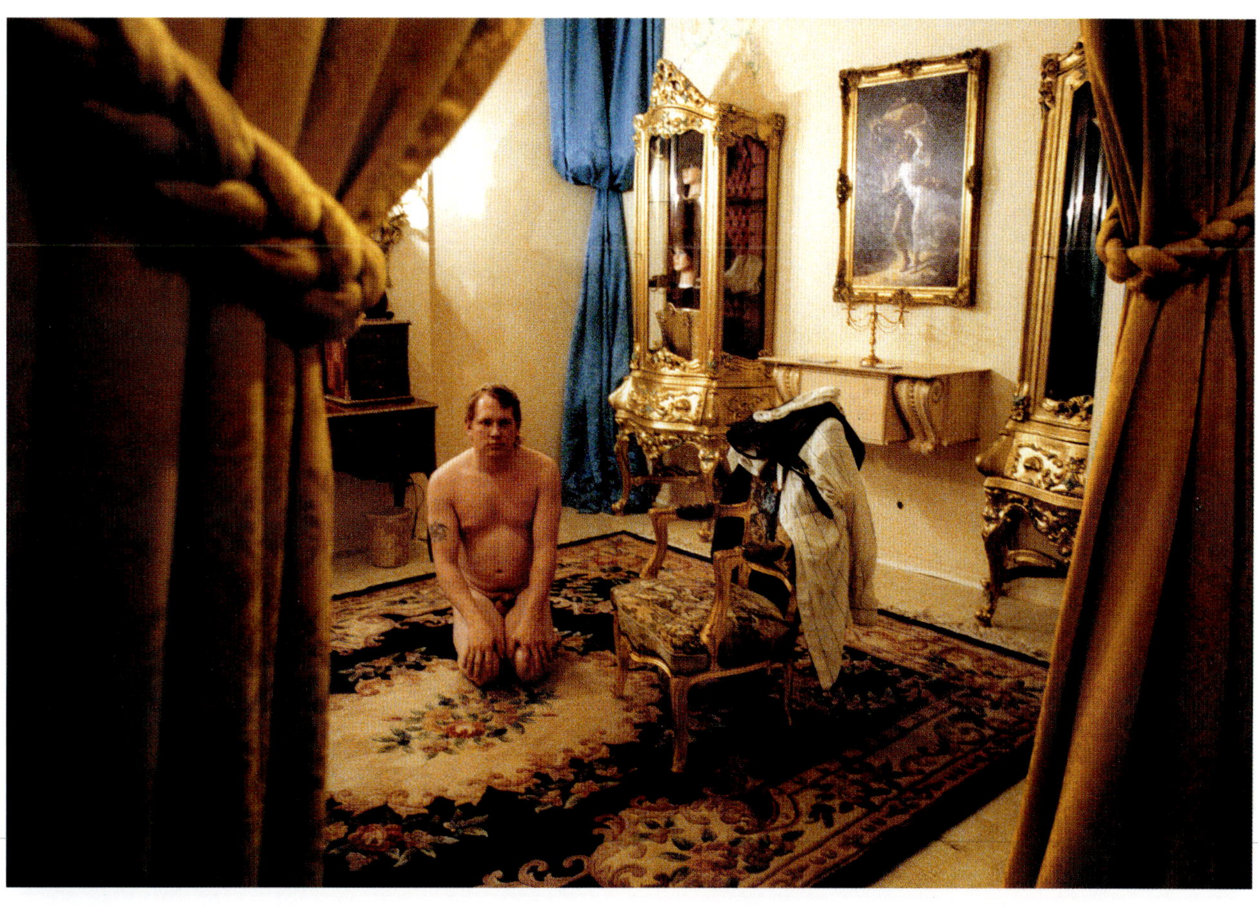

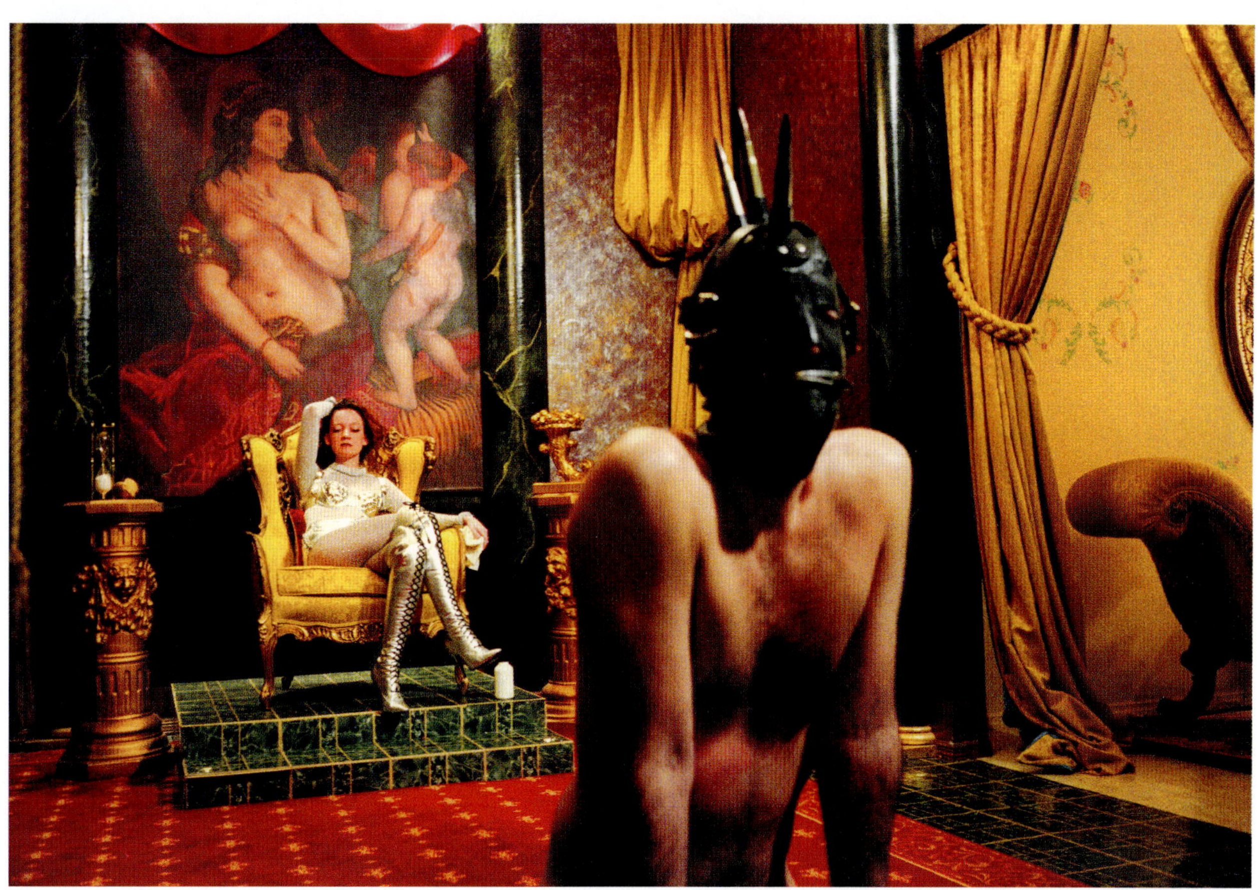

THIS PAGE: photographs by Susan Meiselas. TOP: ***Pandora's Box, Awaiting Mistress Natasha, The Versailles Room, New York City*****, 1995. BOTTOM:** ***Pandora's Box, Mistress Catherine After the Whipping I, The Versailles Room, New York City*****, 1995.**

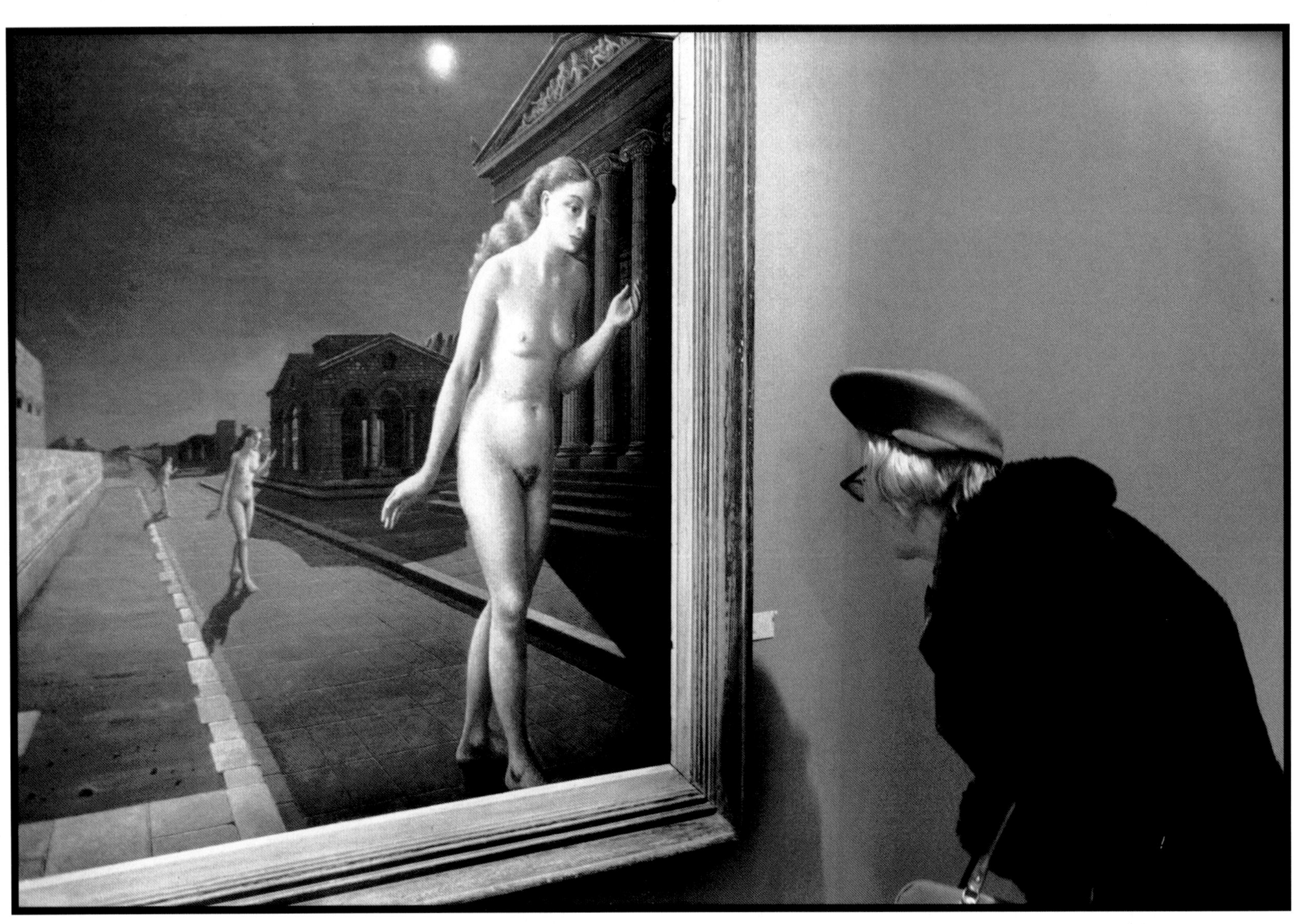

Martine Franck, ***Exhibition, Pompidou Center,*** Paris, France, 1977; from ***Aperture*** 151, 1998.

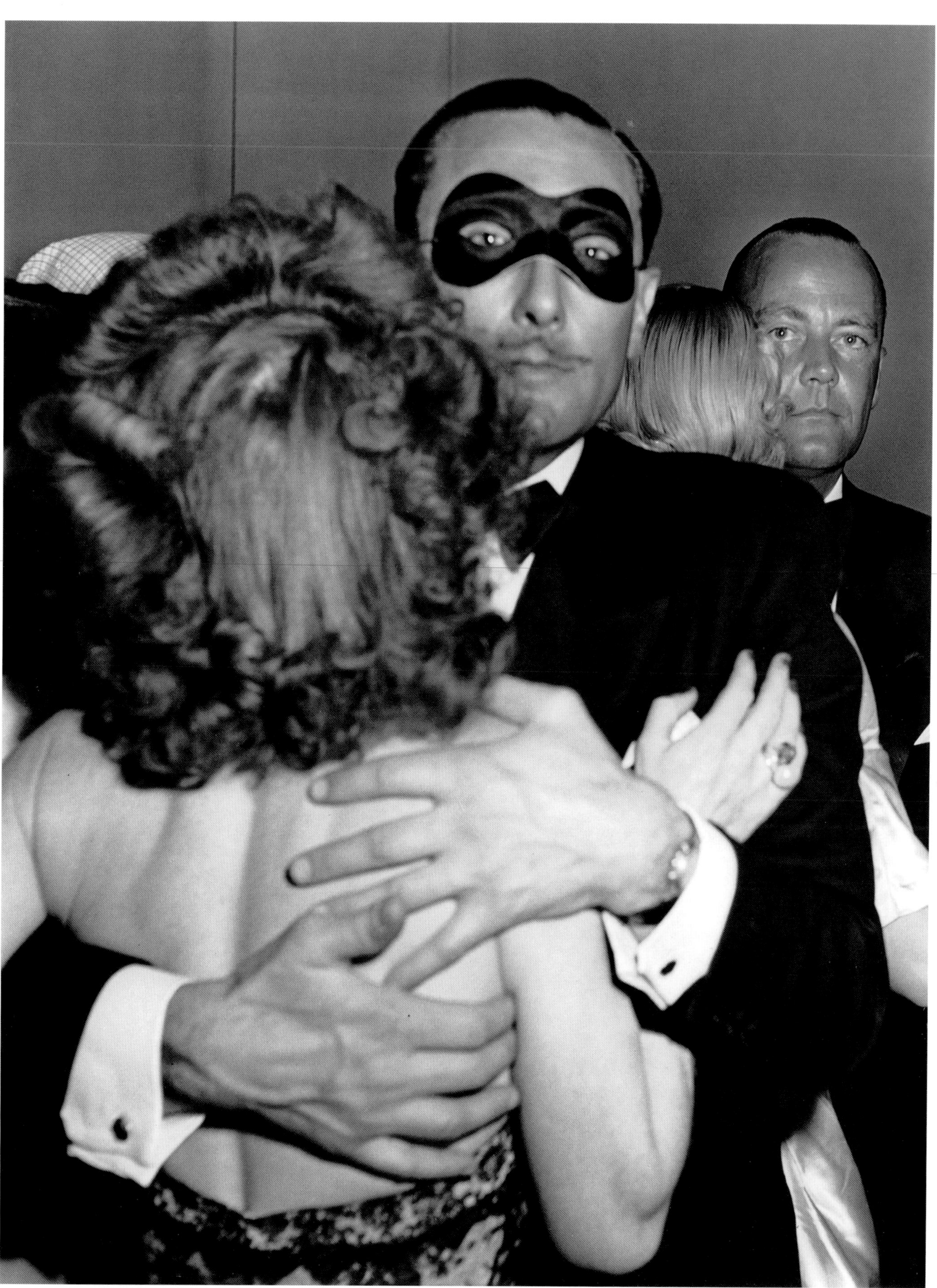

Robert Capa, *Carnival,* Zürs, Austria, February, 1950; from *Robert Capa: Photographs* (Aperture, 1996).

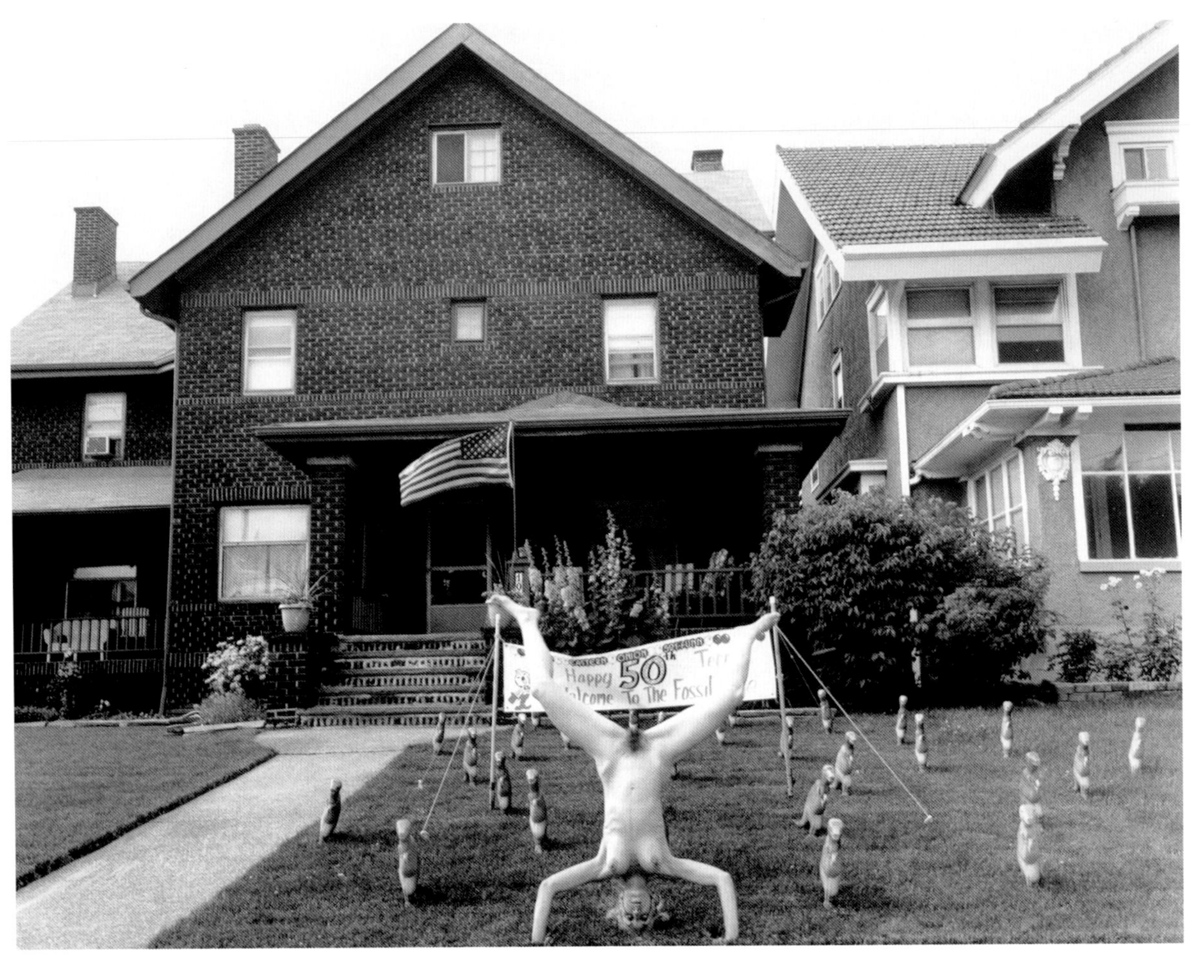

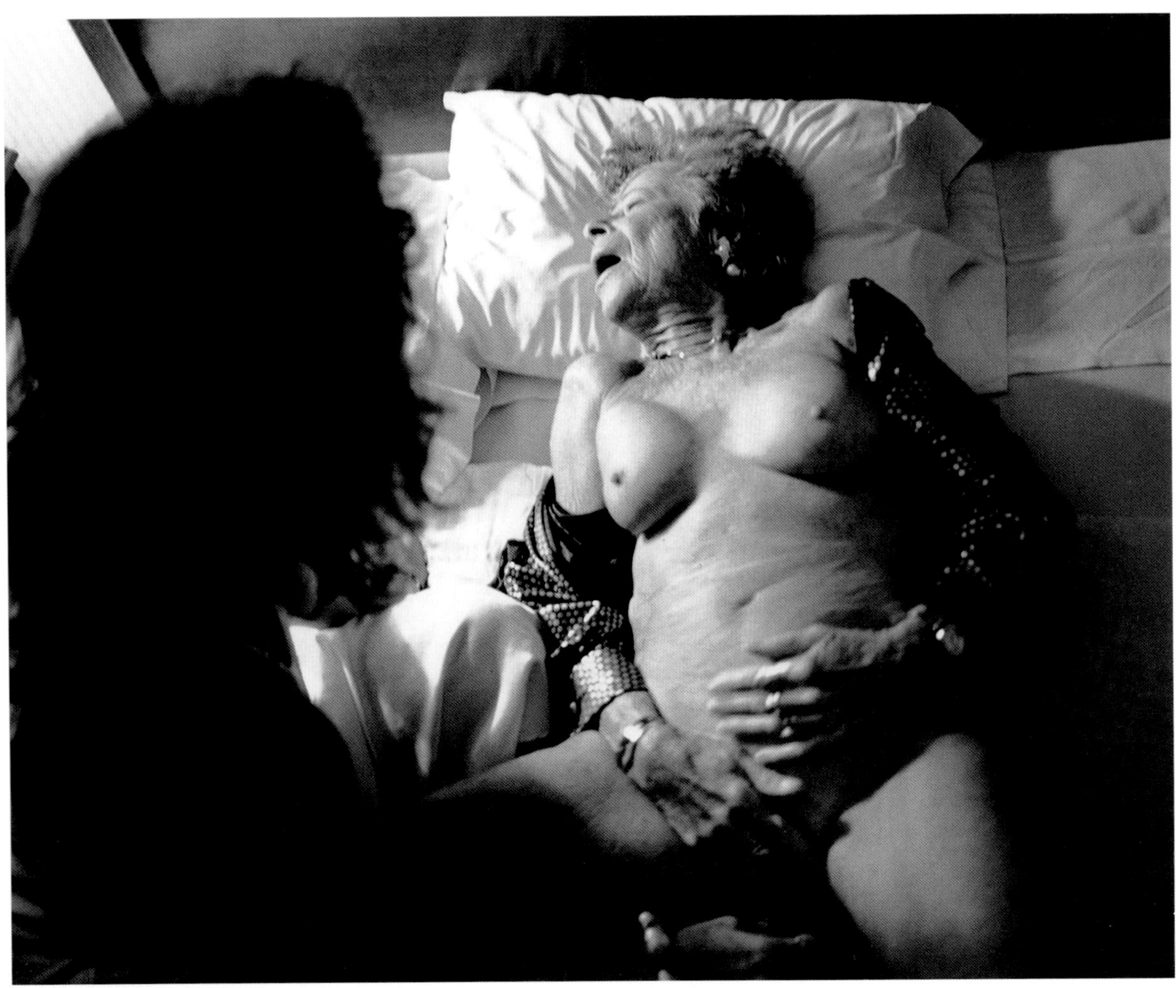

THIS PAGE: photographs by Donna Ferrato. **TOP:** *Performance artist Katherine Chronin, Lakewood, Ohio*, 2001. **BOTTOM:** *Eve finds her g-spot*, 2000.

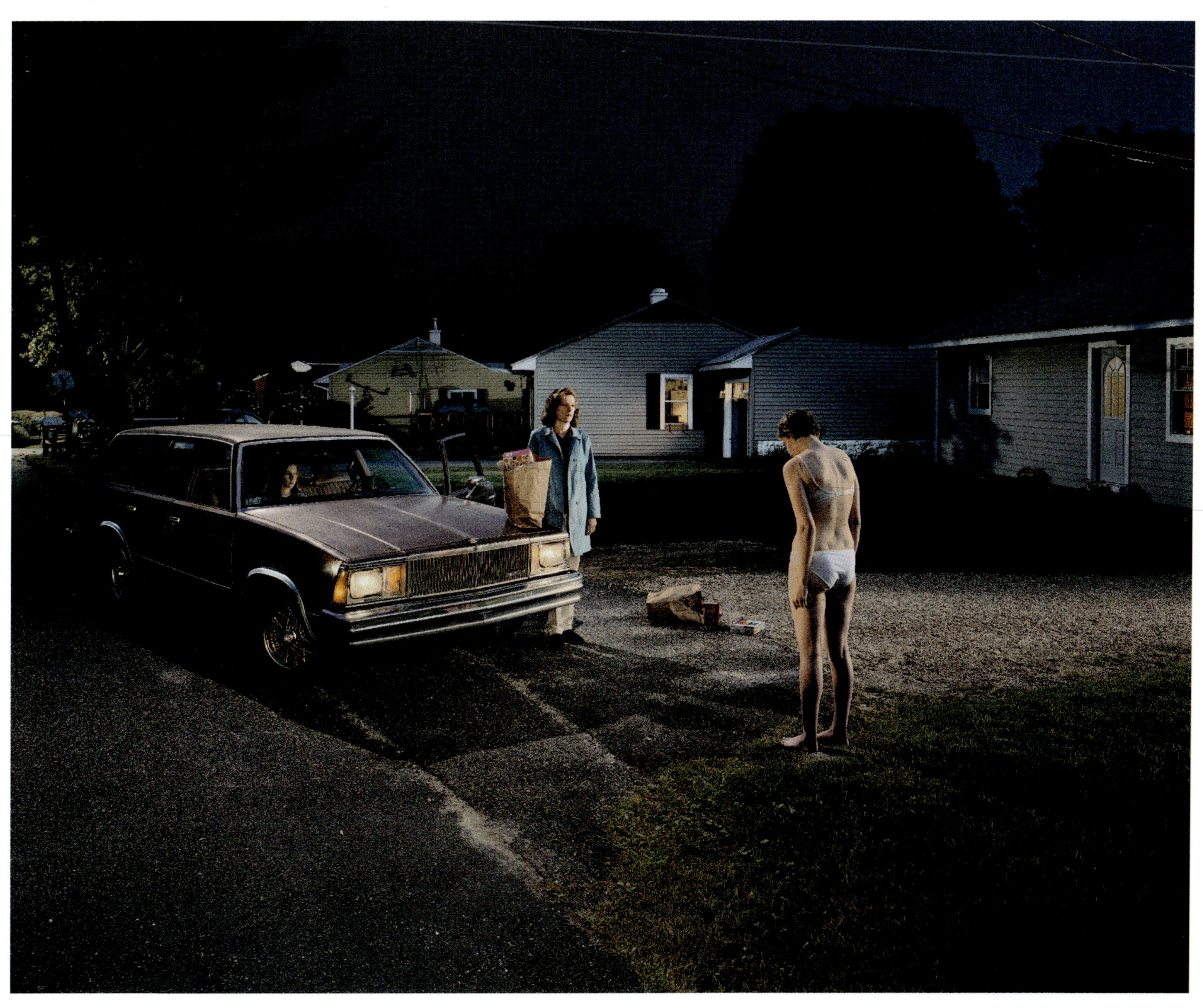

Gregory Crewdson, *Untitled (penitent girl)*, 2001–02.

PART IV

The Evolution of an Ideal

And sometime then there will be a history of how anything or everything comes out from every one, comes out from every one or any one from the beginning to the ending of the being in them.

—Gertrude Stein, *The Making of the Americans*

In 1936 Charis Wilson, at the age of twenty-two, posed for her fifty-year-old lover Edward Weston, in a series of photographs that might be grouped as the "dune nudes." The pictures were taken one morning near Oceano, California, and in a rare glimpse of a masterpiece from the subject's point of view, she described the moments of their creation:

> Altogether it was a magical place. The silence and emptiness, the beauty of the wind-sculptured forms, the absence of any living things beside ourselves—all these combined to give me an exhilarating sense of freedom. As soon as the sun warmed things up, I took off my clothes and went diving down a steep slope. . . . I was reminded of the childhood games of statues as I kept returning to the top of the bank to relaunch myself, and each slide down ended in a more abandoned position.

By one definition, art is what artists make. Therein lies the implication that the more that is known about the life of a great artist, the more that can be discovered about the nature of his or her work—about the creative process itself. In such a context, few artists have been better served than Weston.

Along with portfolios appearing from time to time in the journal, Aperture's contribution to the Weston iconography involves seven monographs. They are of course profoundly beautiful publications, but what most sets these monographs apart are the accompanying texts: writings that invoke the voices of Weston's admirers, friends, family, and lovers. These texts include Ben Maddow's classic biography of the photographer in *Edward Weston: His Life*; Charis Wilson's remembrances for *Edward Weston: Nudes* (excerpted above) and for *California and the West*; and a biographical essay by Susan Morgan in the 1995 monograph devoted to his portraits. Aperture's chief collaborator throughout has been Weston's youngest son, Cole, who recreated to perfection Edward's prints for publication, and who contributed his own recollections to the Weston saga.

And it was a saga, quintessentially American. No one told it better than Weston himself in his *Daybooks*. Although there are fragments from earlier and later in the photographer's life, these autobiographical writings span his most creative and productive years. In his huge, scrawling handwriting, Weston recounted his difficulties with money, marriage, conscience, and his devotion to his four sons. And there were rollicking accounts of life among artists, including those of the Mexican Renaissance such as José Orozco, Diego Rivera, and Tina Modotti—perhaps the greatest of Weston's many loves.

But it is in the moments of revelation arising from his work that Weston's journals rise to greatness. "I am not limiting myself to theories," he wrote. "Dare to be irrational—keep free from formulae, open to any fresh impulse, fluid." And elsewhere: "I have come to realize life as a coherent whole, and myself as a part, with rocks, trees, bones, cabbages, smokestacks, torsos, all interrelated, interdependent—each a symbol of the whole." Such fragments barely hint at the delights of the *Daybooks*, in which Nancy Newhall's editing in itself reached a level of brilliance. In the gathering of voices that have enriched Aperture publications, Nancy's insights offered prescient guideposts to future generations of editors.

Her essay in the debut issue of *Aperture*, "The Caption: The Mutual Relation of Words/Photographs," defined a new conception of the caption, which she called formally the *additive caption*. In contrast to the caption as title, miniature essay, or narrative, she wrote, the additive caption "leaps over facts and adds a new dimension. It combines its own connotations with those in the photograph to produce a new image in the mind of the spectator—sometimes an image totally unexpected and unforeseen, which exists in neither words nor photographs but only in their juxtaposition."

During his editorship, Minor White experimented with image/word possibilities through poetry, dialogues, and other devices. The technical essays of the early issues were quickly abandoned, as were the advisories on "how to look at" or "read" photographs. As Michael Hoffman's editorial tenure progressed, he continuously sought out writers, critics, poets, and especially the viewpoints and comments of contributing photographers.

Aperture's place in the critical canon is largely defined by its mission of being true to the "artist's intent." Thus the goal is to deepen the viewer's encounter with the images and their creators:

to provide, as Michael once put it, "an entry point into the work." The other dimensions of criticism—explication, analysis, and, automatically for some critics, abuse—are usually left to other venues.

In Aperture's history, the marriage of image and word has met with notable successes, often achieved with agonizing effort—none more successful, nor more agonizing, than with that master of architectural photography, Clarence John Laughlin.

Laughlin was born on a Louisiana plantation in 1905 and remained a resident of New Orleans throughout his life. His 1948 book *Ghosts Along the Mississippi*, a portrayal of architectural survivals and relics of the Old South, was extraordinarily successful, and caught the attention of both Minor and Michael. Letters these two exchanged in 1966 abound with descriptions of Laughlin's eccentricities, even as they pushed toward the creation of an exhibition and monograph devoted to the photographer.

On his first visit to Laughlin's apartment in a rundown building on New Orleans's Vieux Carré, Michael found himself in a gray room lit by a single yellow bulb, covered with dust, and surrounded by walls and stacks of books—more than fifteen thousand of them. Laughlin was, Michael said, "certainly one of the most well-read people in the entire universe." And he clearly had his own tastes. As Michael recalled, "His refrigerator was filled with cans of Spam, like some creation of Andy Warhol's. He had almost no money, and traveled by bus to work in a darkroom in the house of a wealthy friend, returning with the prints in a tray. He was an absolute master printer, although he used Sears & Roebuck varnish on them, which cracked horribly." The prints, which Michael was there to see, were brought out parsimoniously, because the artist wished to discuss each one—endlessly. The place, circumstances of the making, the atmosphere . . . Michael would leave the room for a break only to return and discover that Laughlin had gone on talking, oblivious to his absence. And so it went over several years, until finally the Laughlin exhibition was mounted in Philadelphia and the Aperture monograph appeared in 1973.

Clarence John Laughlin: The Personal Eye would remain one of Michael's favorite books not only because of the imagery, but also because of Jonathan Williams's accompanying text, which characterizes Laughlin as "all phantasmagoria and gumbo—Archimboldo, 'The Invasion of the Body Snatchers,' Grandville, Belle Grove Plantation, the Wizard of Oz, and skillet cornbread . . . *Bizarrerie*." The essay reads like a jukebox blaring a pastiche of jazz riffs, Cajun jigs, Eric Satie, and through it the rich, tempestuous sense of the artist emerges. Williams's text was that rarity of Newhall's ideal: merging word and image into a new medium.

Michael had embarked on a search for the images and artists, both past and present, that he believed needed to be brought before the public. There continued the endless pressure to raise funds and subventions, and to work with the myriad details and decisions of design and production. The Laughlin experience illustrates the enormous consumption of time each project required. Michael needed editorial help, and he also began to recognize that it was time for fresh perspectives. Although he chafed under the criticisms, Aperture was viewed by many as a publishing house limited to formal, classical, and above all "mystical" and "artistic" imagery deriving from the ascetic aesthetics of Stieglitz, Minor, and Michael himself. Aperture's most severe critics called it "cultish" and "incestuous."

Carole Kismaric had been one of the outstanding visual editors at Time-Life Books, involved with popular series on science, human behavior, and American history. She also was part of the editorial team that created the company's influential "Photography" series. Researched, written, edited, and designed to the highest standards, the publications of Time-Life Books nonetheless offered little creative scope to the individual, and when Michael invited her to work at Aperture, Carole was ready for a change.

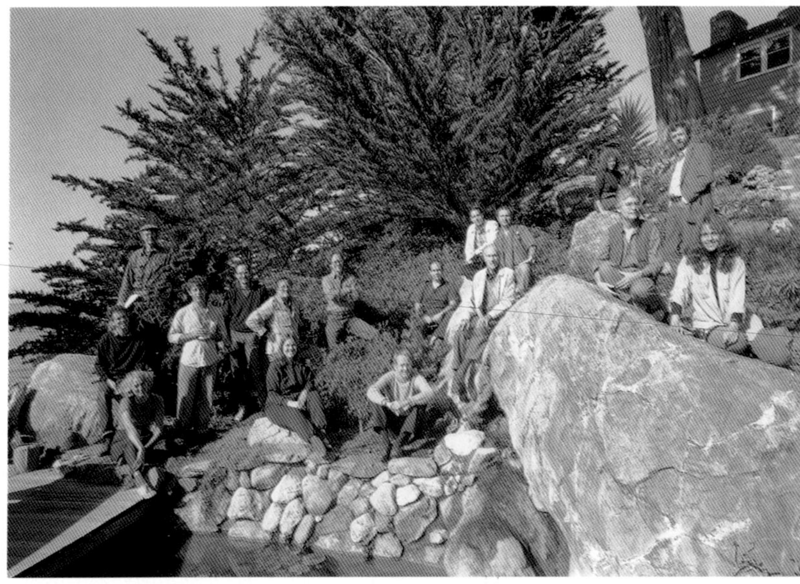

Participants of "Photography 1982," a symposium sponsored by Aperture at the Esalen Institute, Big Sur, California. Photograph by John Grimes.

"I had thought little about photography as art," Carole recalled years later. "I understood it as a powerful communicating device that had changed, and was continuing to change, our societies and our culture. But I thought, 'I've spent years communicating to millions of people with the books Time-Life was doing. Why not communicate to a few thousand about things of quality, of intellectual challenge?' I was supposed to stir things up."

She was also supposed to bring a much-needed degree of professionalism into the editorial process, which Michael freely admitted he lacked. One of her early tasks was sifting through the backlog of submissions, and one group of photographs in particular led to her own vision of what photography, and Aperture, could accomplish.

What I remember most profoundly is looking at this one portfolio of Jerome Liebling's photographs of cadavers and starting to cry. I was so *present* to the fragility of those cadavers; they were truly beautiful, and most people could not bear to look at beauty penetrating into this dimension of truth. . . . What I care about in photography is that it shows me something I've never seen before, that it documents our world and our experience of the world. But I've also been interested in the crossover—how the documentary experience extends in other dimensions of experience.

Aperture had never published anything like Liebling's cadavers. That singular experience enabled Kismaric and Hoffman, despite their differing approaches to the medium, to discover what Proust called the "consanguinity of spirit," which lets even the most opposite characters transcend differences. And Carole and Michael were indeed opposite characters, a study in complementary contrasts.

Michael was barely of medium height, with black hair and dark eyes, and rather stocky. He was extremely energetic and physically strong—ever burdened with tote bags and briefcases full of Aperture publications, maquettes of prospective books, and project proposals. He was always on the lookout for a deal. Carole was tall, slender, extremely elegant and gracious. They almost naturally fell into good cop/bad cop relationships with artists and writers. Michael could be a witty and utterly engaging conversationalist—but he also had a quicksilver temper and an amazing range of histrionic effects, from sweetly cheerful to full-fledged tantrum. Carole was invariably civil, simultaneously sympathetic and empathic. She could charm the birds down from the trees; Michael often sent them fleeing for cover.

Carole brought from Time-Life an extensive network of contacts among photographers and writers. She infused the journal with images and ideas relating to political and social issues that had been largely missing in *Aperture* since the death of Dorothea Lange in 1965. She also tapped into a new generation of documentarians with a grasp of deeper currents of the culture ranging from the exotic to the mundane: Danny Lyon's Hell's Angels and Texas convicts, Chauncey Hare's technologically alienated home life, Larry Fink's social gatherings, Garry Winogrand's and Tod Papageorge's street scenes found places alongside images by Atget, Strand, and Bullock.

From this point, at Carole's instigation, *Aperture* subscribers would begin to have an entirely new experience—and among their numbers were those who, accustomed to unperturbing images of classical and romantic beauty, were not pleased. The Liebling cadavers, the homoerotic interpretation of Yukio Mishima by the Japanese master Eikoh Hosoe, and in particular the searing war images by Don McCullin brought storms of protests and subscription cancellations. Unexpectedly, the numbers of cancellations were balanced by a newly awakened interest among a more venturesome audience. The journal continued, slowly, to grow.

Confident in Carole's stewardship of the journal and book projects, Michael was free to pursue his dream of transforming Aperture into a community of like-minded souls who would share his quest for "life beyond the ordinary." Naming it the Silver Mountain Foundation, he envisioned a residential environment where individual creativity would be nurtured by communal living. His intangible hopes for Silver Mountain never materialized, but his expanded vision led to tangible results. It was during these few years in the early 1980s that Aperture created the Paul Strand Archive, the Photogravure Workshop, the Internship Program, and a gallery to exhibit the prints of published photographers. And Aperture, now officially a foundation, finally found a permanent home.

Housed in the five-story building that Shirley Burden had purchased for Aperture at 20 East 23rd Street in Manhattan, the new headquarters brought to an end Aperture's thirty-year wanderings. The second-floor gallery was a long-cherished dream of Burden's, but it wasn't the only legacy of this member of a collateral branch of the legendary Vanderbilts. He was an accomplished artist in his own right. Following a brief career as a filmmaker in Hollywood, Burden had devoted himself to photography after World War II. He was a deeply religious man who brought a gentle vision to his subjects. He was also shy and unassertive, and his books were published with Aperture only at Michael's insistence.

The late 1970s and early 1980s were a crucial period because the long struggle to have the medium recognized as an art form was being resolved. This was only in part due to the accomplishments of the artists. Collectors, connoisseurs, galleries, and museums were creating a new market. Prices were rising for the works of dead masters, in particular, but also for critically recognized members of the new generation. "Art photography" was beginning to be profitable. Still, a new art form—and photography had existed for only a few generations—remains a novelty until it is firmly placed within a tradition. It needs a history.

In this connection, Michael was undertaking seminal monographs of the medium's past. One of the most triumphant resulted from a visit to New York in 1980 by Mark Haworth-Booth, then at the beginning of his long career as curator of photographs at the Victoria & Albert Museum in London. He brought with him a proposal for an ambitious project, *The Golden Age of British Photography: 1839–1900*. Haworth-Booth's selection for the book ranged from Chauncey Hare Townshend, William Fox Talbot, and Roger Fenton through the early artistic ventures of Oscar Rejlander; the Victorian portraiture of Julia Margaret Cameron and Lewis Carroll, down to the early struggle for photography as an art waged

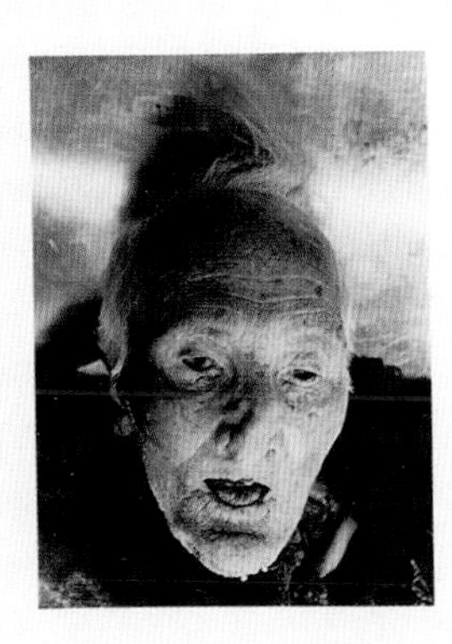
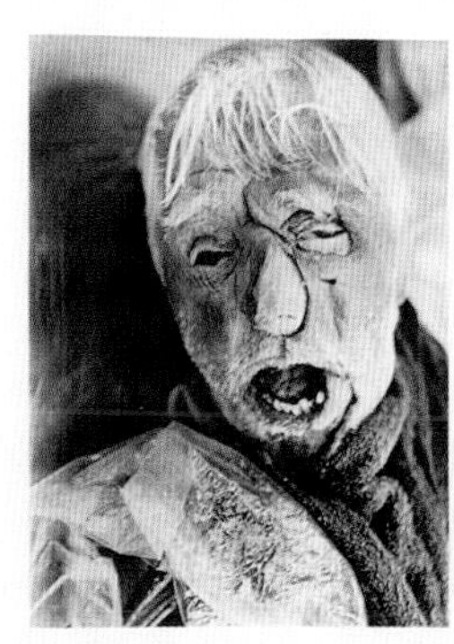

The Liebling cadavers, Eikoh Hosoe's homoerotic work, and in particular the war images by Don McCullin brought storms of protest and subscription cancellations. Unexpectedly, the numbers of cancellations were balanced by a newly awakened interest among a more venturesome audience.

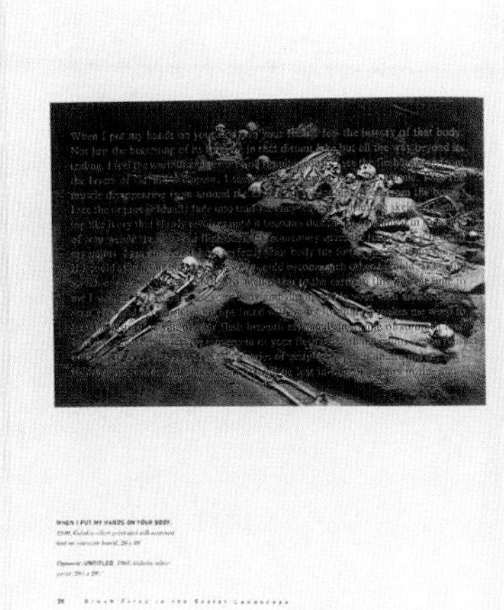
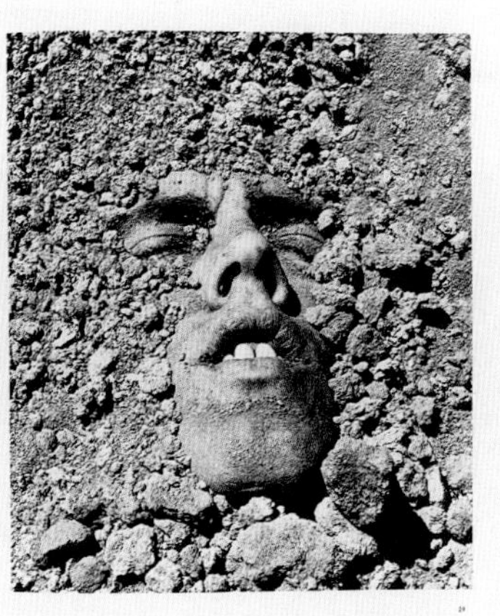
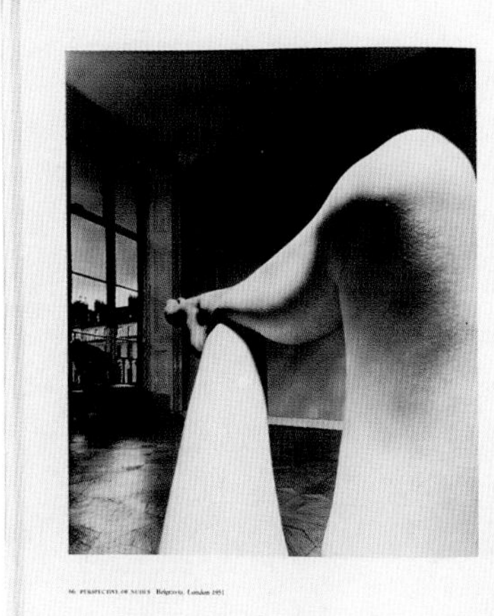
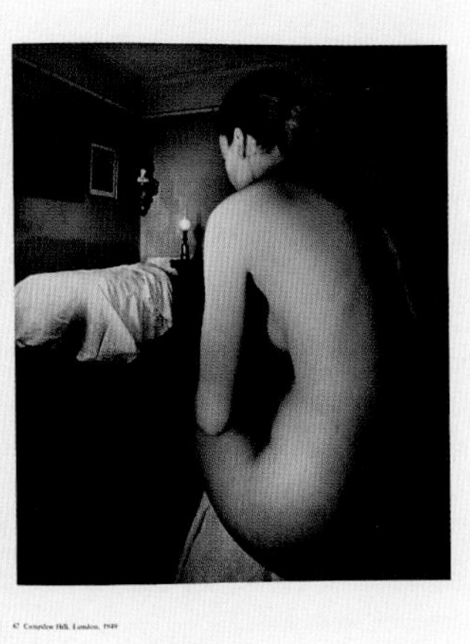

TOP: *Aperture* 79, 1977, pages 72–73: photographs by Jerome Liebling.
MIDDLE: *Aperture* 137, 1994, pages 28–29: photographs by David Wojnarowicz.
BOTTOM: *Aperture* 99, 1985, pages 66–67: photographs by Bill Brandt.

by P. H. Emerson. *The Golden Age* was more than a revelation of overlooked photographers; it was also a major addition to critical history. Haworth-Booth, who also wrote the book's introductory essay, would go on to become one of Aperture's most prolific contributors.

Michael's understanding of the need for a historic tradition also found expression in elegant monographs devoted to the studies of cathedrals by Frederick Evans; to the portraiture of North American Indians by Edward Curtis; and to the largely neglected, and perhaps greatest, twentieth-century portraitist, August Sander.

Equally important to Michael was bringing the medium's artists to a wider public through inexpensive, small-format books. A selection of Henri Cartier-Bresson's acclaimed photographs introduced the Aperture "History of Photography" series in 1976, later retitled "Masters of Photography." For the first time, audiences unable to afford Aperture's more costly monographs had access to well-rendered images by Stieglitz, Strand, Weston, Eugène Atget, André Kertész, Man Ray, and others—a total to date of eighteen volumes in the series.

In the 1970s, Aperture also made its early ventures into what had been a prohibitively expensive domain of publishing: color photography. Stephen Shore's vision of mainstream America—its seldom appreciated highways, byways, gas stations, small towns—was one of the early color efforts. This volume, *Uncommon Places*, was followed by Shore's magnificent *Gardens at Giverny: A View of Monet's World*. The search for printers capable of reproducing high-quality color, at a nonbankrupting price, had Aperture's production expert Steve Baron journeying from Hong Kong to Italy, with numerous stops in between.

Meanwhile, Kismaric's efforts with the journal led to discoveries of photographers with that most subtle of qualities: the literary sensibility. British photographer Bill Brandt revealed a gift for the *genius loci* in his studies for *Literary Britain*. And America's literary heartland, the Deep South, inspired two artists whose photography came to light almost simultaneously in Aperture publications.

One of the best-loved storytellers of the twentieth century, Eudora Welty had at the beginning of her writing career carried a camera into the homes, churches, and neighborhoods of her black friends and acquaintances in Mississippi. The subjects in Welty's photographs were treated with the same encompassing sense of kinship and warmth as they are in her short stories and novels.

William Christenberry was born in Hale County, Alabama, and his grandparents' farm bordered that of the pseudonymous "Ricketts" family, the subject of Walker Evans's and James Agee's Depression-era collaboration, *Let Us Now Praise Famous Men*. Christenberry was a lifelong fan of Agee, inspired by the author's famous supplication: "If I could do it, I would do no writing at all here. It would be photographs; the rest would be fragments of cloth, bits of cotton, lumps of earth, records of speech, pieces of wood and iron, phials of odors, plates of food and of excrement." And indeed, the photographer Christenberry made use of painting, found objects, and sculpture in his large, mysterious, sinister environmental work, "The Klan Room." The expressive range of Christenberry's talents, as well as his deep-seated dread of Klan influence in the South, were represented in resonant color reproductions in an Aperture monograph and in the journal.

The photographer whose literary gifts have most decisively influenced Aperture over the years was based in the West, near Colorado Springs. A former professor of literature, Robert Adams, and his wife Kerstin, were ardent conservationists, peace activists, and supporters of animal rights in an area where some of the most transcendent vistas of American nature were blighted by some of the worst excesses of American culture. Near his home were both a plutonium-producing nuclear-bomb factory and a nuclear power-plant; the landscape was disfigured by urban sprawl. Adams documented these blights upon land and lives. He also possessed a true landsman's poetic instinct in his photographs of pristine prairies and grasslands, and scenes evoking universally felt moments in a series called "Summer Nights." Adams's perfectly composed images demand pause and considered attention. Michael was to become one of Adams's most devoted supporters; Aperture has published no fewer than six monographs of his work, as well as portfolios in the journal. Adams also brought to the medium his gifts as a critic with two volumes of essays: *Beauty in Photography: Essays in Defense of Traditional Values* and *Why People Photograph*.

Michael once remarked, "When you look backward too much, you get turned into a pillar of salt." By 1980, he felt a need for personal renewal. Inspired in part by Dorothy Norman—who had had close personal relationships with Mahatma Gandhi and Prime Ministers Jawaharlal Nehru and Indira Gandhi—Michael set out for a prolonged pilgrimage to India. His only companion was the Temple edition of Dante's *Divine Comedy*. His travels and the poem worked their wonders, each with rippling implications for Aperture in the ensuing years.

The most significant event in Michael's Indian journey was the first of many encounters with the Dalai Lama, beginning a close association that would subsequently lead to Aperture's publications *Tibet: The Sacred Realm, Photographs 1880–1950* and *Tibet Since 1950: Silence, Prison, or Exile*, two historic monographs documenting life before and after the Chinese invasion and occupation. *Journey to Enlightenment*, with photographs and narrative by Matthieu Ricard, celebrates the life and teachings of the Tibetan spiritual master Khyentse Rinpoche. Other volumes devoted to the photographers and imagery of India became staples of the

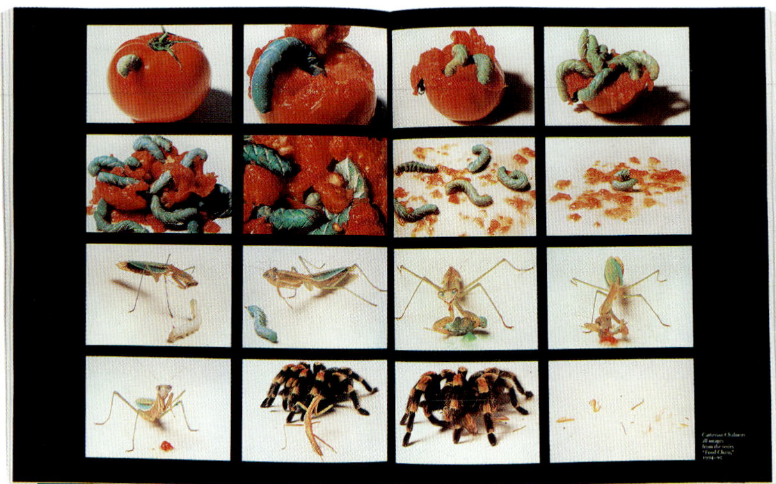

"I've felt almost a sense of obeisance to these ghosts, these spirits that I've had the privilege of being related to, a responsibility in my act of service to provide for a continuation of their qualities, of their ideas."

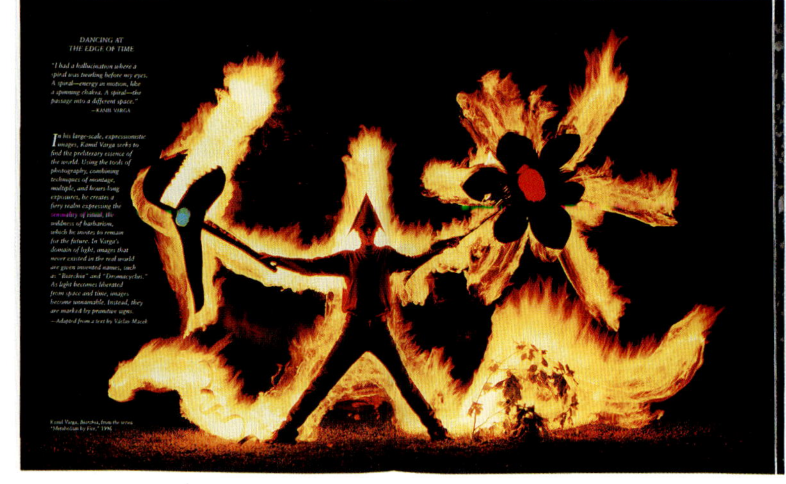

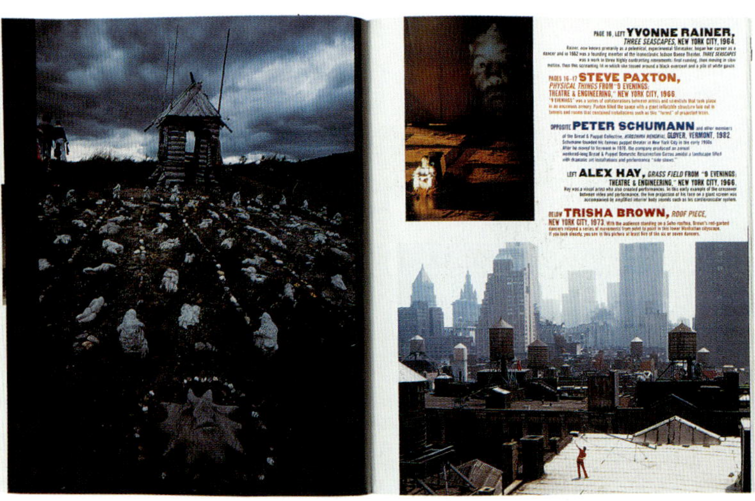

TOP: ***Aperture*** **143, 1996, pages 32–33: photographs by Catherine Chalmers.**
MIDDLE: ***Aperture*** **152, 1998, pages 50–51: photograph by Kamil Varga.**
BOTTOM: ***Aperture*** **164, 2001, pages 18–19: photographs by Peter Moore.**

Aperture library. Michael, who felt he had found a second home on the subcontinent, seldom let a year pass without visiting it.

Michael had read Dante at college, but the long hours spent in the poet's company during his first Indian journey led to a lifelong study. New interns at Aperture to whom he gave copies were shocked to find that reading the epic seemed to be a prerequisite for a successful apprenticeship (in later years, Michael would add the gargantuan *Mahabharata* to the list of required reading). As he once remarked to Robert Adams, "I go back to Dante because he seems to offer a key in the search from darkness to light."

His own energies refreshed, Michael felt that Aperture, too, was ready for revitalization. He and Kismaric believed that there was a need for more meaningful dialogue among the arts, and together they organized an extraordinary conference of poets, performance artists, graphic artists, curators, writers, and critics, along with photographers William Christenberry, Ray Metzker, Linda O'Connor, Frank Gohlke, Sigfried Halus, and Raymond Depardon. The group convened at the Esalen Institute on California's Big Sur coast in November 1982. In an ensuing manifesto, they recognized a "growing climate of public restraint, the complexities and dangers of the age, the prevalence of mechanization and dehumanizing technique, [which] encroach upon the individual, the society, and the human adventure itself." Within this context, the group statement continued, "an artist is an awakener: to the surrounding world, to dimensions of the human spirit, and, when necessary, to the need for action."

In subtle ways, the conference guided Aperture's direction during the remainder of the decade and beyond. After Kismaric left Aperture in 1984 to pursue new creative challenges, a soft-spoken, dynamic young Englishman, Mark Holborn, was named editor. Michael enabled Holborn to pursue his passion for Japanese art and photography in three unprecedented publications, *Black Sun: The Eyes of Four*, featuring the photographs of Masahisa Fukase, Eikoh Hosoe, Daido Moriyama, and Shomei Tomatsu; *BA.RA.KEI.: Ordeal by Roses*, Hosoe's controversial tribute to Mishima; and a volume devoted to the fantastic theater of Butoh. Marilyn Bridges's amazing aerial studies of ancient earthworks were featured in the monograph *Markings*. Holborn also helped shepherd Nan Goldin's *The Ballad of Sexual Dependency* through publication even as she brought its source, an uproarious, emotional slide show, with commentary, into Aperture's Burden Gallery.

After Kismaric and Holborn, there was a considerable turnover of Aperture editors and guest editors: a succession of highly talented individuals, each of whom left their mark. These included Charles Hagen, Steve Dietz, Nan Richardson, Lawrence Frascella, Rebecca Busselle, Peggy Roalf, Michael Sand, and Andrew Wilkes. Under their helms through most of the 1980s, and then into the 1990s, the journal shifted to thematic approaches. These issues were devoted to such subjects as the relationship of photography and drawing, including a number of rapid-fire sketches by Cartier-Bresson; to technology and transformation; to connoisseurs and collecting; to fashion photography; and to varieties and experiments in communal living.

It was during this period that *Aperture* also became a truly international journal of photography. Michael's powers of persuasion had reached new heights when he wrested from the Communist bureaucracy in Czechoslovakia the masterpieces by a long-overlooked genius, Josef Sudek, for the exhibition and monograph *Poet of Prague*. The most influential and innovative photographers would be represented in issues of the journal devoted to France, Italy, Germany, Japan, Cuba, and Spain. India was a continuing subject of Aperture monographs, including the mammoth volume in tribute to the country's golden anniversary of freedom from colonial rule, *India: A Celebration of Independence*.

Editorial stability was achieved—and editorial content grew yet more adventurous—when Melissa Harris, who had first joined Aperture in 1989, took over the journal, as well as selected book projects, in 1992. Melissa brought to the work a unique background that ranged from teaching multimedia collaboration at Yale University (her alma mater) to her editing job at *Artforum* magazine. Along with her breadth of interests in the arts, she also brought to Aperture deeply felt concerns about political, social, and moral issues. Harris challenged complacency and sanctimony as no previous editor had done. Early on, censorial objections were raised—and dismissed—by her fearless compilation issue/monograph "The Body in Question." Later, Melissa brought to publication Eugene Richards's dark yet compassionate chronicle of drug addition; Sally Mann's poignant portrayals of childhood; Mary Ellen Marks's edgy photo-essays; Donna Ferrato's exposé of domestic violence; Letizia Battaglia's probing of mafioso evil rife in Sicily; the chaotic dynamism of bordertown life in *Juárez: The Laboratory of Our Future*, a photographic anthology with texts by Charles Bowden, Eduardo Galeano, and Noam Chomsky; and an issue and monograph devoted to the life, work, and terrible affliction from AIDS of the artist David Wojnarowicz. A champion of the dauntless eye, Harris also fostered definitive monographs on geniuses of other media, including dancer-choreographer Merce Cunningham and the controversial, worthy heir of Italian *commedia dell'arte*, Nobel laureate Dario Fo.

For editors, curators, and spectators, the power of fine photography is in large measure the power of surprise: "What I have never seen before," as Carole Kismaric put it. This has nothing to do with the pursuit of faddish "newness" or of shock value for its own sake—all too often the purview of "art biz" in modish galleries. Surprise, as John Szarkowski has pointed out, is primarily about enlargement of vision and experience.

Space allows mention of only a few instances of such surprises in recent Aperture history. Among them: Young British photographer Nick Waplington, whose color profiles of working-class families in Nottingham unveiled a new dimension of intimate theater in documentary photography. Robert Glenn Ketchum's color landscapes of the Tongass helped save the last North American rainforest from untrammeled development. Michiko Kon's constructions from the wares of fishmongers of Japan brought new wit to still lifes. Mimmo Jodice's lens refocused the mythical impressions of ancient Mediterranean civilization and the romance of present-day Paris. Joel-Peter Witkin's comic-grotesque tableaux, which have been featured in the magazine, transmogrified studio photography. Graciela Iturbide unveiled dreamlike encounters with the commonplaces of Mexican life. And Neil Folberg, in *Celestial Nights*, created new thresholds of mystical contemplation.

And of the wordsmiths' contributions. . . . Arthur Miller on his wife Inge Morath's photography; Czeslaw Milosz on Czech photographer Josef Koudelka; Larry McMurtry on the rodeo scenarios of Louise Serpa; Adam Gopnik on Parisian life and times. There were the self-scripted playlets of Duane Michals, the self-captioned album of Allen Ginsberg. Writers who expanded the encounter with photographic experience notably included Szarkowski, John Berger, Susan Sontag, and Andy Grundberg. Insights from kindred media were offered up by David Byrne, Karen Finley, and John Waters. Acclaimed literary figures include Annie Proulx, Paul Bowles, Reynolds Price, Marguerite Duras, and V. S. Naipaul. And finally, there have popped up surprising contributors across a spectrum from Muhammad Ali to Aung San Suu Kyi.

Aperture's list of artists and writers is as varied and distinguished as contemporary world culture has to offer. These brief mentions are a fraction of the hundreds who have appeared in the journal and monographs. Such a plethora of omissions!

With the fiftieth anniversary approaching, Michael reflected on his own experience with Aperture as what he called the "evolution of an ideal." It is an ideal never articulated to anyone's intellectual satisfaction, but manifests in the artists and their work.

Evolution is a process of increase: of numbers, of complexity, of diversity. Evolution, in a word, is about *more*. To understand its workings, especially in terms of something as ambiguous as an ideal, it may be helpful to trace a lineage: in this instance, from the photo-reportage of Aperture's activist-founder Dorothea Lange, to photography's preeminent turn-of-the-twenty-first-century chronicler, Brazilian Sebastião Salgado.

The parallels are obvious. Both Lange and Salgado have recorded the lives of workers, their families, and displacing forces beyond their control. Both are artists of the highest order, even as they

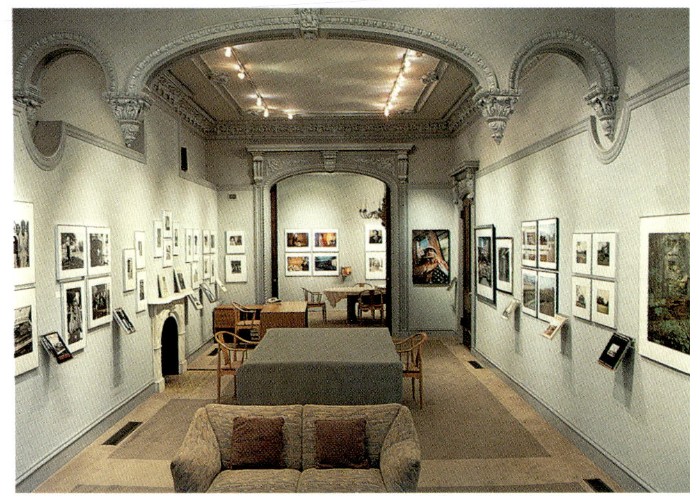

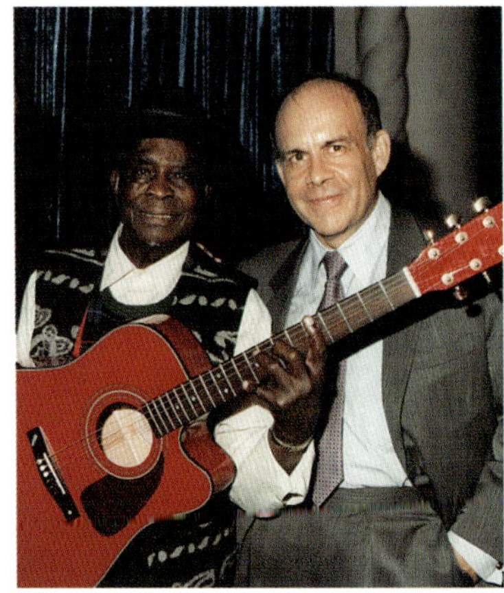

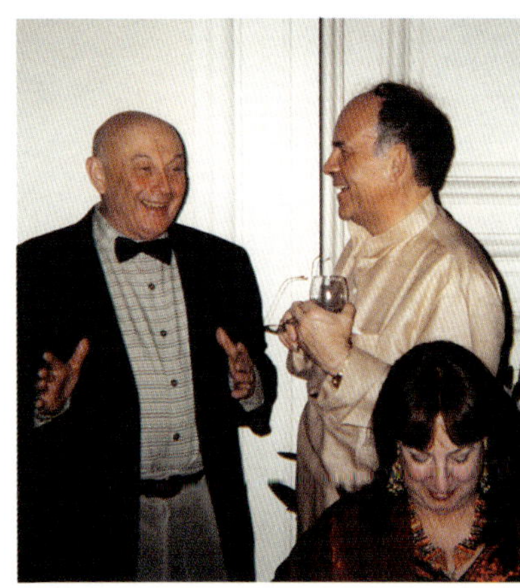

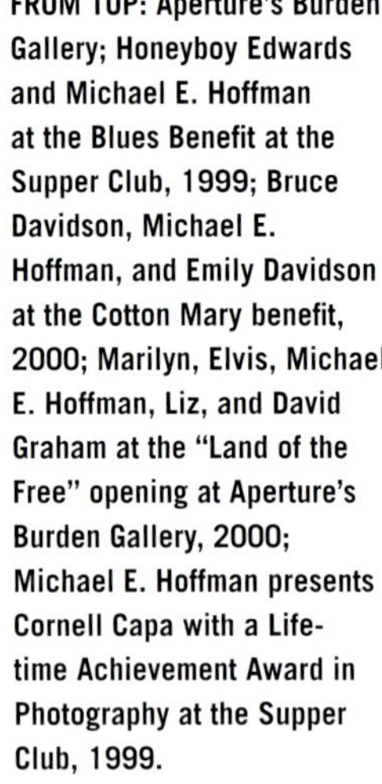

FROM TOP: Aperture's Burden Gallery; Honeyboy Edwards and Michael E. Hoffman at the Blues Benefit at the Supper Club, 1999; Bruce Davidson, Michael E. Hoffman, and Emily Davidson at the Cotton Mary benefit, 2000; Marilyn, Elvis, Michael E. Hoffman, Liz, and David Graham at the "Land of the Free" opening at Aperture's Burden Gallery, 2000; Michael E. Hoffman presents Cornell Capa with a Lifetime Achievement Award in Photography at the Supper Club, 1999.

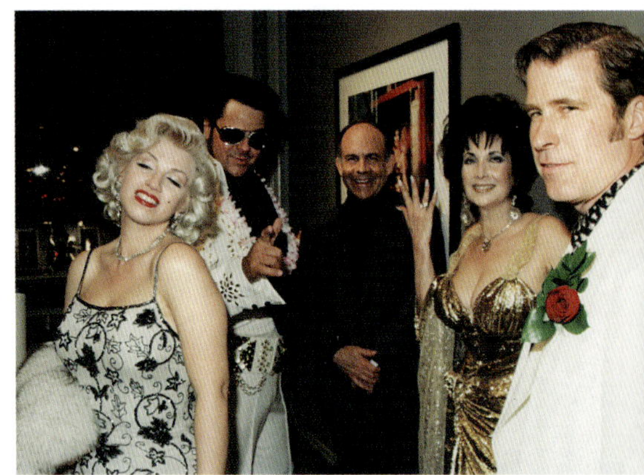

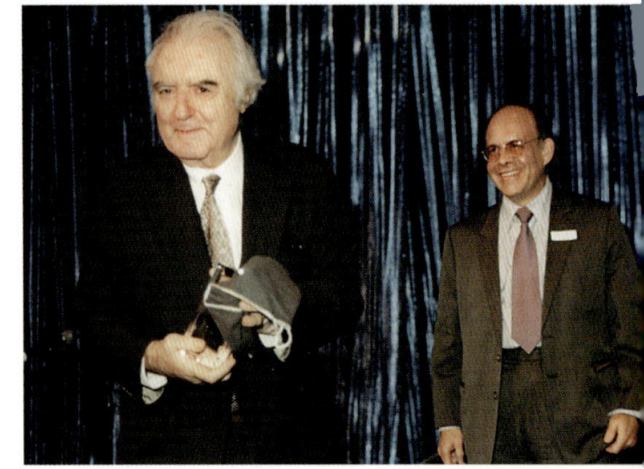

have wedded their imagery to social science; both have worked in close partnership with their spouses (for Lange, the social scientist Paul Taylor; for Salgado, the designer and manager of his projects, Lélia Wanick Salgado). Lange ranged across the United States during the peak years of the Depression; her subjects included the urban unemployed, tenant farmers, and families driven from farmlands by ecological disaster. Salgado has ranged the globe. If his subjects, like Lange's, are workers and migrants, they are far more than victims of temporary circumstance. They have been irresistibly swept up in Tolstoyan shifts of history.

For *Workers: An Archaeology of the Industrial Age*, Salgado took his cameras into the plantations, factories, fishing villages, mines, slaughterhouses, oil fields, and shipyards in nearly a score of countries. His camera vision ranged from panoramas of tens of thousands of antlike miners in the gold-ore pits of Brazil to candid eye contact with young women on the tea plantations of Central Africa. *Workers* occupied Salgado for nearly seven years. He devoted the next six years to *Migrations*, traveling to forty countries where humanity by the tens of millions has been forced into the life of refugee, exile, and migrant by war, repression, poverty, and environmental catastrophe.

Migrations was published at the beginning of the new millennium, and it was also in 2000 that Melissa Harris undertook an evolutionary leap in the content of the journal. It was in response, she wrote in an editorial, "to the shifting boundaries between media, and to the remarkable range of cross-cultural experiences that photography now addresses." With a bold transformation in design by Yolanda Cuomo, the new *Aperture* was to be increasingly diverse, with the "potential to motivate, to incite, to infuriate, to enrapture, to change minds, to change lives."

Even as Michael was reflecting upon "the evolution of an ideal," he was grumbling about his own personal evolution. Now in his fifties, he complained that he was becoming a curmudgeon. In fact, as old friends such as Haworth-Booth observed, quite the opposite was happening. Although his temper could still be mercurial, Michael was in fact becoming . . . well, almost mellowed. In 1998, Michael and Melissa were married. Two years later, Michael's first grandchild, Isabel Katharine, the daughter of Michael's son Matthew and his wife, was born in December 2000.

With the beginning of 2001, momentum gathered for the publications, exhibition, and other events marking Aperture's fiftieth anniversary. Michael and Melissa were determined that the occasion should be focused upon the future. Melissa and her staff sent out requests for new work to more than one hundred artists. The Burden Gallery was closed to make space for laying out, selecting, and sequencing images. At the Millerton complex, longtime archivist and master conservator Anthony Montoya oversaw printing and framing of selected images. Wendy Byrne was at work designing and re-designing journal issues devoted to the occasion. And throughout the New York headquarters, staff and interns were involved in fund-raising, publicity, scheduling, and the endless details of finance and bookkeeping. Meanwhile, the Foundation's trustees were keeping watch, appropriately trustful but not without some anxiety: they, too, had reputations at stake. Michael, as ever, was involved in every single detail.

Then, in mid August of 2001, Michael was taken seriously ill and admitted to New York Hospital. Throughout the following weeks, including the horrible September of the terrorist attacks on Manhattan's World Trade Center, he fought the illness. Still, at Aperture, the work continued, always awaiting Michael's approval or changes. For nearly four decades, he had decided upon the selection and sequencing of photographs, the design, the printing, the hanging of exhibitions. It was inconceivable that Michael would not be back. But on November 23, the meningitis diagnosed exhausted even his seemingly invincible life force. Michael died of complications from the disease at age fifty-nine.

It seemed unbelievable, unthinkable, then and it still does months later, at the time of this writing. That Michael died. More than the passing of a single man, it was as if a roomful of animated, irreplaceable, utterly alive people had suddenly vanished, never to return. The shock, of course, was felt deeply at Aperture, but the work went on. The fiftieth anniversary took on special meaning as a tribute to the man who had made it possible.

On a personal note, I began the interviews with Michael which were to be the basis for this essay in February 2001 at Esalen. The next sessions took place at his Shekomeko farm in late July. On our final day of discussions, relaxing in the late afternoon with Leonard Cohen's music in the background, I put to him a question I had raised often during our twenty-five years of collaboration and friendship: "Michael, why did you do this, devote your life to Aperture?" In the past, he'd shrugged it off, usually with: "I was unemployable anywhere else." On this occasion, he did answer, and spoke of Stieglitz, Minor, Ansel, Nancy, Weston, and the other Founders and shaping artists of Aperture's beginnings. He spoke carefully, as if he had been thinking about it for some time:

> I've felt almost a sense of obeisance to these ghosts, these spirits that I've had the privilege of being related to, a responsibility in my act of service to provide for a continuation of their qualities, of their ideals.

And that was what he intended for Aperture's fiftieth anniversary, to be a celebration of trust, of continuity, and above all of service to those artists who will make photography's future.

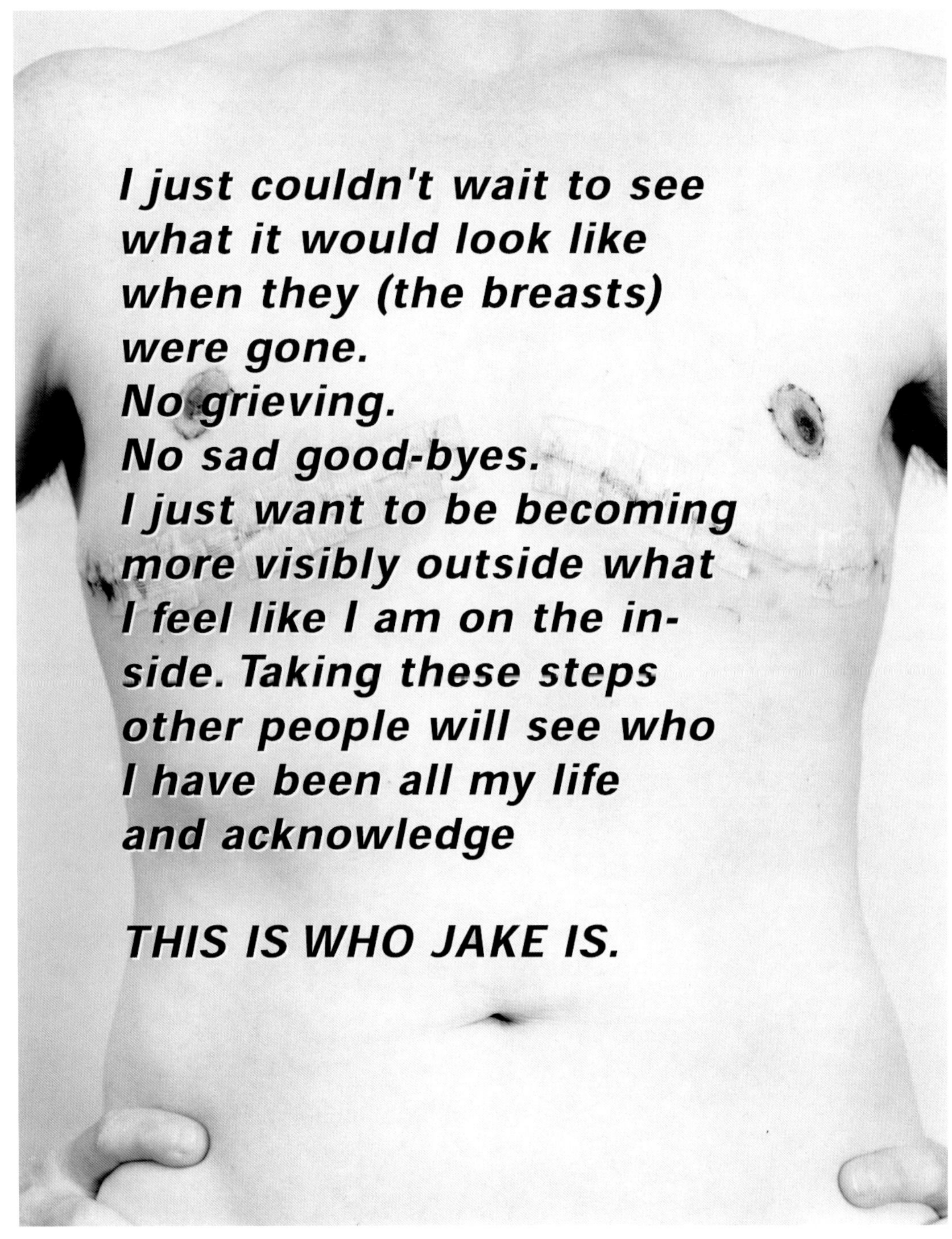

Clarissa Sligh, *I Just Couldn't Wait to See*, 2000.

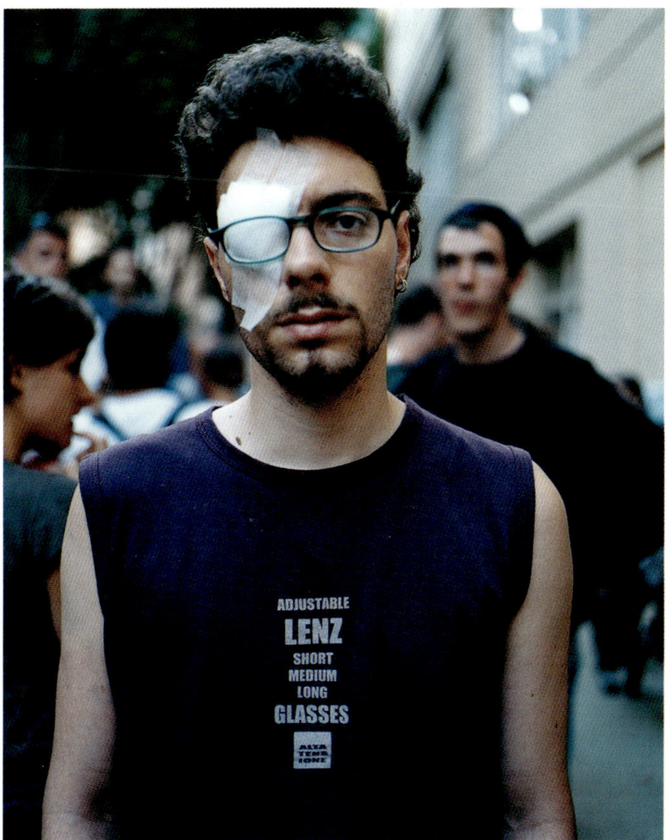

The most important reason for me to come to Genoa is to tell people on the radio what really happens here, because official media do not tell the truth. **—Man, Italy**

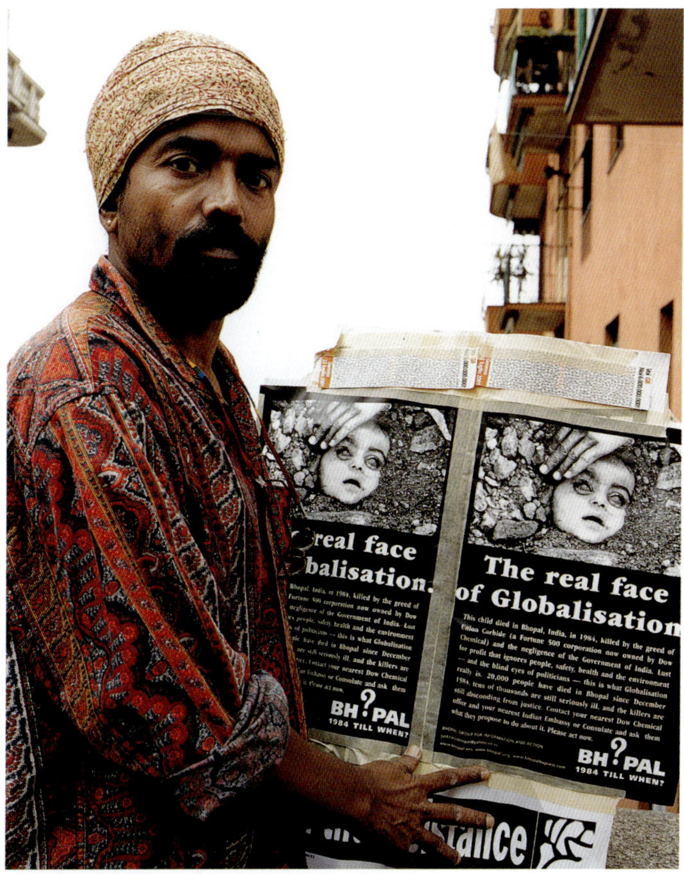

People are still dying in Bhopal. Over 20,000 have died and those born after the disaster have growth and menstrual problems.

Over 120,000 are still suffering from chronic diseases of the eyes, brain, reproductive and immune systems.

Five thousand metric tons of chemicals were dumped into the ground inside and outside the factory—it's gone into the drinking water, the only source of drinking water for ten communities.

Union Carbide evades justice and now it has sold itself to Dow Chemical. **—Man, India**

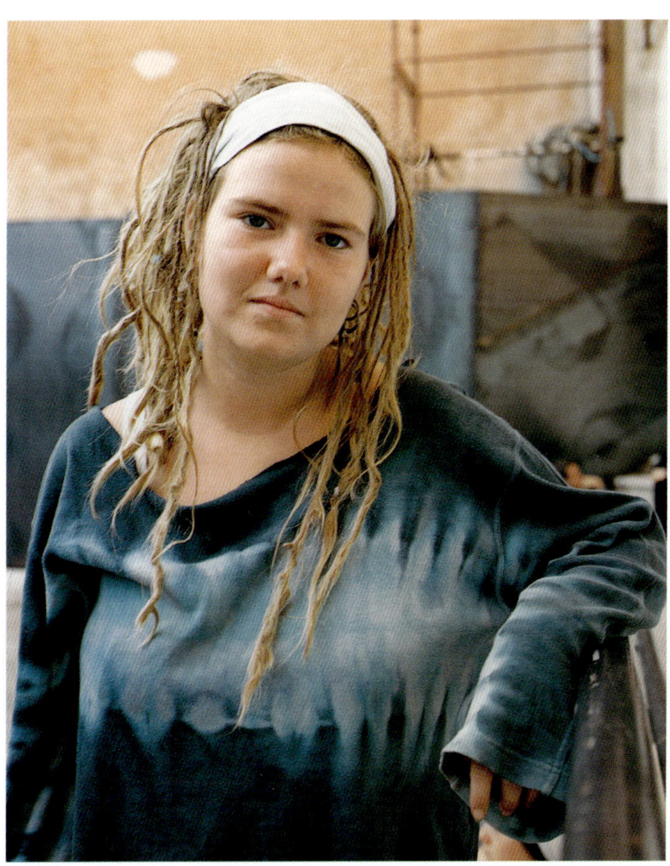

For me, ecology and equality of all peoples are the same subject.

If you have a factory and employ thousands of people under the lowest conditions or you are dumping chemicals it's the same—you have no respect for life.

The economy is ruling the world.

—Declined to reveal nationality

Joel Sternfeld, photographs July 2001, from his book *Treading on Kings: Protesting the G8 in Genoa,* 2002.

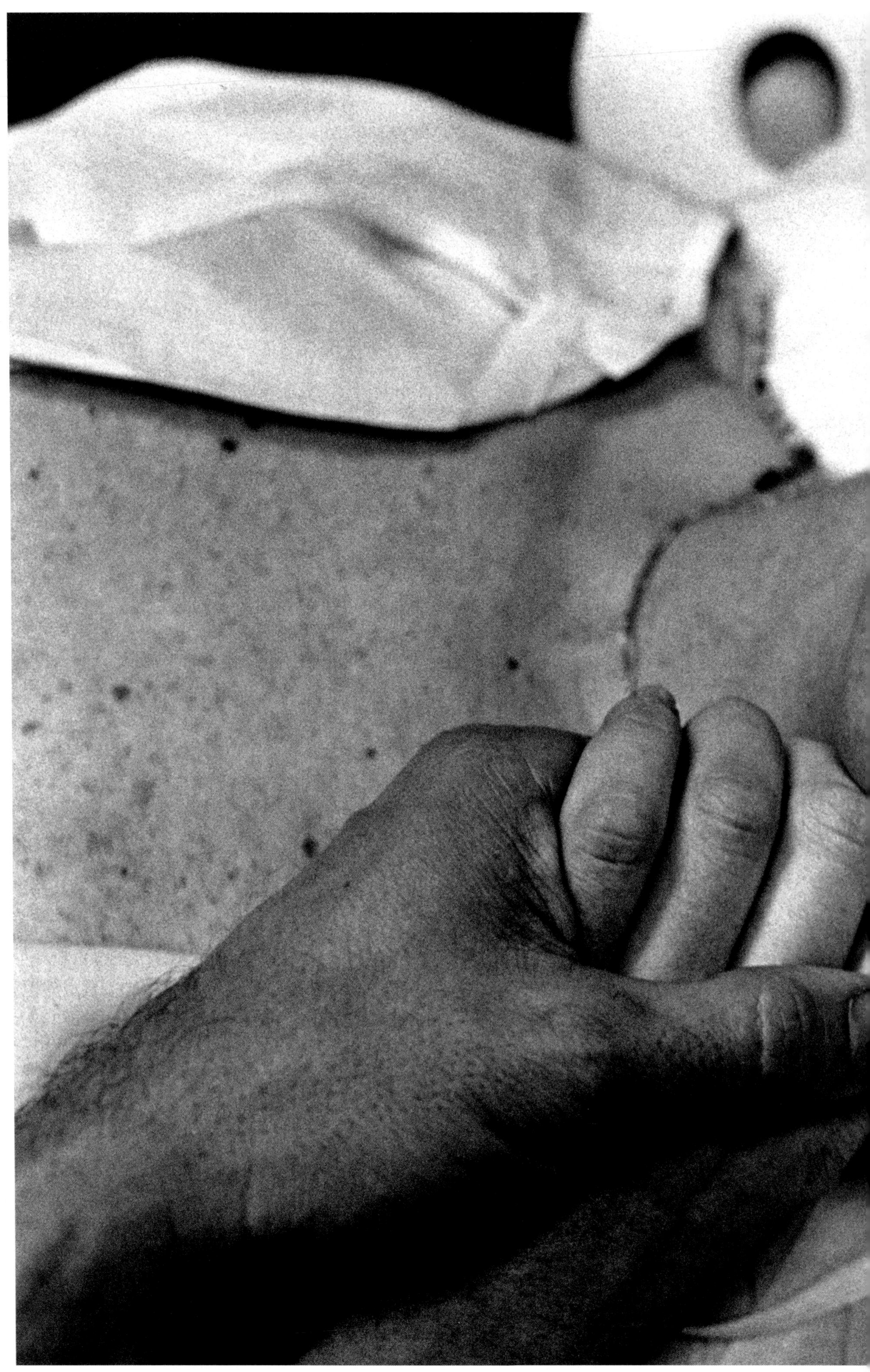

Eugene Richards, Final chemotherapy treatment, Boston, 1979; from *Exploding into Life* (Aperture, 1986).

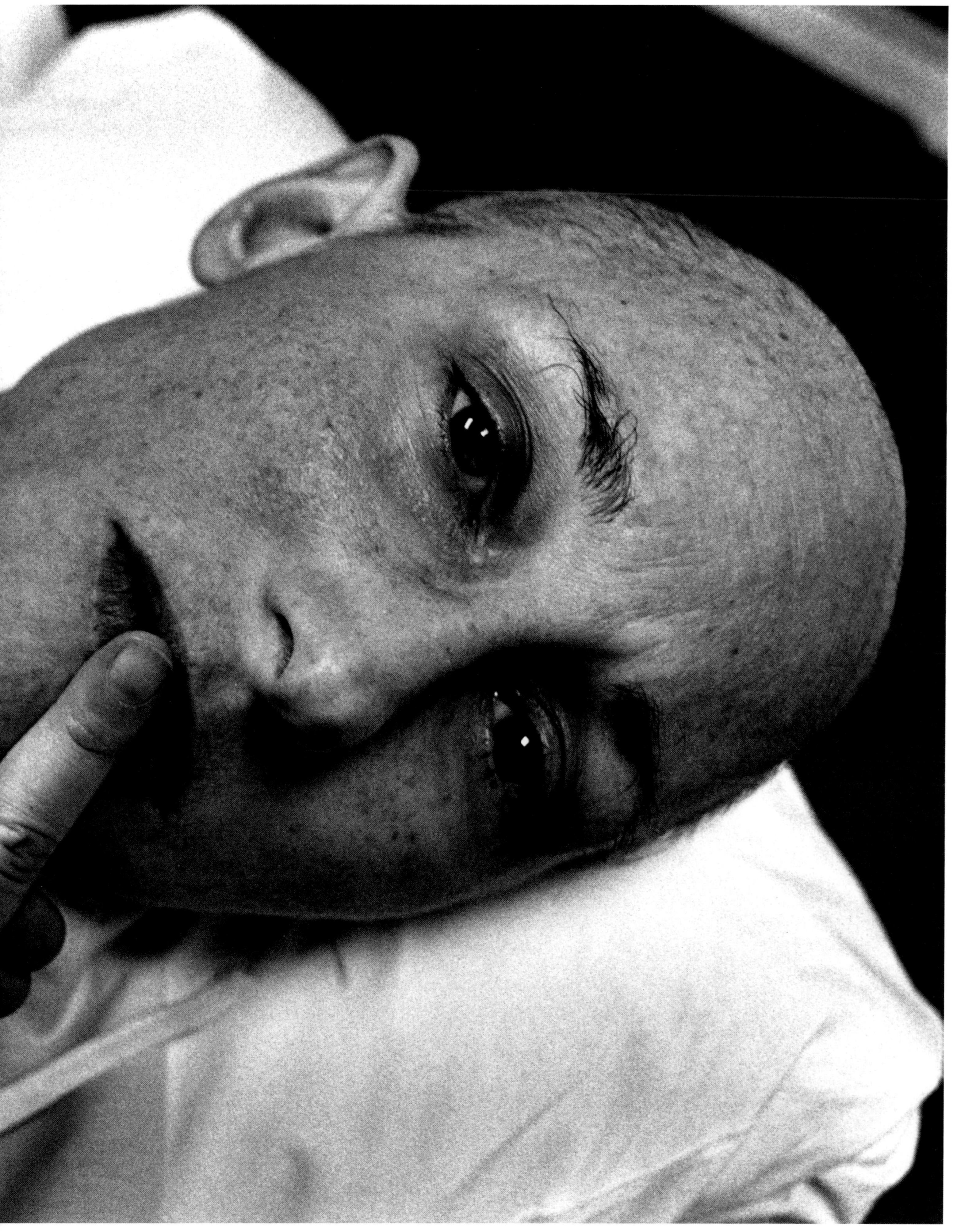

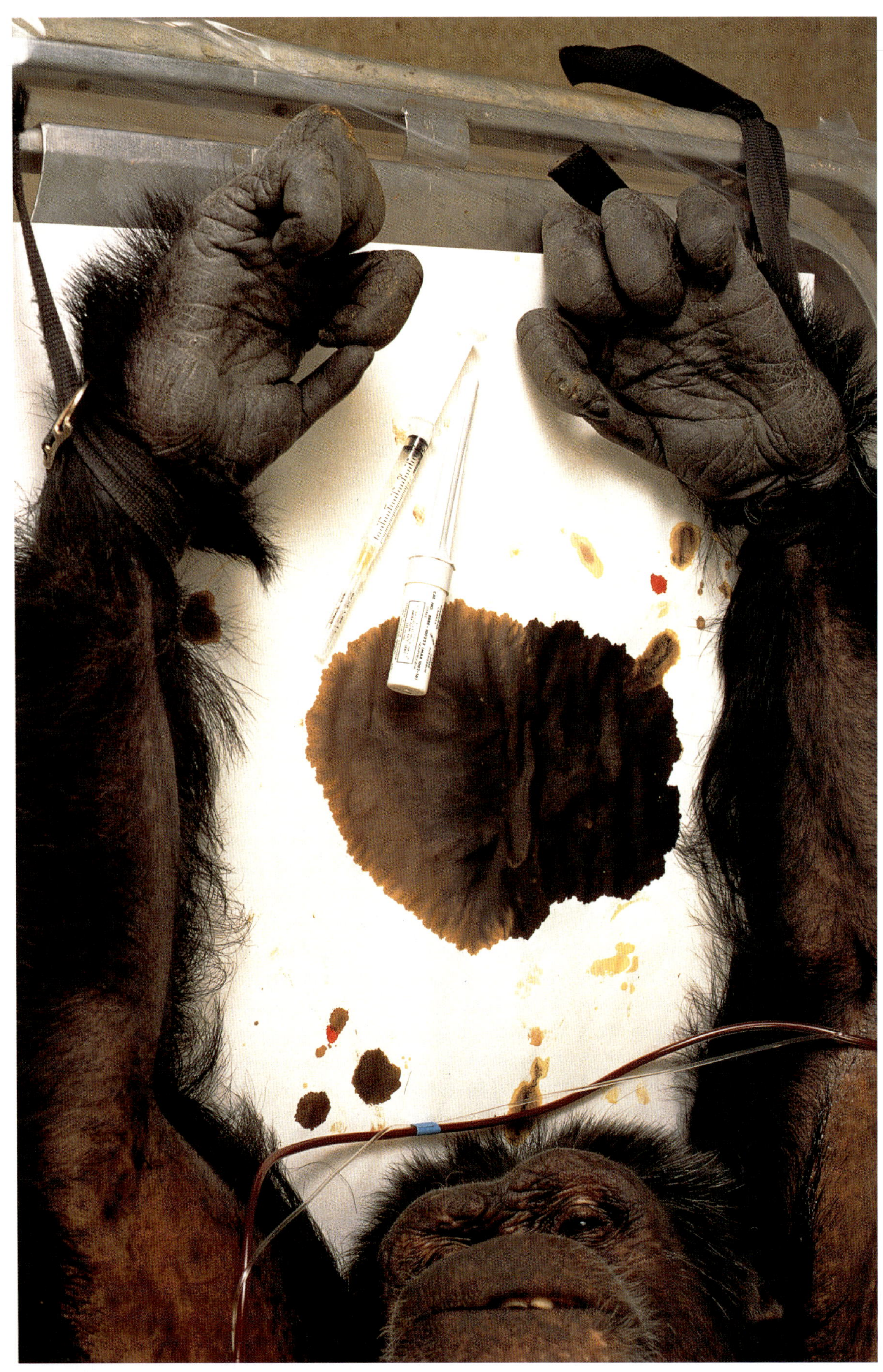

Michael Nichols, At a medical research facility in New York, blood plasma separation is performed on one of its chimps, n.d.; from *Brutal Kinship* (Aperture, 1999).

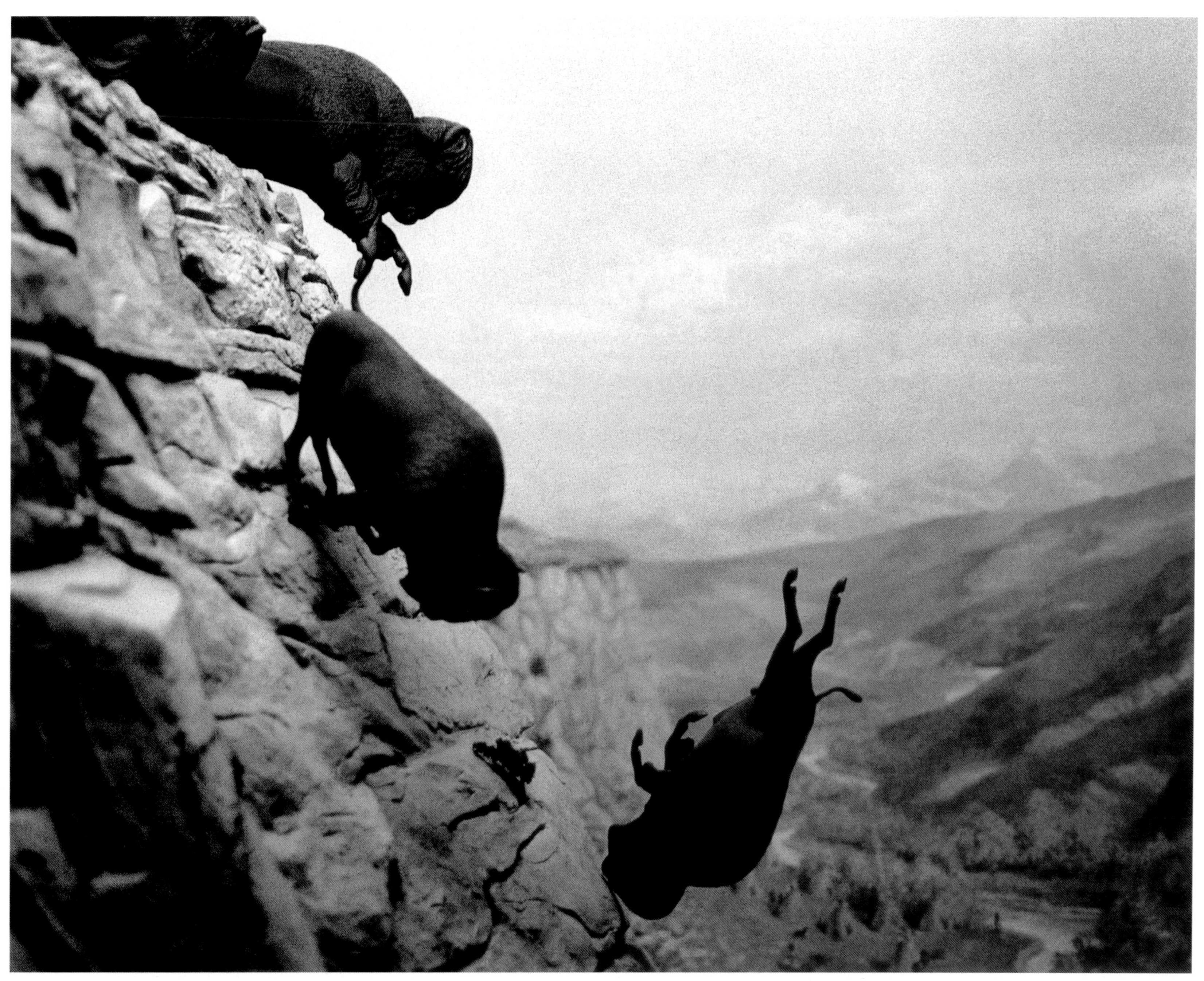

David Wojnarowicz, *Untitled*, 1988–89; from *Aperture* 137, 1994.

For work to be really alive to me, it has to engage with the world. I may talk about spiritual matters, I may talk about transcendental things. But to me, you don't have those qualities without engaging in heaven and hell, because you don't know one without the other. And I don't mean to get into a Calvinist dichotomy here, or even to suggest that I see things totally in terms of darkness and light. Not at all. It's only a metaphor for my concerns.

I think the greatest photographic work is that which has somehow engaged with the depths and the heights of the possibilities of our experience. . . .

—Michael E. Hoffman, from an interview with Robert Adams, *Aperture* 129, 1992

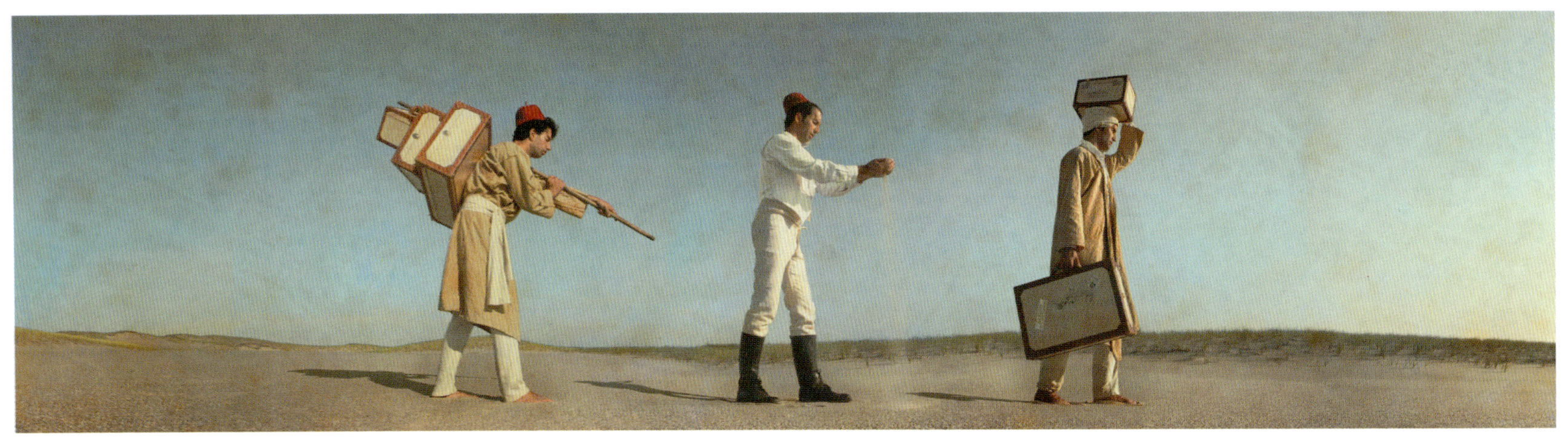

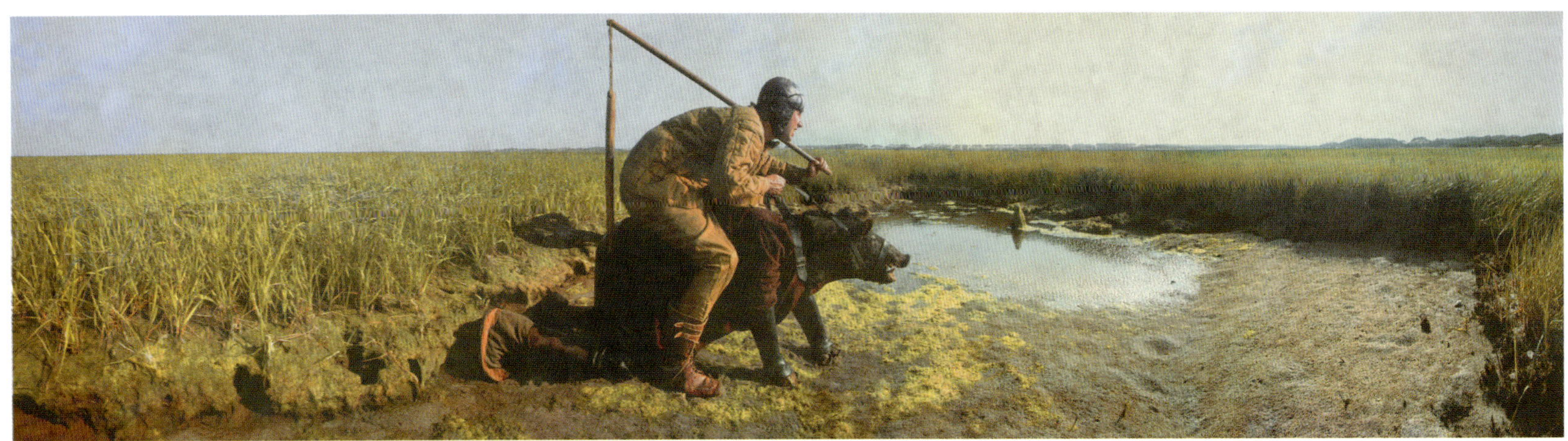

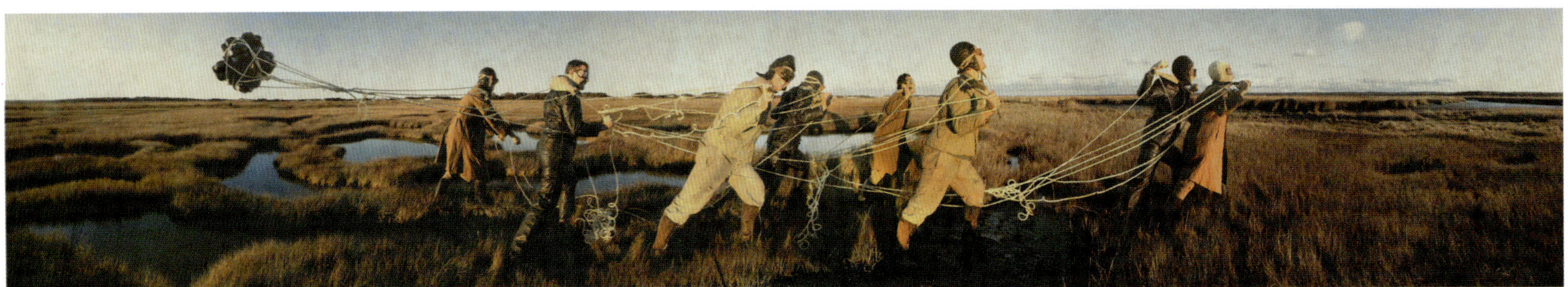

THIS PAGE: photographs by Nicholas K. Kahn and Richard S. Selesnick. TOP: *Luggage*, 2001. MIDDLE: *Rider*, 2001. BOTTOM: *The Black Sun*, 2001.

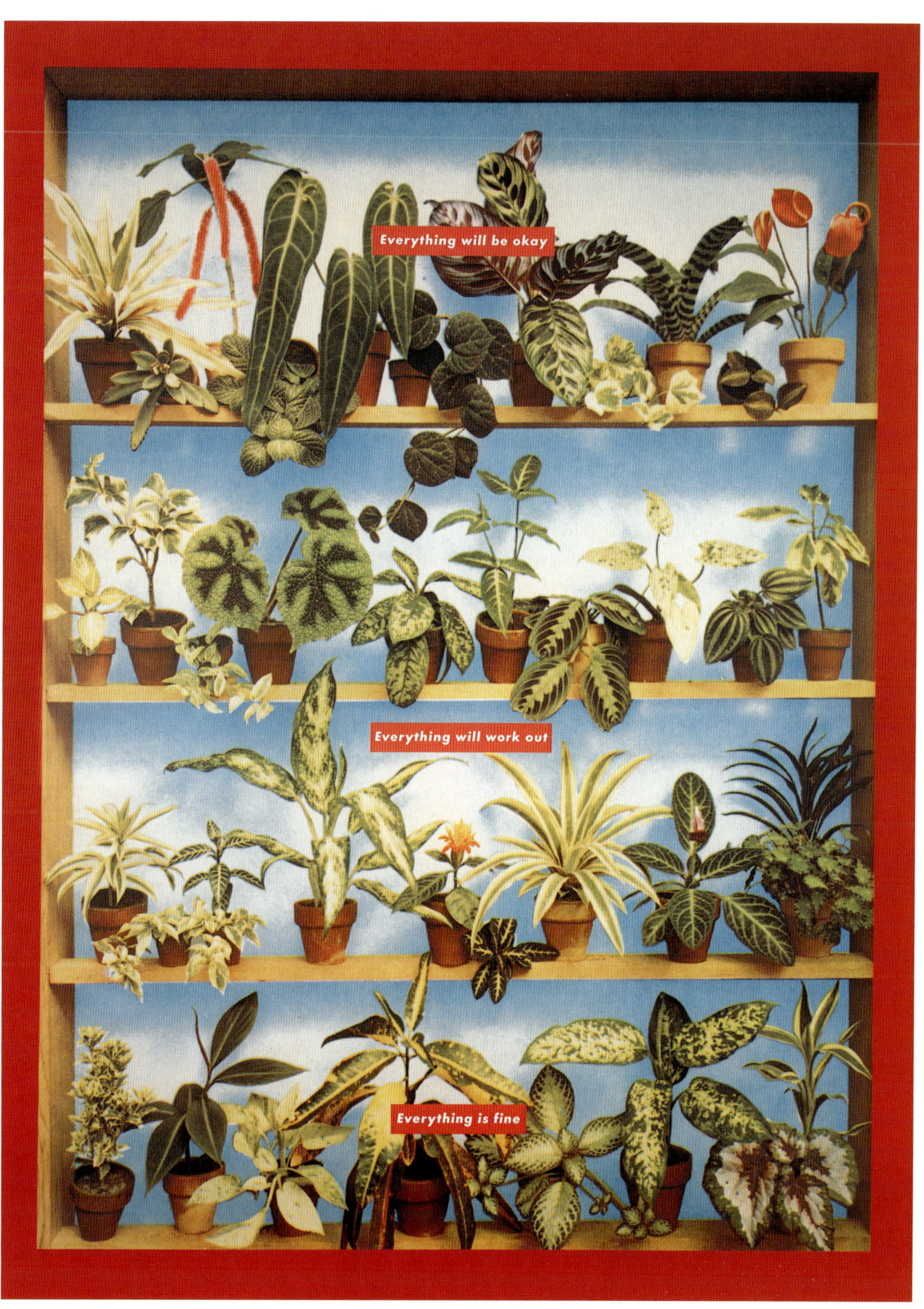

Barbara Kruger, *Untitled (Everything will be okay / Everything will work out / Everything is fine)*, 2001.

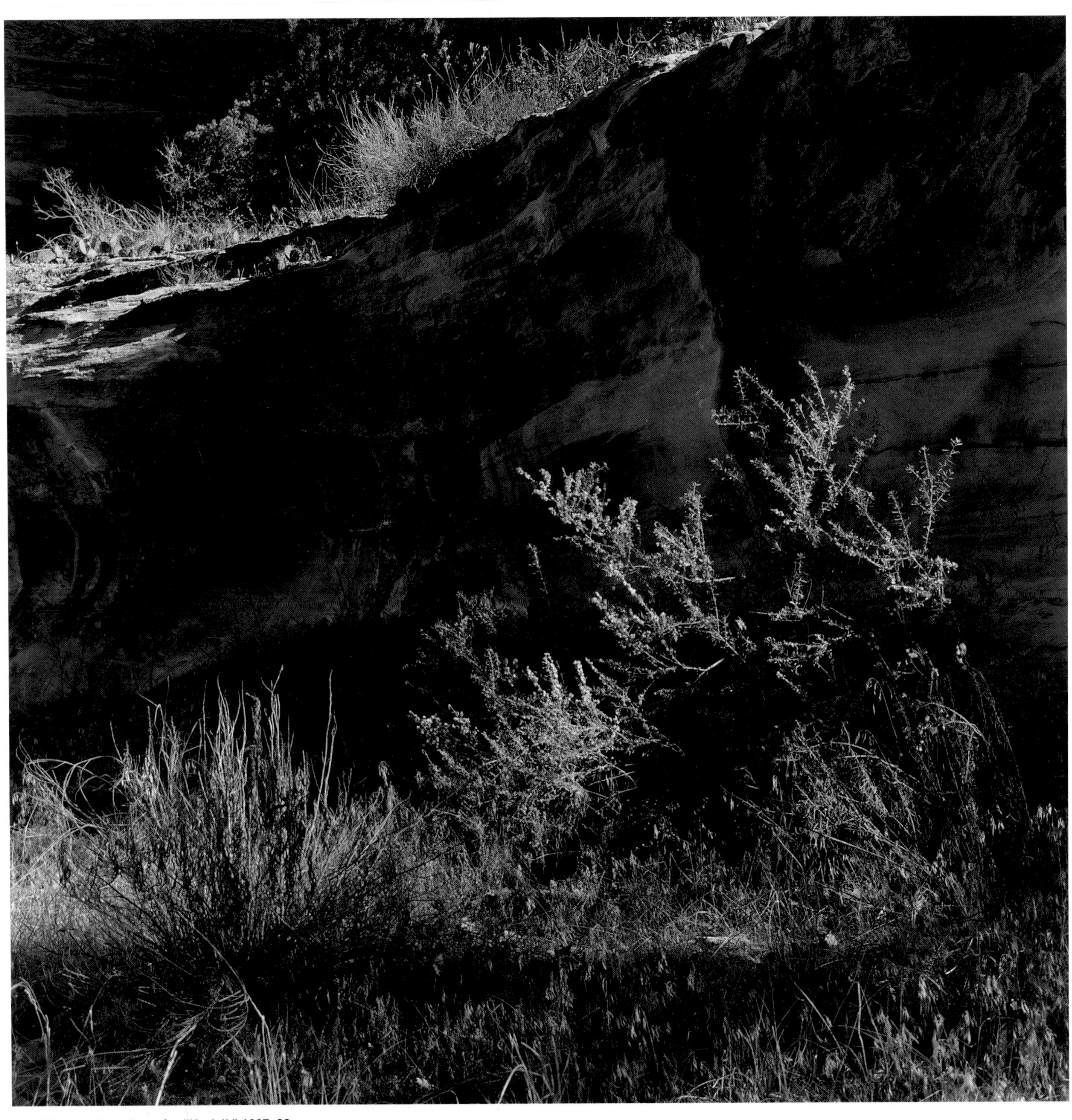

Ray K. Metzker, from the series "Moab II," 1997–98;
from *Ray K. Metzker: Landscapes* (Aperture, 2001).

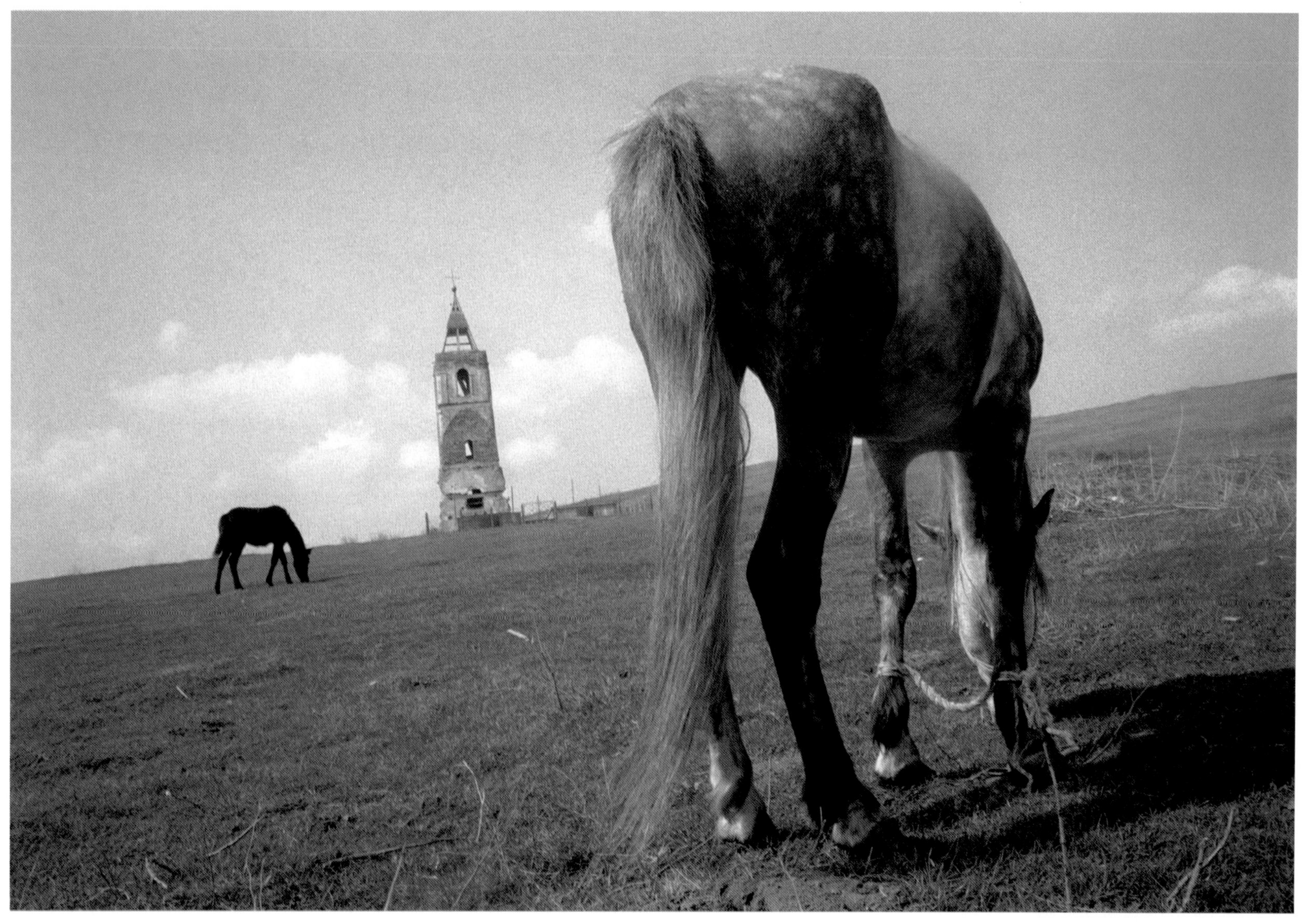

Josef Koudelka, *Transylvania*, 1999.

One view of photography is that it is a zen-like act which captures reality with its pants down—so that the vital click shows the anatomy bare. In this, the photographer is invisible but essential. A computer releasing the shutter would always miss the special moment that the human sensibility can register. For this work, the photographer's instinct is his aid, his personality a hindrance.

—Peter Brook, *Aperture* vol. 13, no. 2, 1967

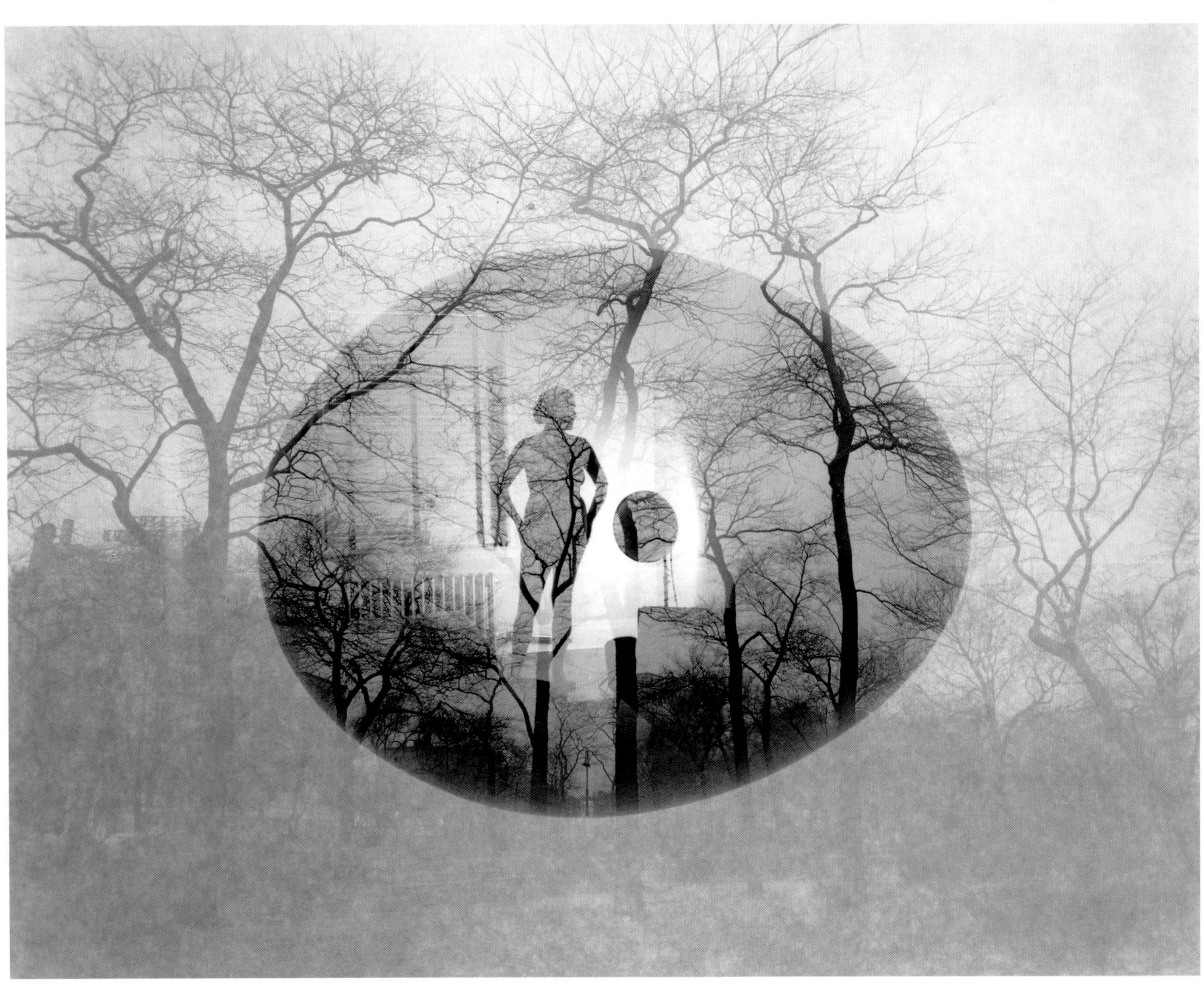

Harry Callahan, *Eleanor*, Chicago, 1953;
from *Aperture* vol. 13, no. 4, 1968.

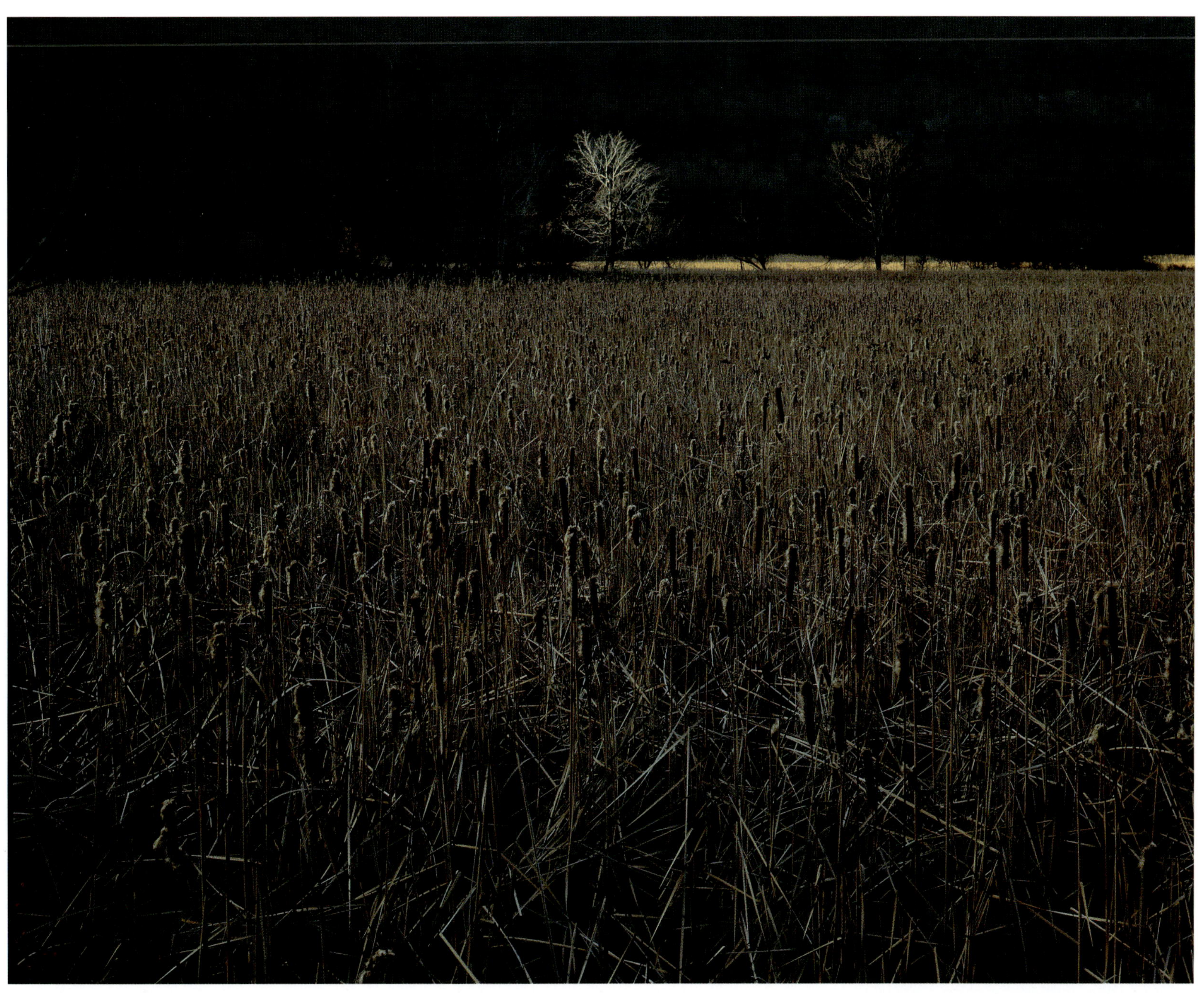

Robert Glenn Ketchum, *December 20, 1983 / 3:30 p.m.*; from *The Hudson River & the Highlands* (Aperture, 1985).

Given the lack of public skills in reading photographs, given that photographic content is sometimes buried in beauty, contemporary landscape photographers are often condemned to making pretty pictures. Dramatic clouds and sifting light can overwhelm more mundane information. Yet who can resist beautiful landscape pictures of one kind or another? Not I. The role of aestheticization is the thorniest issue within the already difficult process of communicating not only how a landscape looks, or seems, but how it *is*, and, most significantly, how it became that way. . . .

—Lucy R. Lippard, from "Outside (But Not Necessarily Beyond) the Landscape," *Aperture* 150, 1998

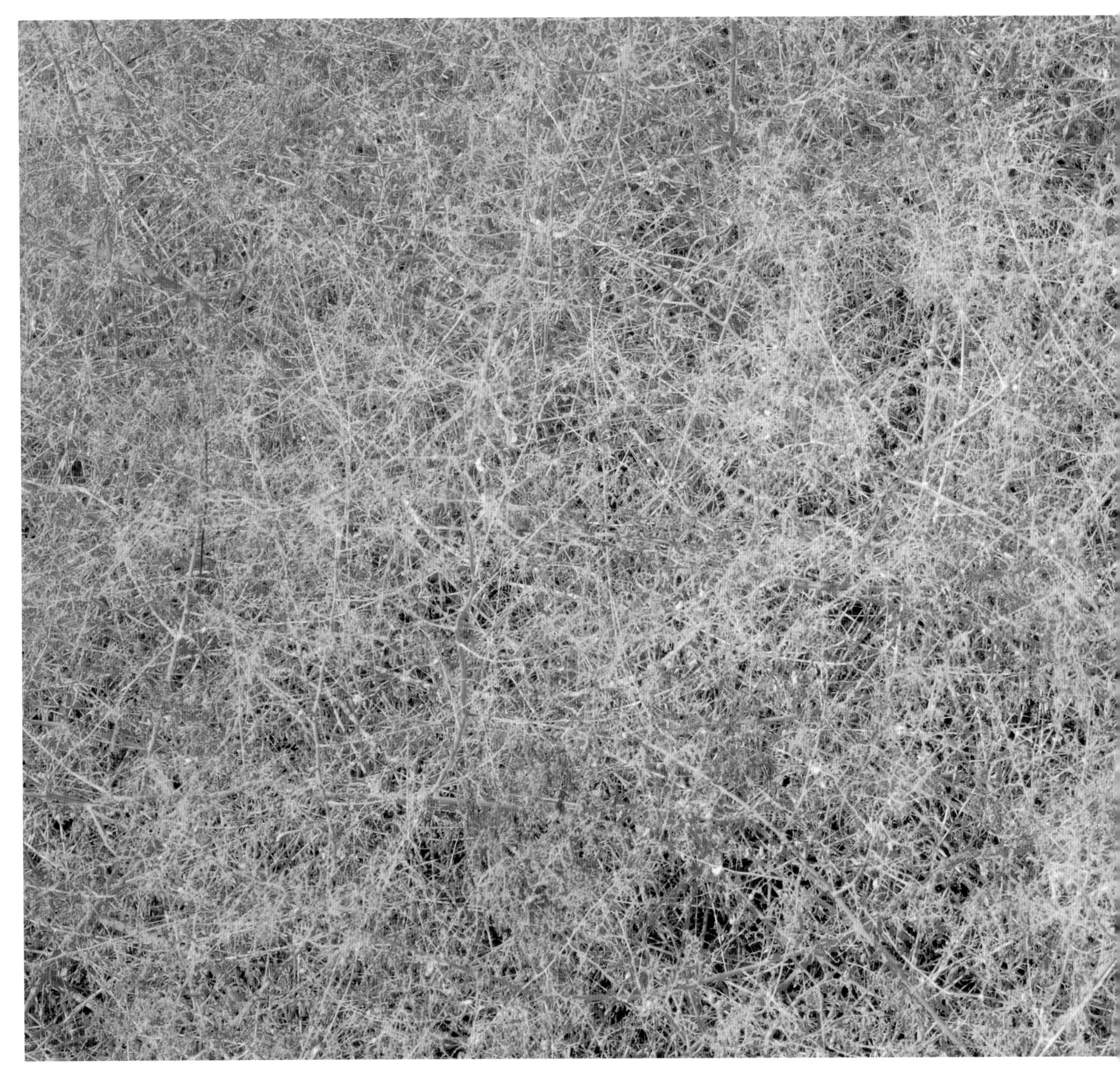

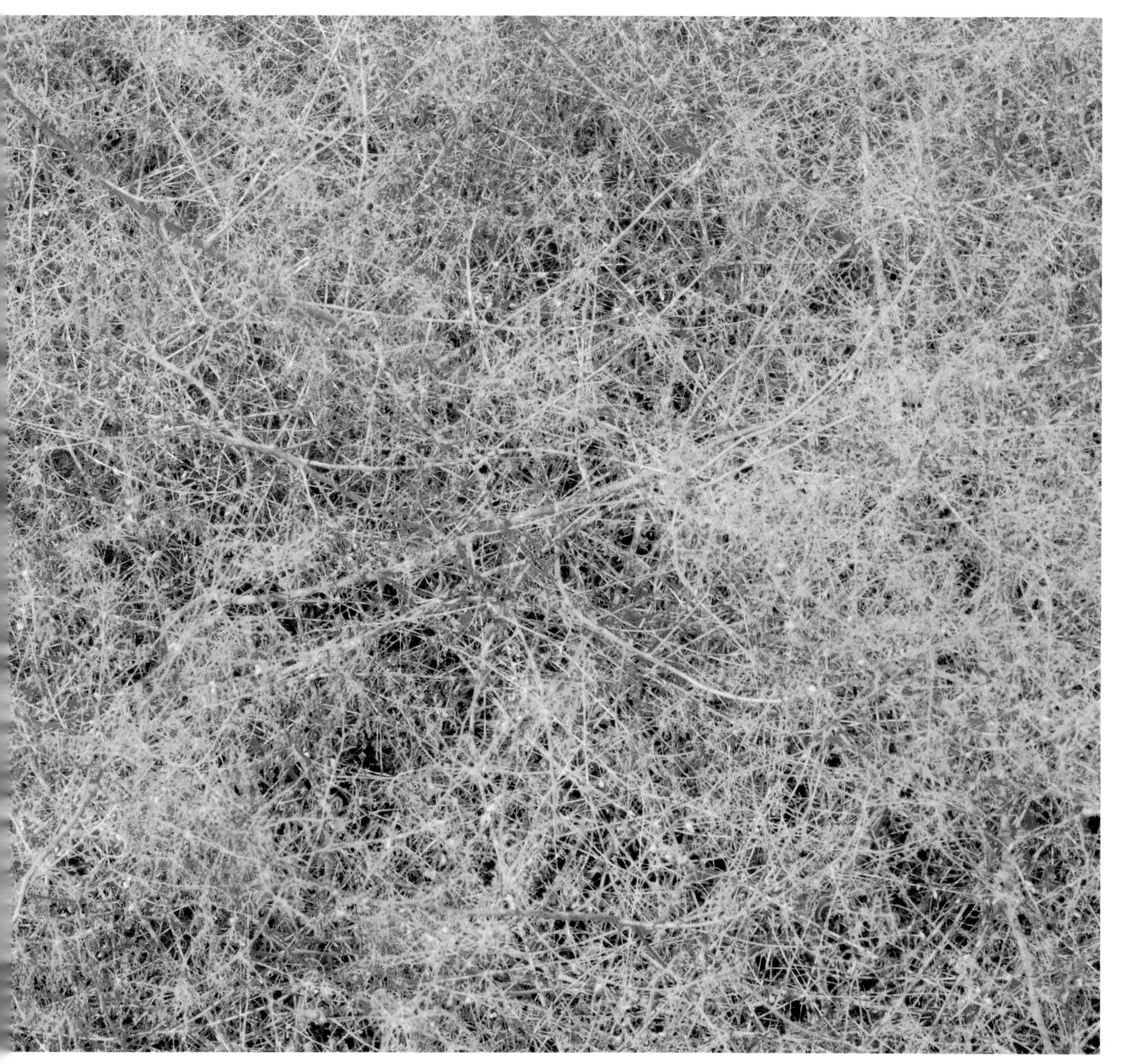

Richard Misrach, *Untitled #731–96*, from "Desert Canto" XXVI, 2001.

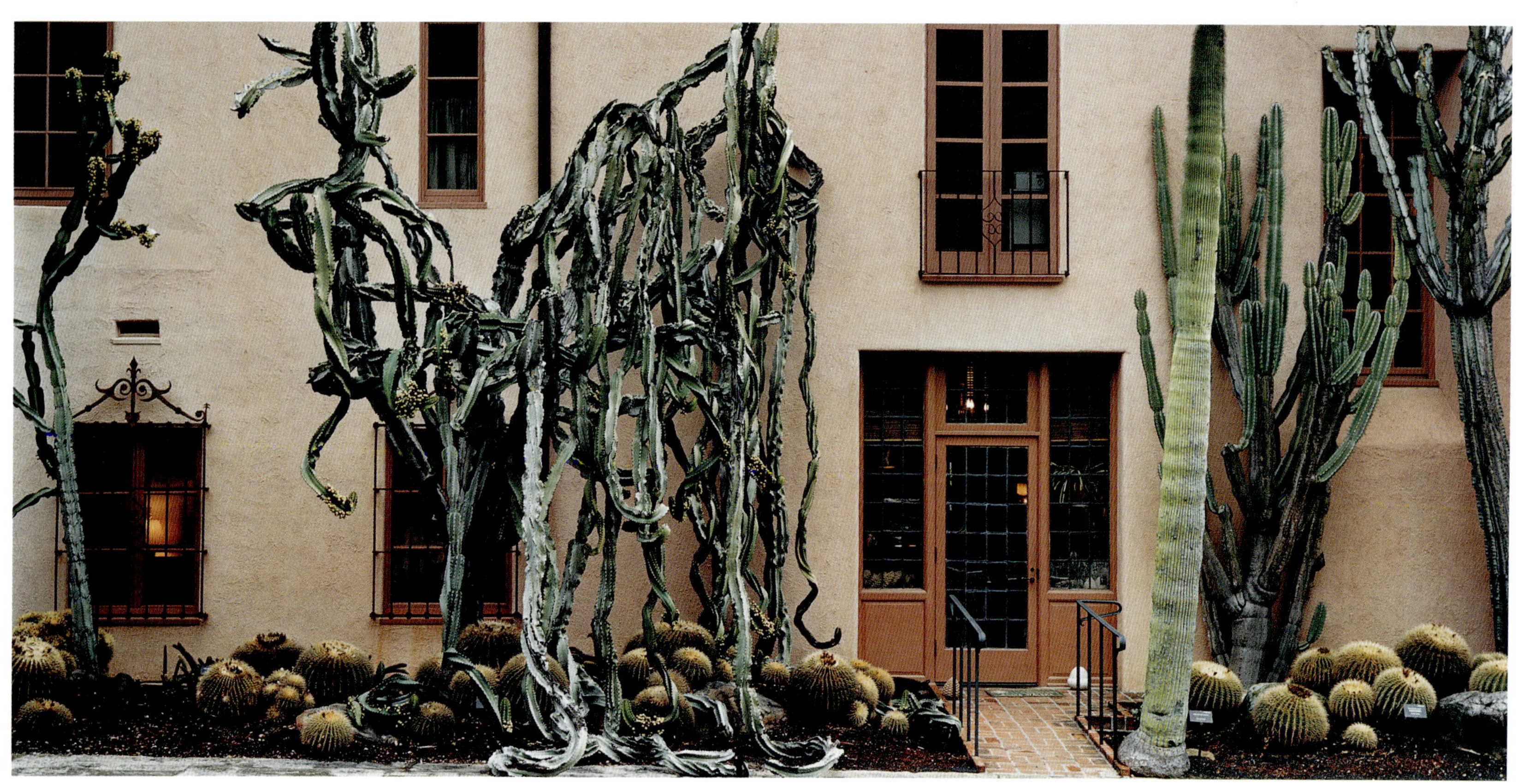

John Pfahl, ***Relaxed Euphoria, Lotusland***, Montecito, California, March, 2000.

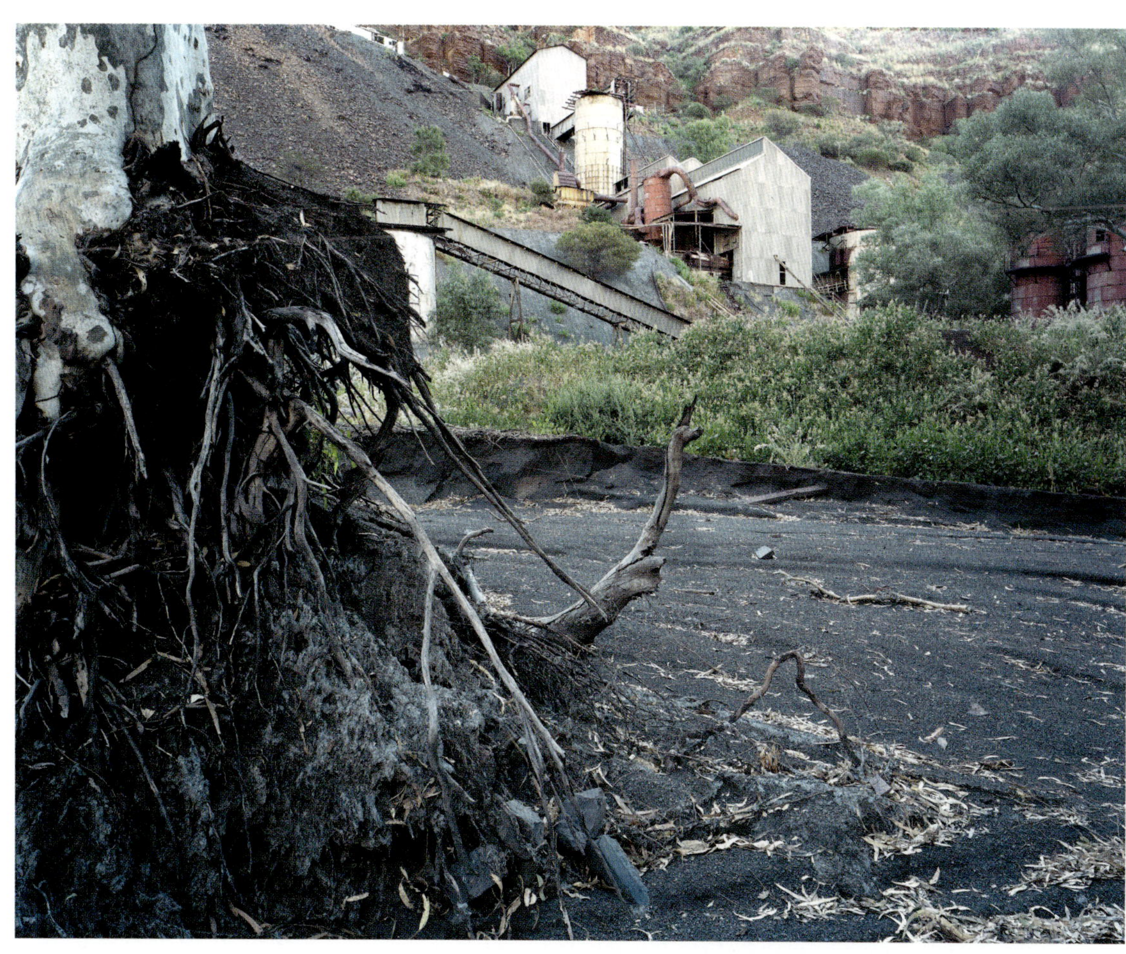

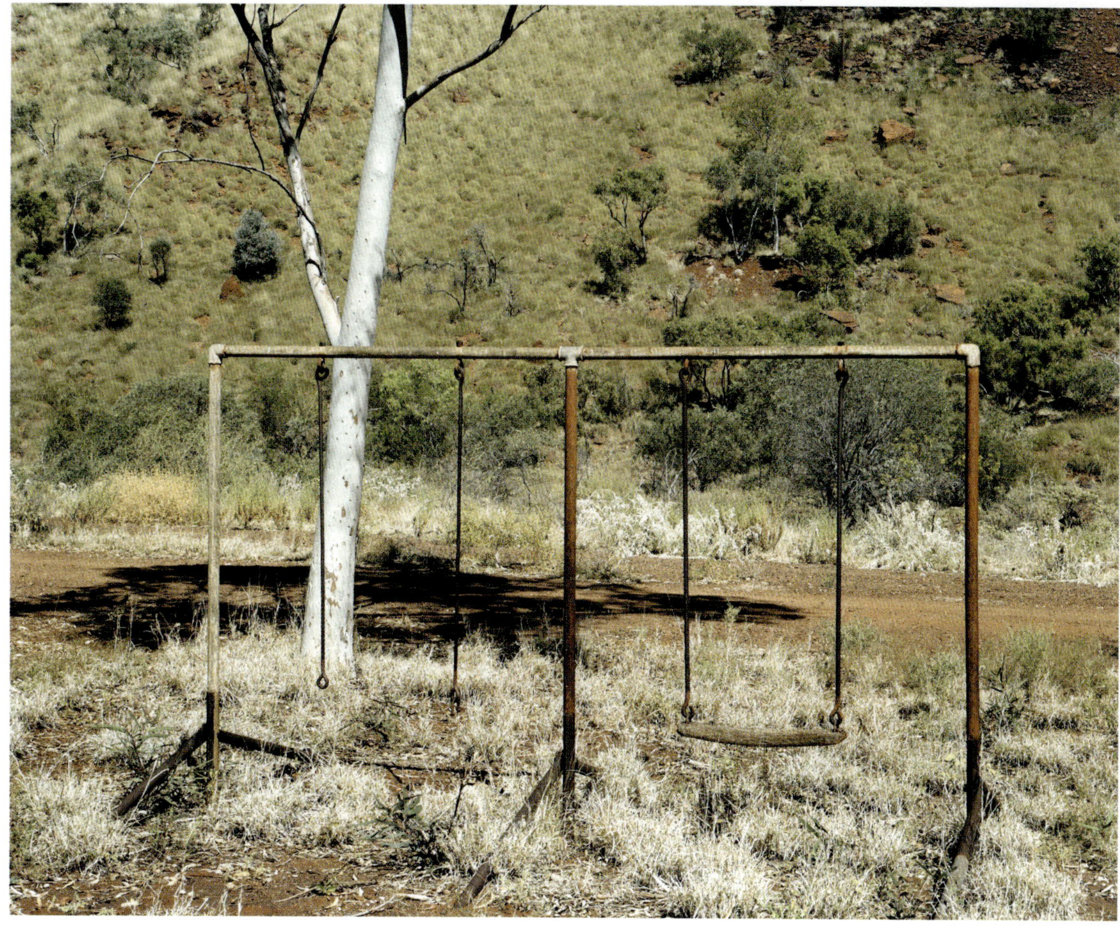

THIS PAGE: photographs by David Goldblatt.
TOP: The Colonial Mine with blue asbestos tailings, Wittenoom, Western Australia,1999. Blue asbestos was mined here from 1953 until 1966, when payable ore ran out. In 1994 it was estimated that some 65,000 tons of the substance were present in the mine's tailings dumps. With each rain some of this material gets washed into the creeks that surround the old workings. No safe level of inhalation of blue asbestos is known. In a susceptible person, one fiber could cause the fatal cancer, mesothelioma. Neither the government nor the mining company have so far indicated willingness to deal with this vast source of potential for harm.
BOTTOM: Children's swings at The Settlement, Colonial Mine, Wittenoom, Western Australia, 1999. The Settlement was close to mining operations and was home to the families of senior officials of the company. Only a caretaker lives on the property now.

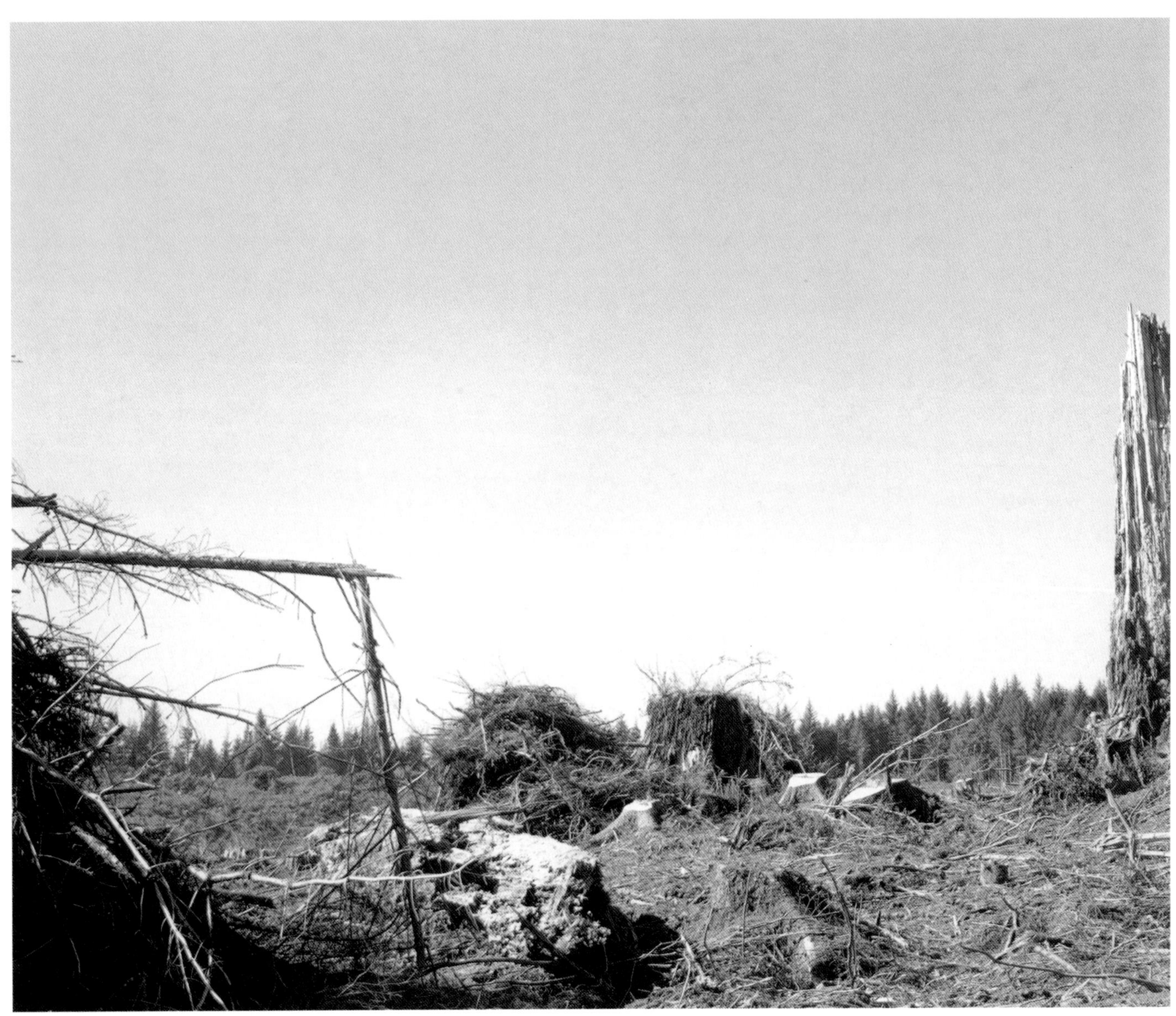

THESE PAGES: photographs by Robert Adams.
***Clearcut*, Coos County, Oregon, 1999.**

Photographers who can teach us to love even vacant lots will do so out of the same sense of wholeness that inspired the wilderness photographers of the past twenty-five years (the deepest joy possible in wilderness is, most would agree, the mysterious realization of one's alliance with it). Beauty,

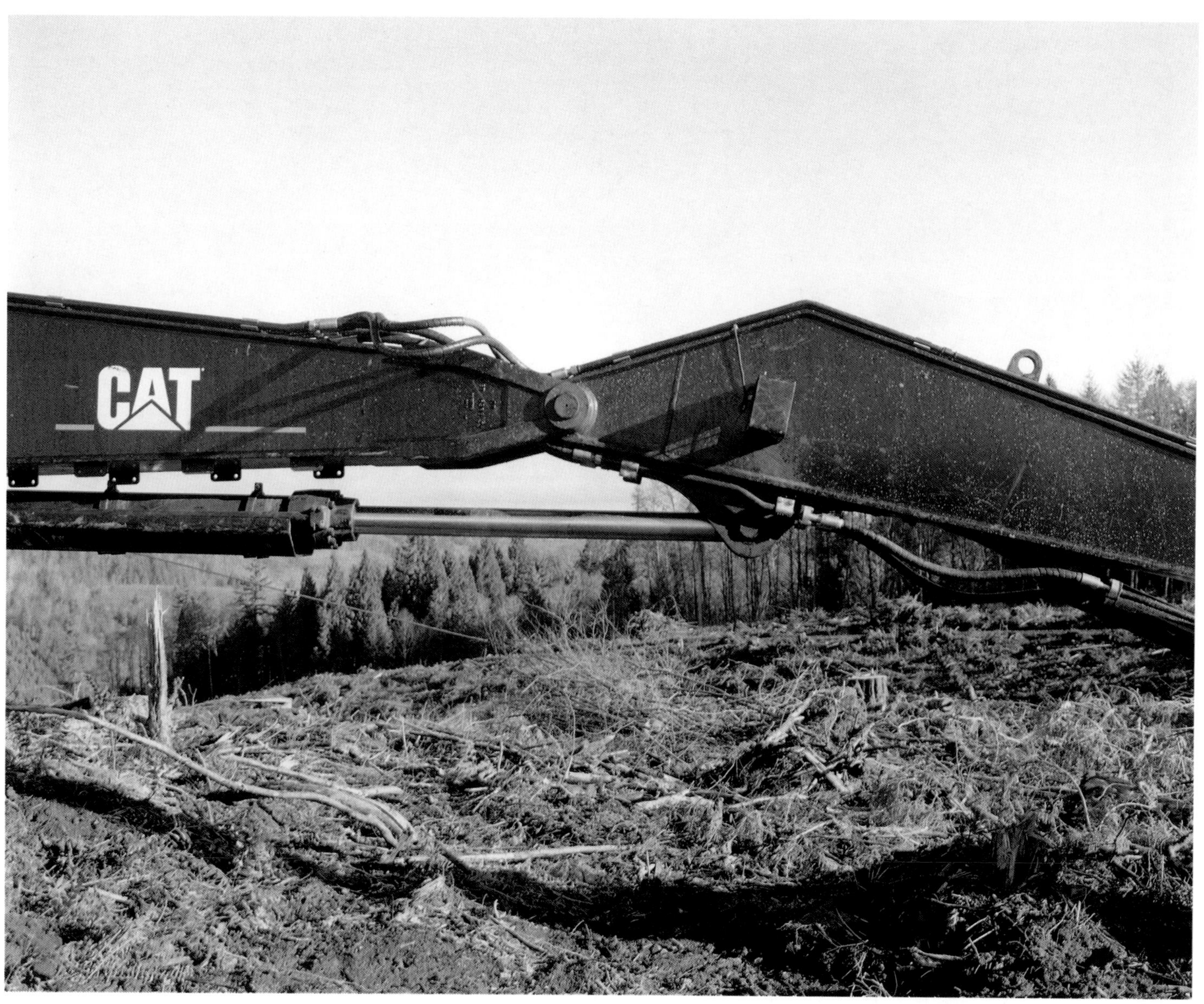

***Clearcut*, Columbia County, Oregon, 2001.**

Coleridge wrote, is based in "the unity of the manifold, the coalescence of the diverse." In this large sense, beautiful photographs of contemporary America will lead us out into daily life by giving us a new understanding of and tolerance for what previously seemed only anarchic and threatening.

—Robert Adams, from "Inhabited Nature," *Aperture* 81, 1978

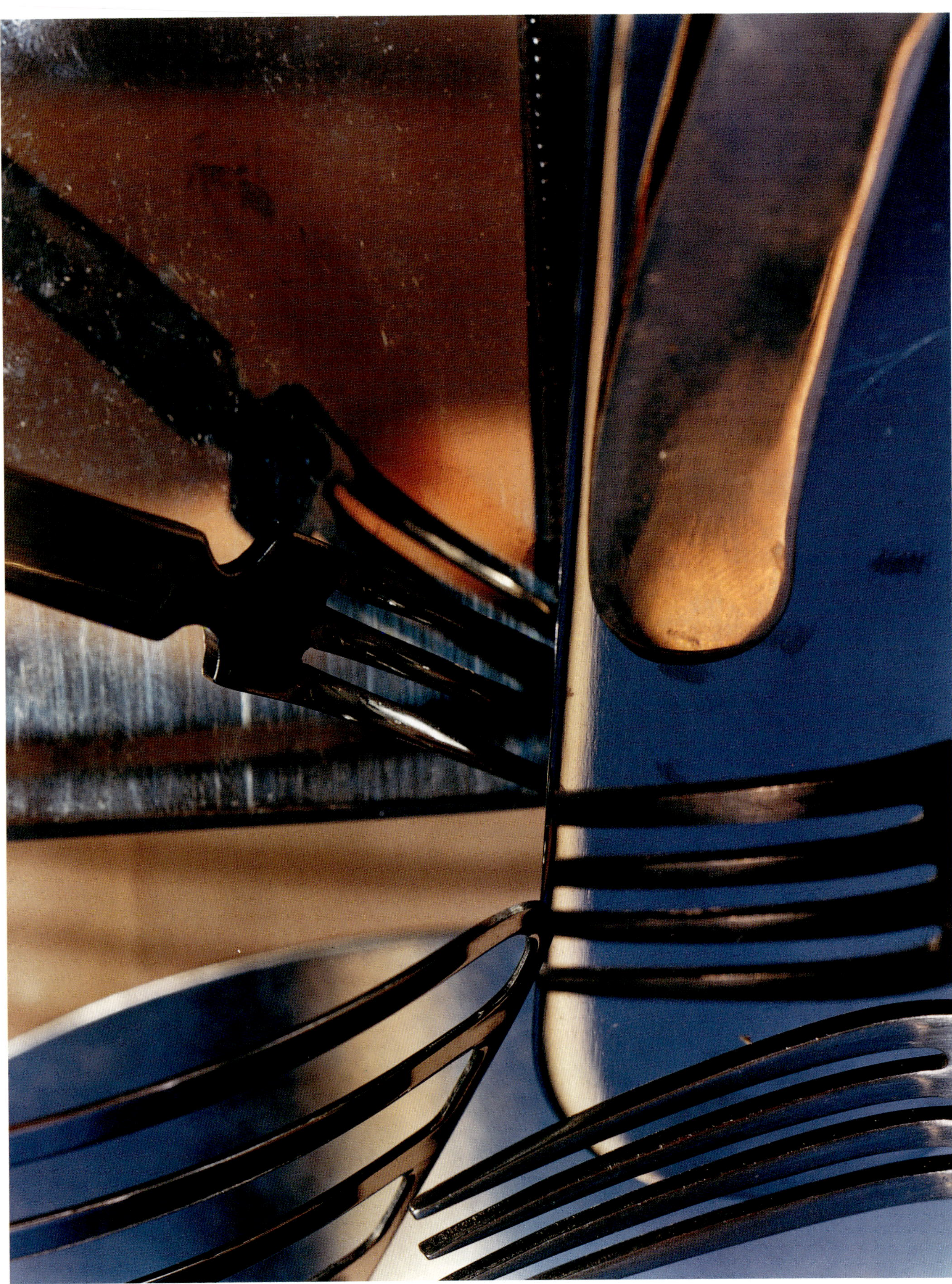

Jan Groover, *Untitled*, 1978.

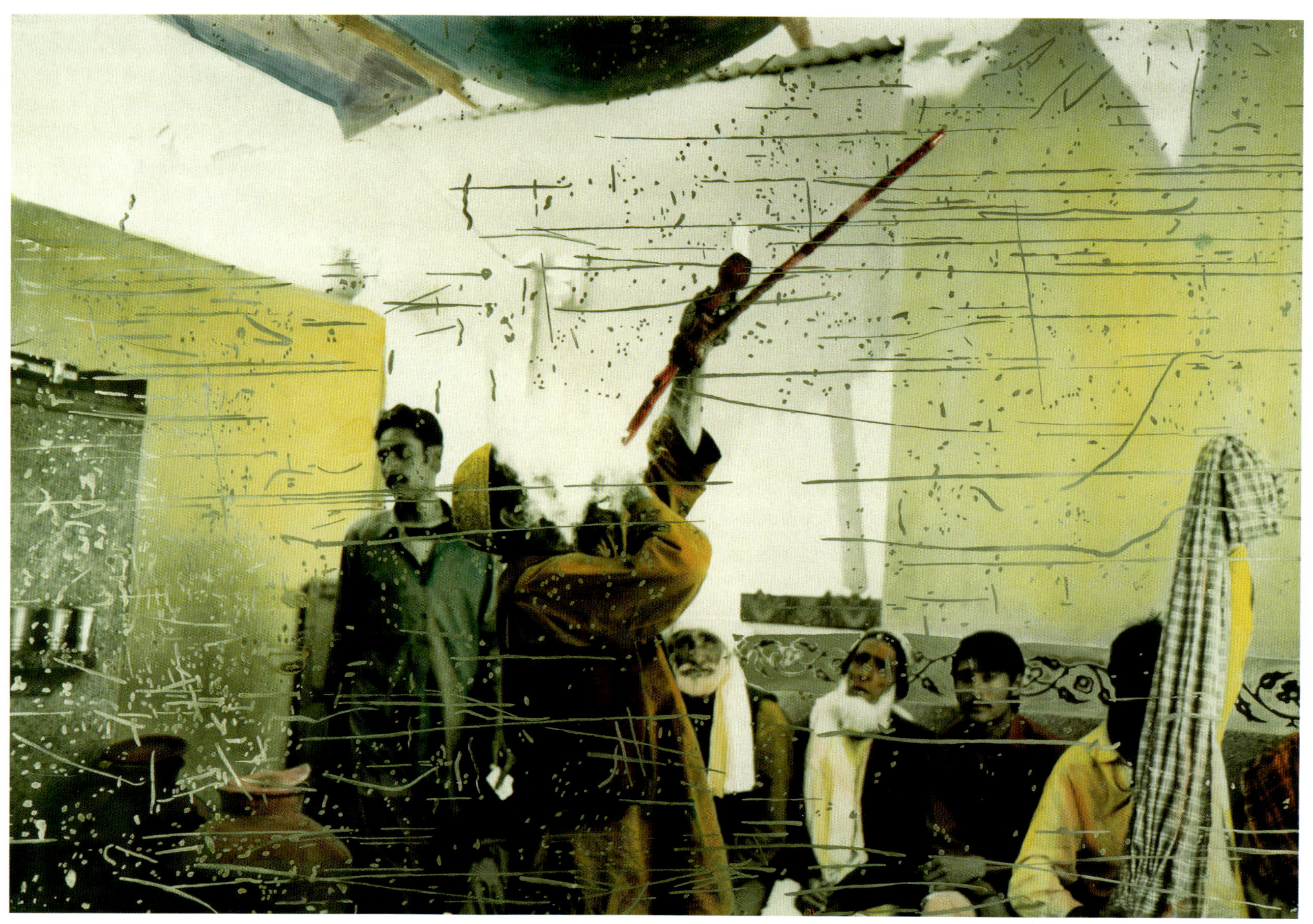

Sigmar Polke, *Quetta, Pakistan*, 1974–1978; from *Aperture* 145, 1996.

Photography's potential as a great image-maker and communicator is really no different from the same potential in the best poetry where familiar, everyday words, placed within a special context, can soar above the intellect and touch subtle reality in a unique way.

—Paul Caponigro, *Aperture* vol. 13, no. 1, 1967

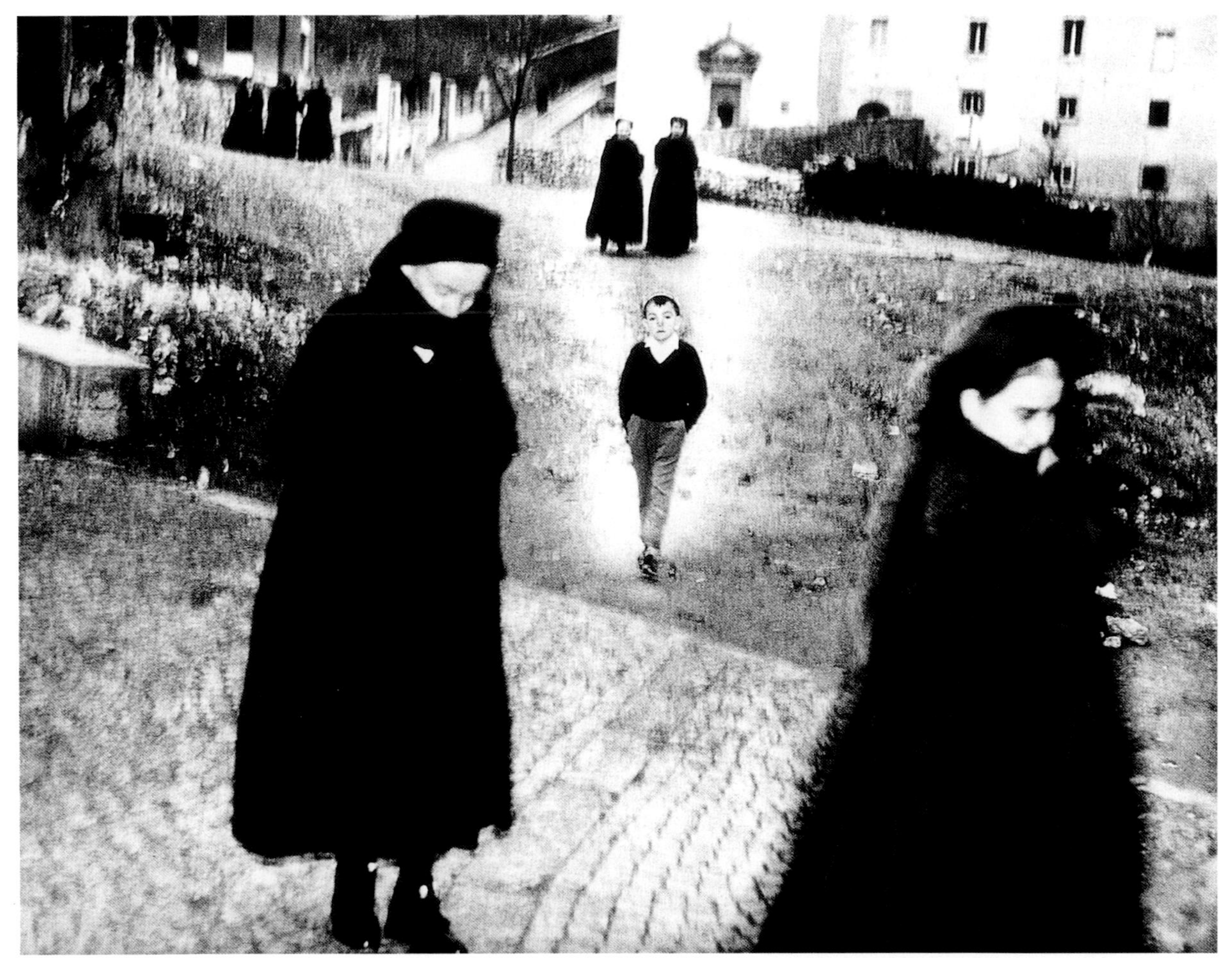

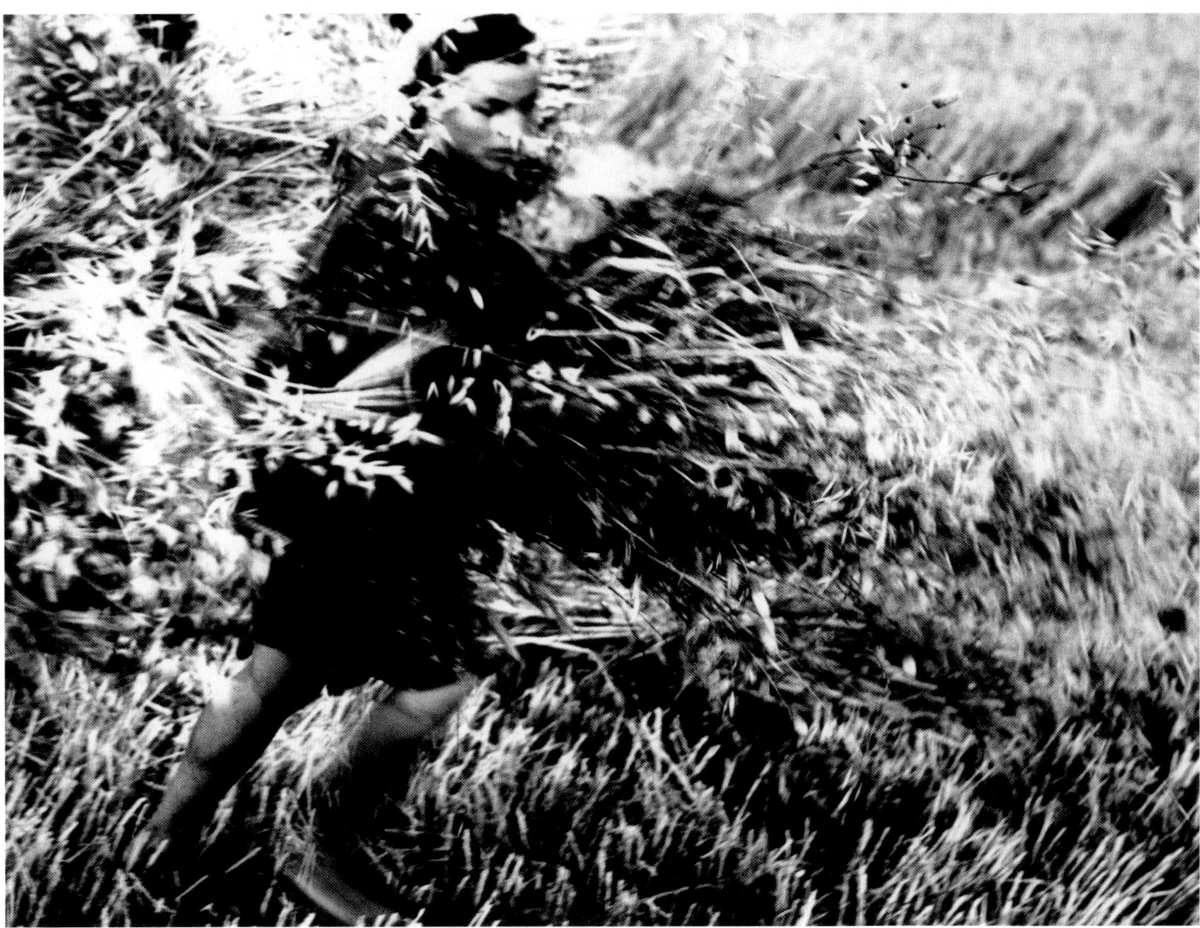

THIS PAGE: photographs by Mario Giacomelli. TOP: from the series "Scanno," 1957–59; from *Aperture* 132, 1993.
BOTTOM: from the series "La buona terra" (The good earth), 1964–65; from *Aperture* 132, 1993.

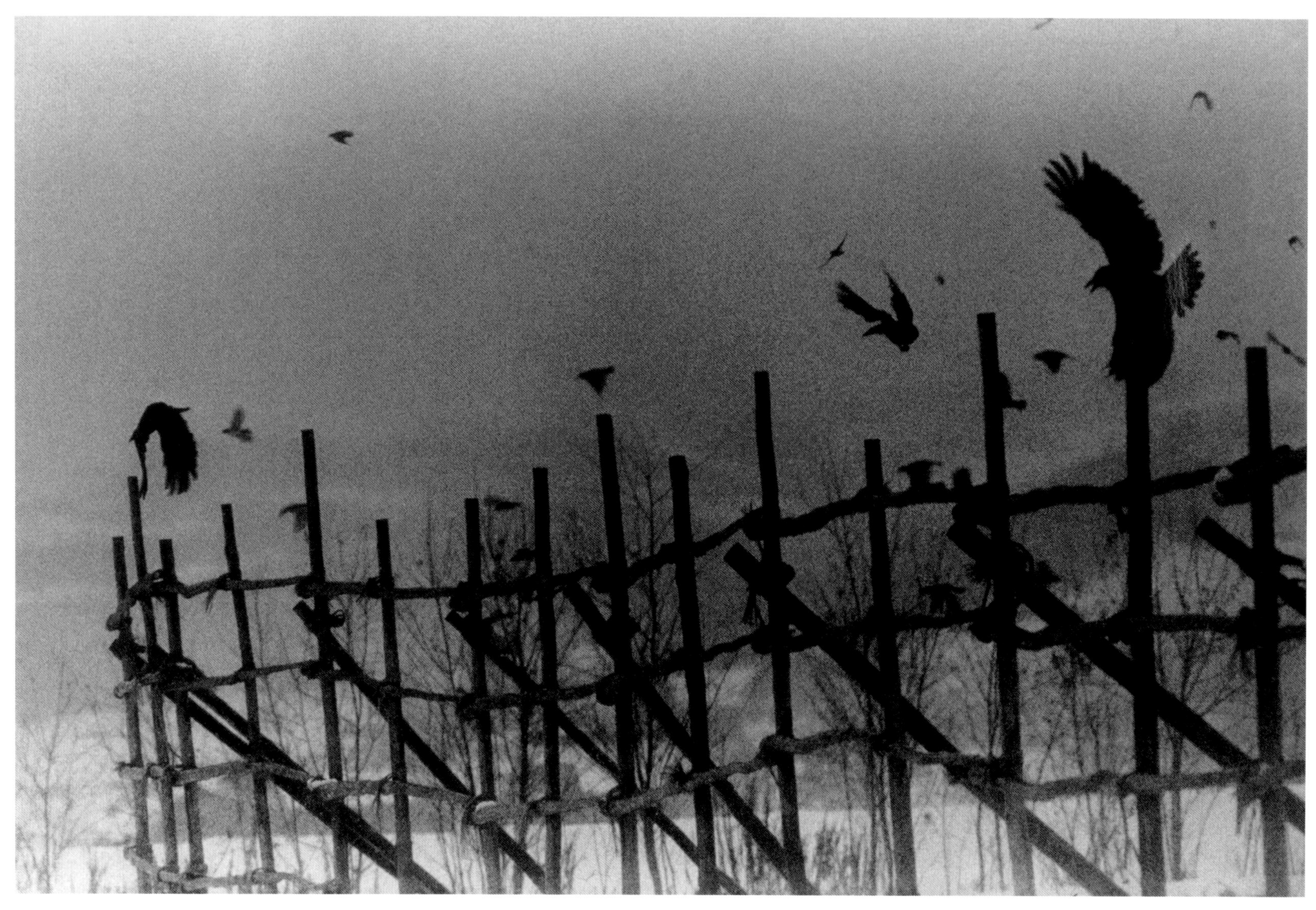

Masahisa Fukase, *Nayoro*, 1977; from *Aperture* 102, 1986.

You see, the extraordinary thing about photography is that it's a truly popular medium. . . . But this has nothing to do with the art of photography even though the same materials and the same mechanical devices are used. Thoreau said years ago, "You can't say more than you see." No matter what lens you use, no matter what the speed of the film is, no matter how you develop it, no matter how you print it, you cannot say more than you see. That's what that means, and that's the truth.

—Paul Strand, *Aperture* vol. 19, no. 1, 1974

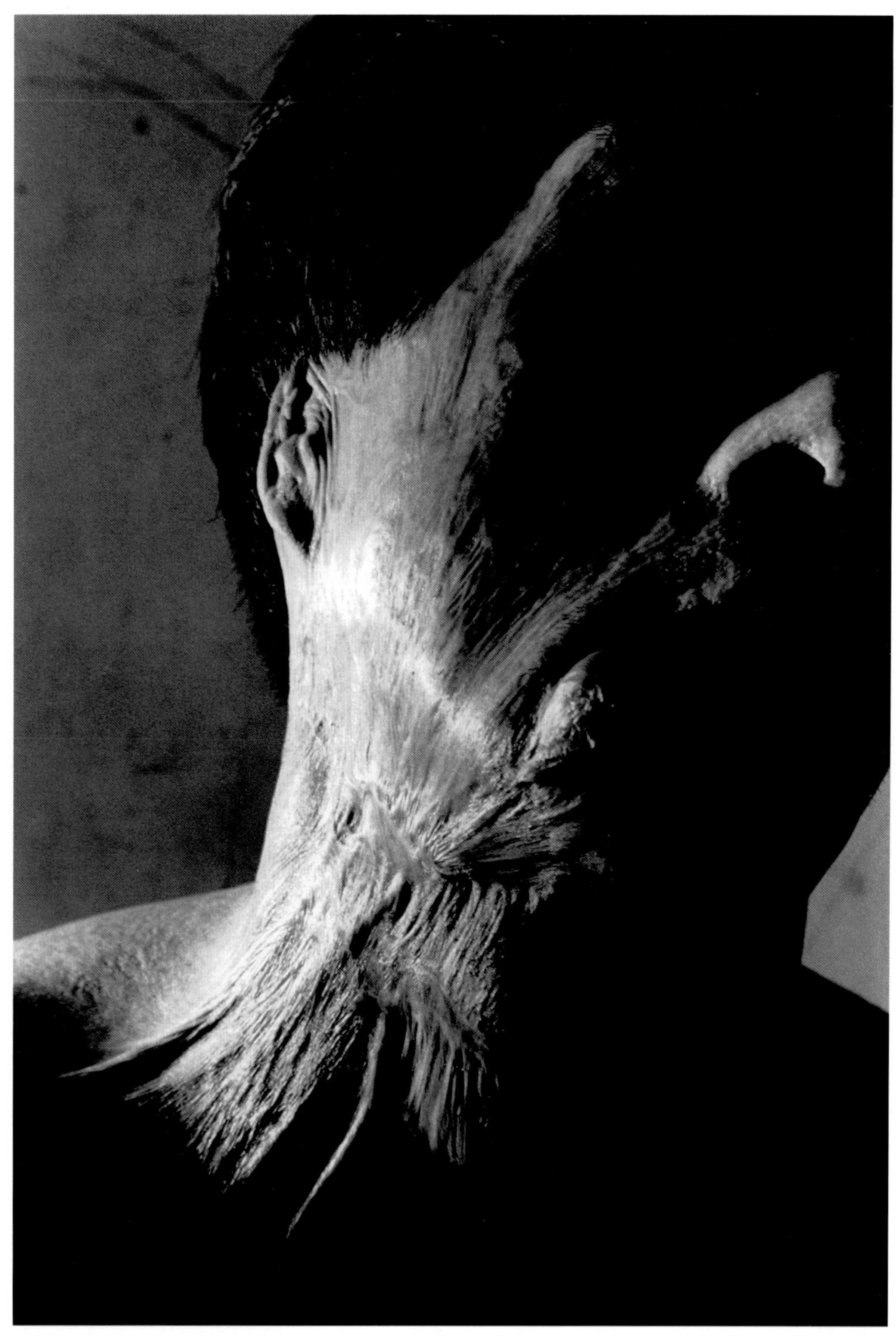

Shomei Tomatsu, *Yamaguchi Senji Who Was Injured 1.2 km from the Epicenter of the Blast,*1962, from the series "11:02—Nagasaki"; from *Aperture* 102, 1986.

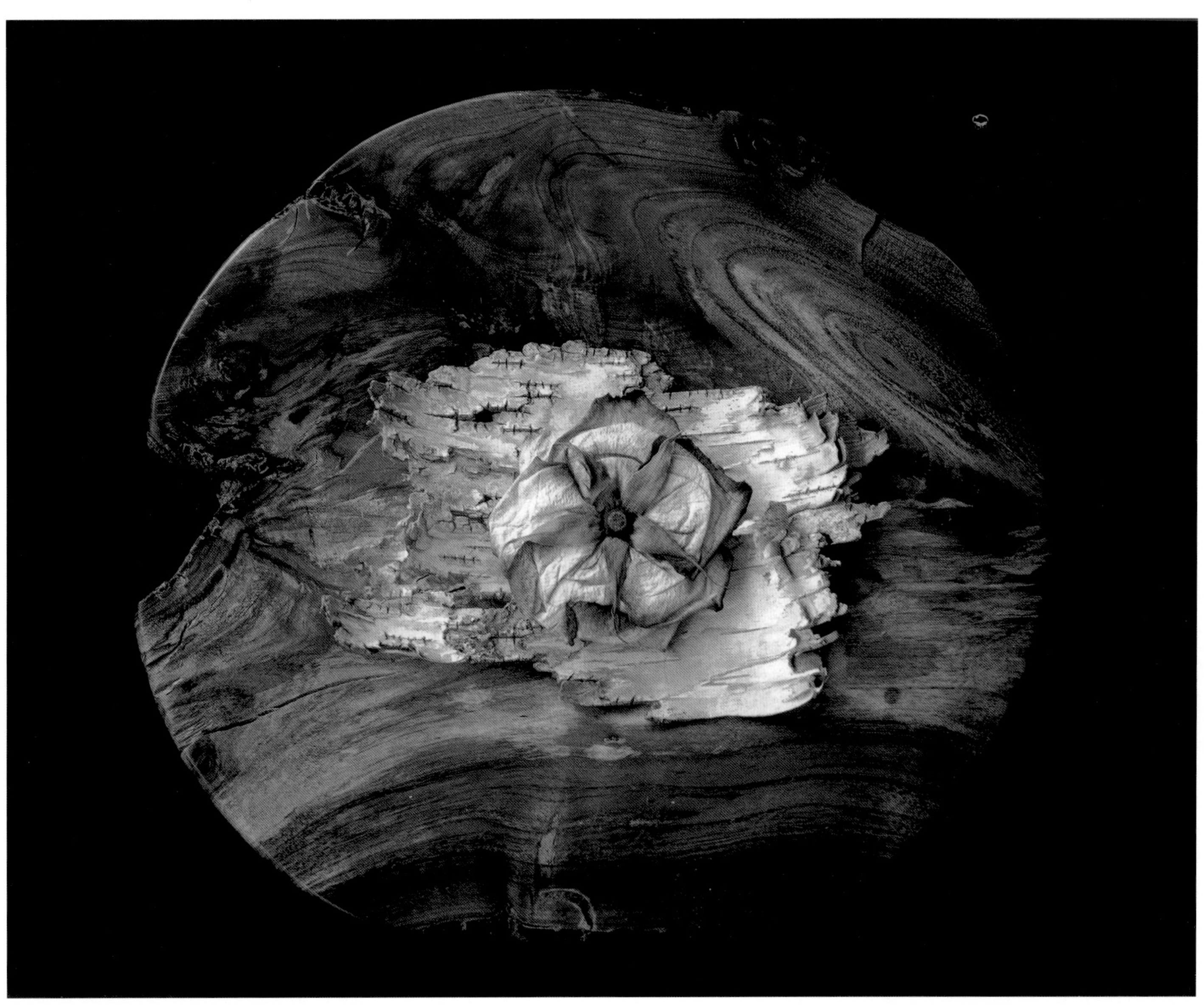

Paul Caponigro, *Inner Night Sky*, 1999.

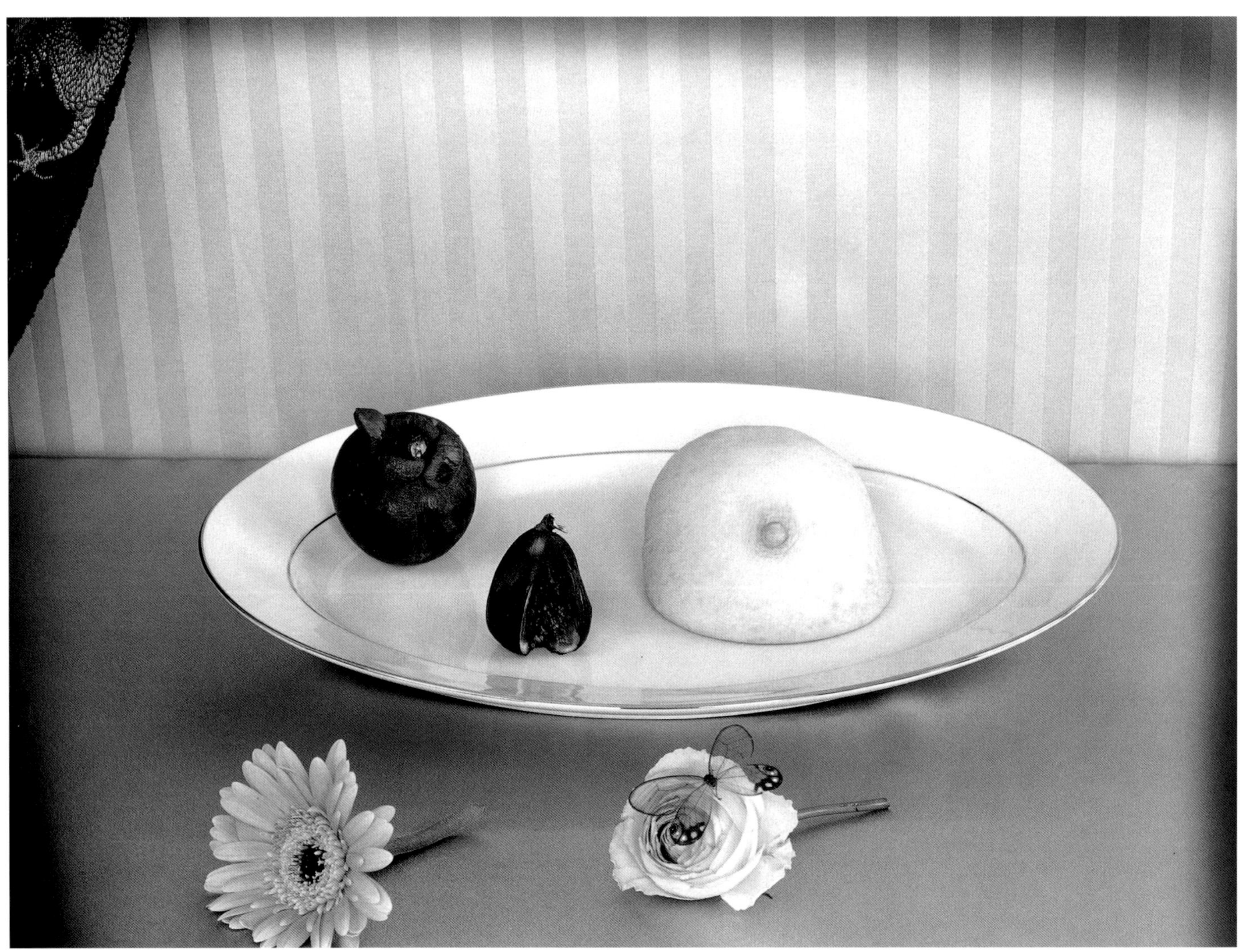

Joel-Peter Witkin, *Still Life with Breast*, 2001.

Postpone judgment! When starting to read, experience or take part in a photograph (or picture of any kind) first put aside both like and dislike. Leave criticism to the last, or better still forget to criticize.

—Minor White and Walter Chappell, from "Some Methods for Experiencing Photographs," *Aperture* vol. 5, no. 4, 1957

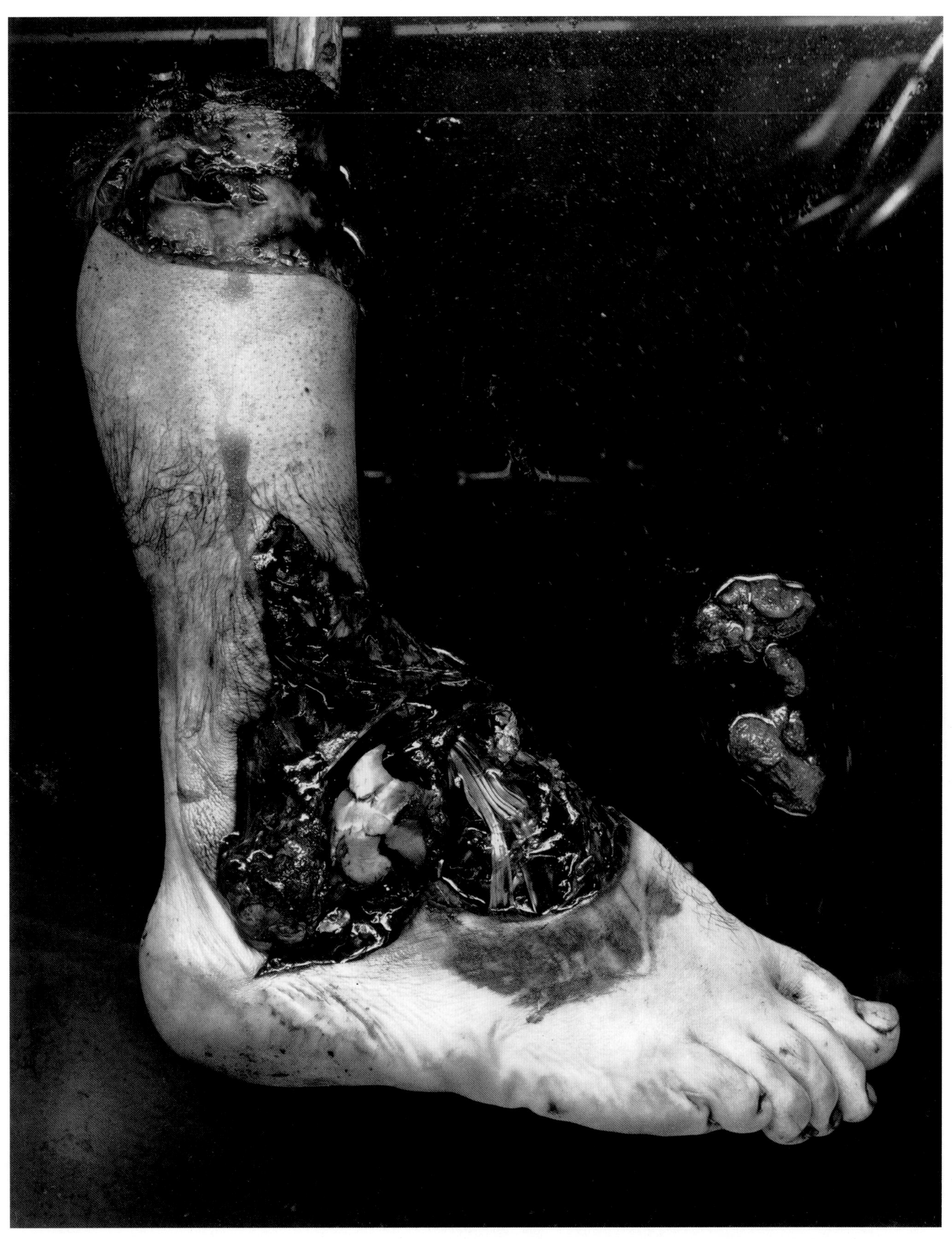

Frederick Sommer, *Untitled (Amputated foot)*, 1939; from *Aperture* vol. 9, no. 3, 1961.

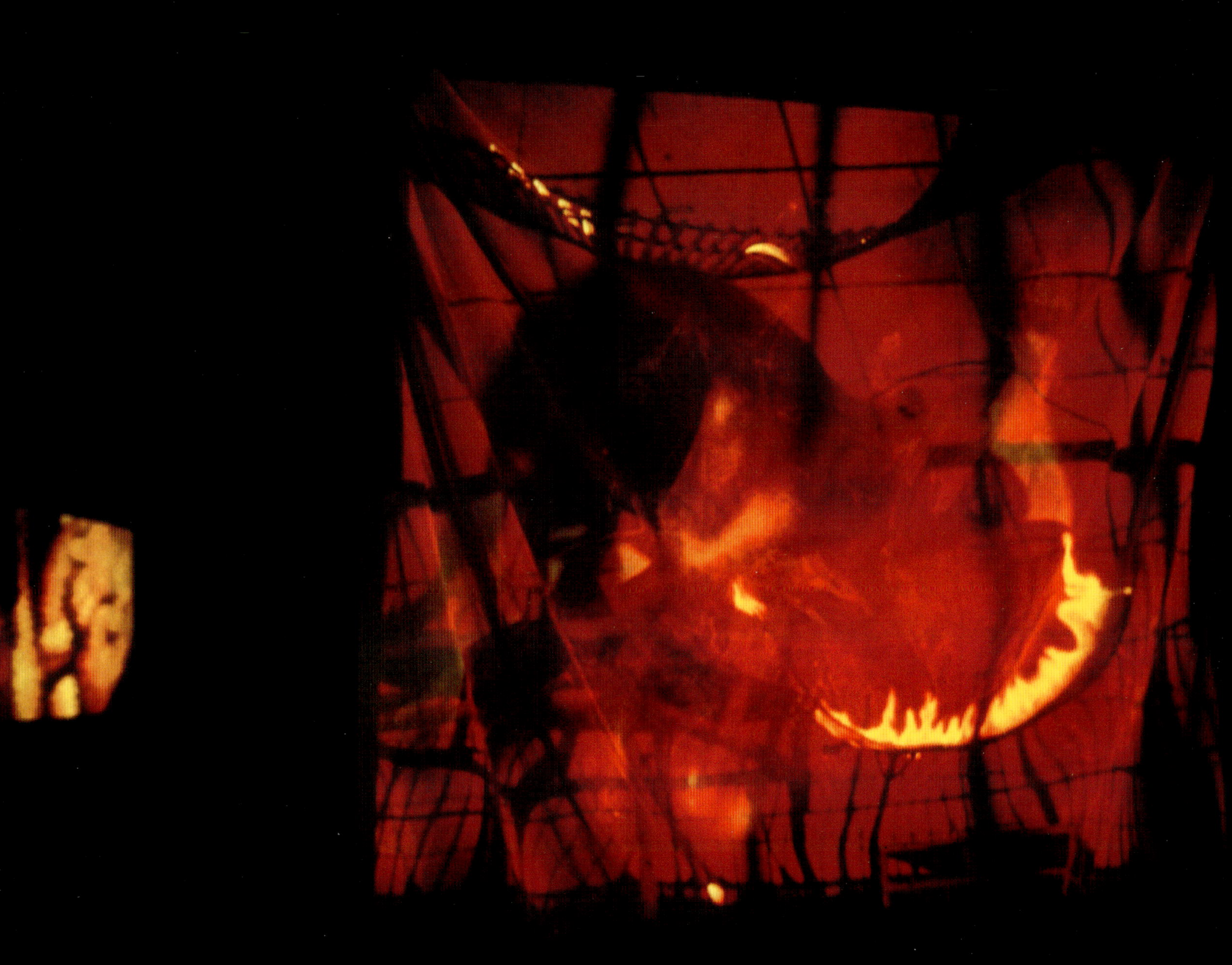

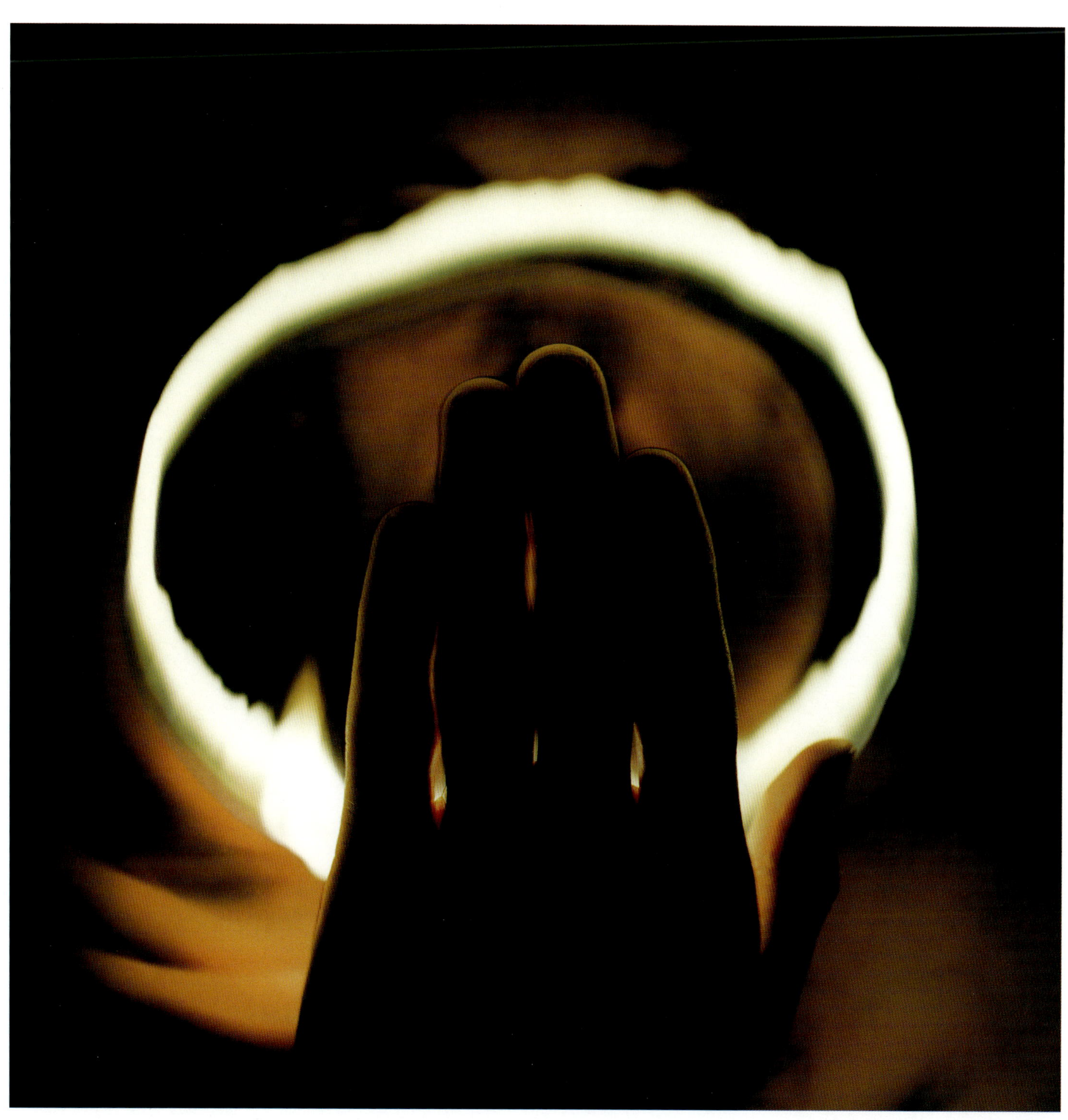

Javier Vallhonrat, *Untitled #18,* from the series "Autograms," 1991; from *Aperture* 155, 1999.

OPPOSITE: Miguel Rio Branco, *Door into Darkness*, 2001.

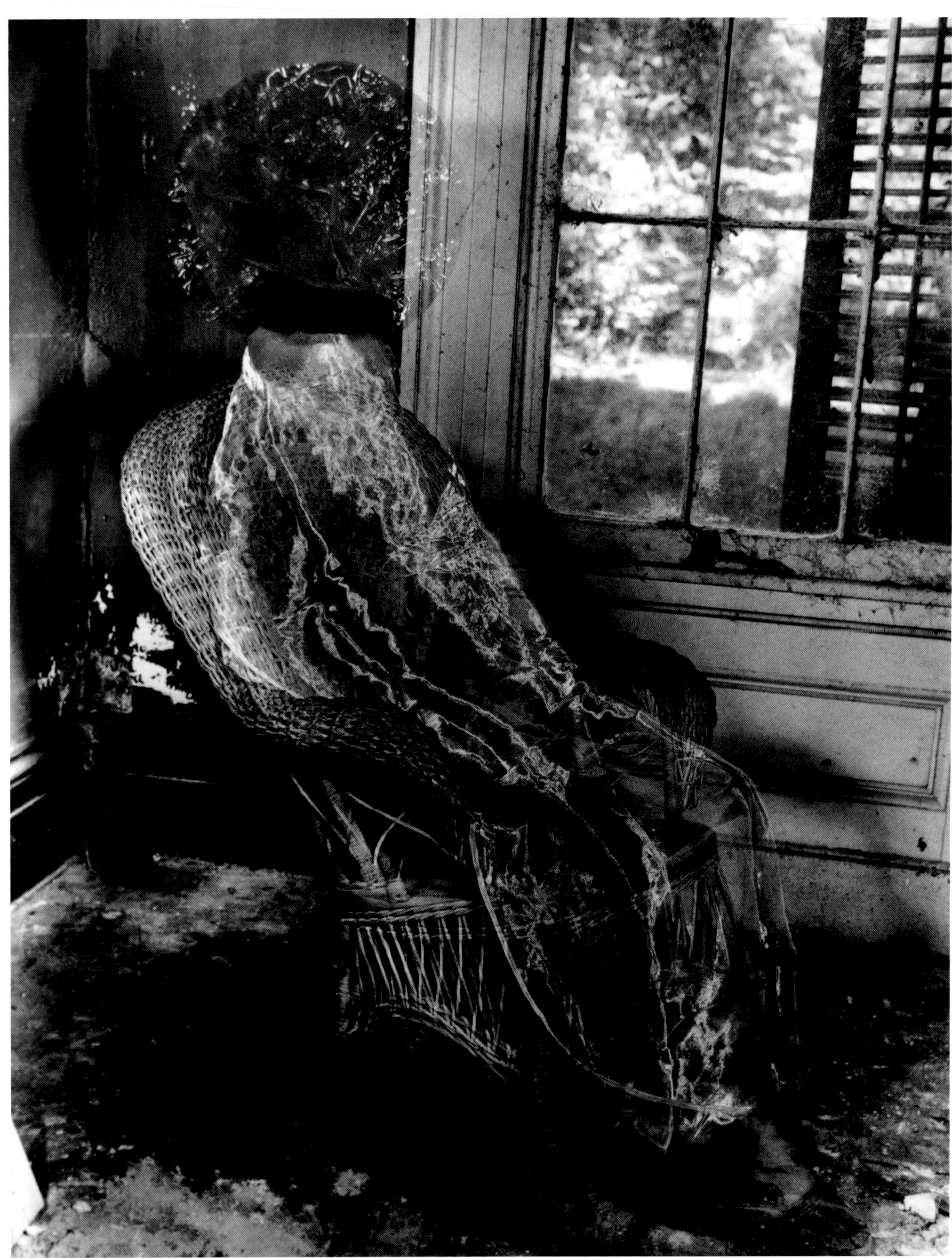

Clarence John Laughlin, *The House of the Past*, 1948; from *Aperture* vol. 9, no. 3, 1961.

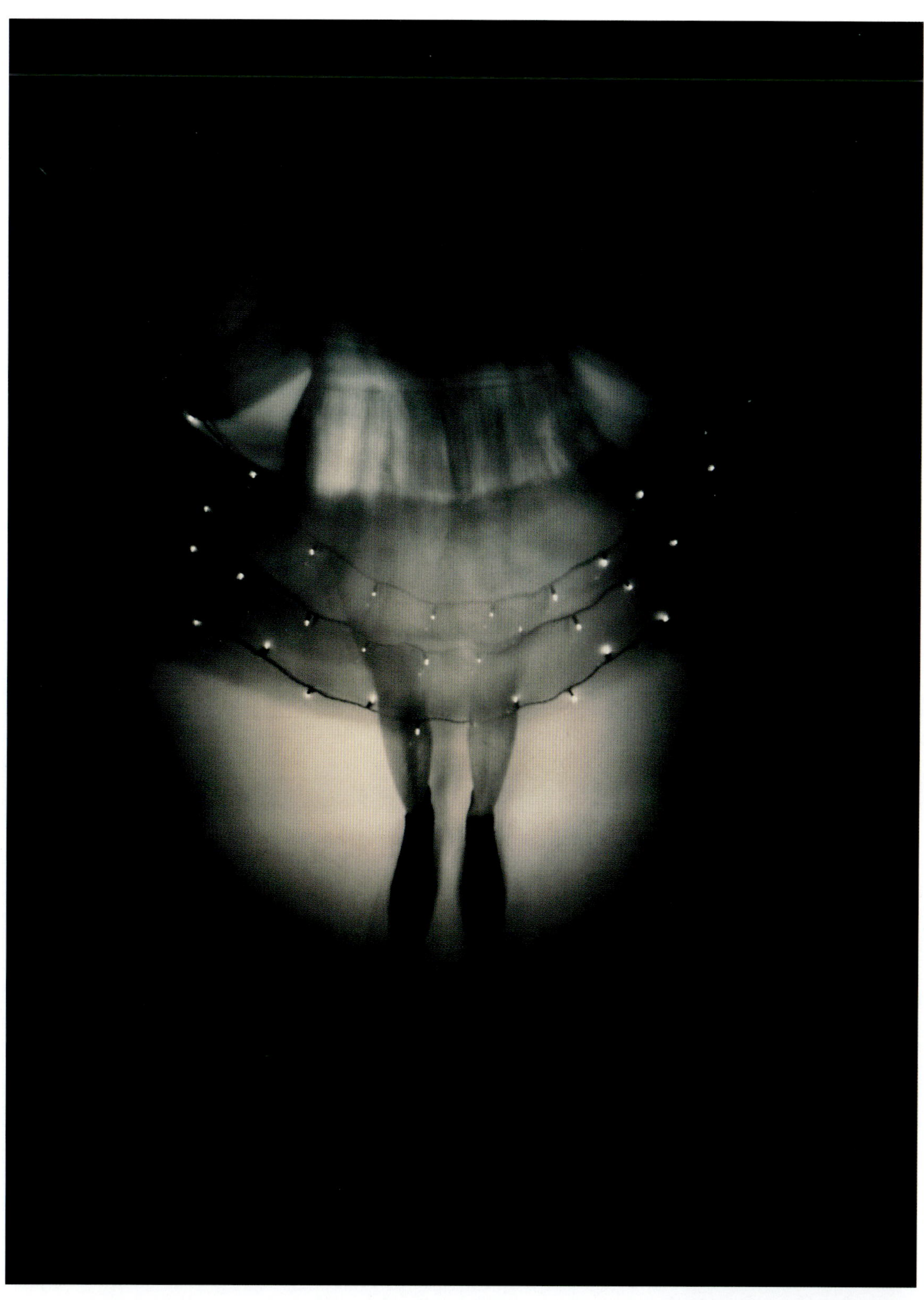

Barbara Ess, *No Title*, 1997–98; from *I Am Not This Body: Photographs by Barbara Ess* (Aperture, 2001).

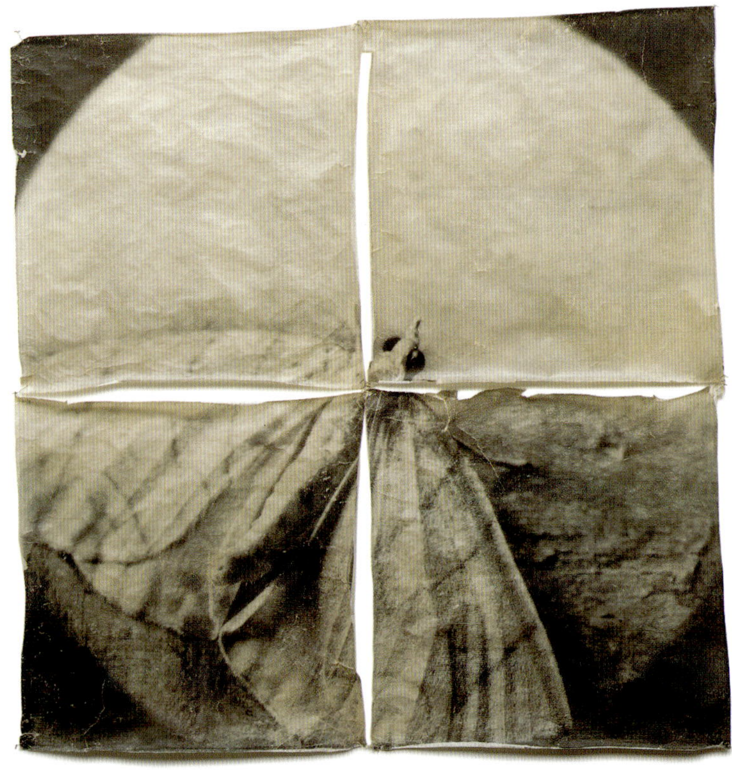

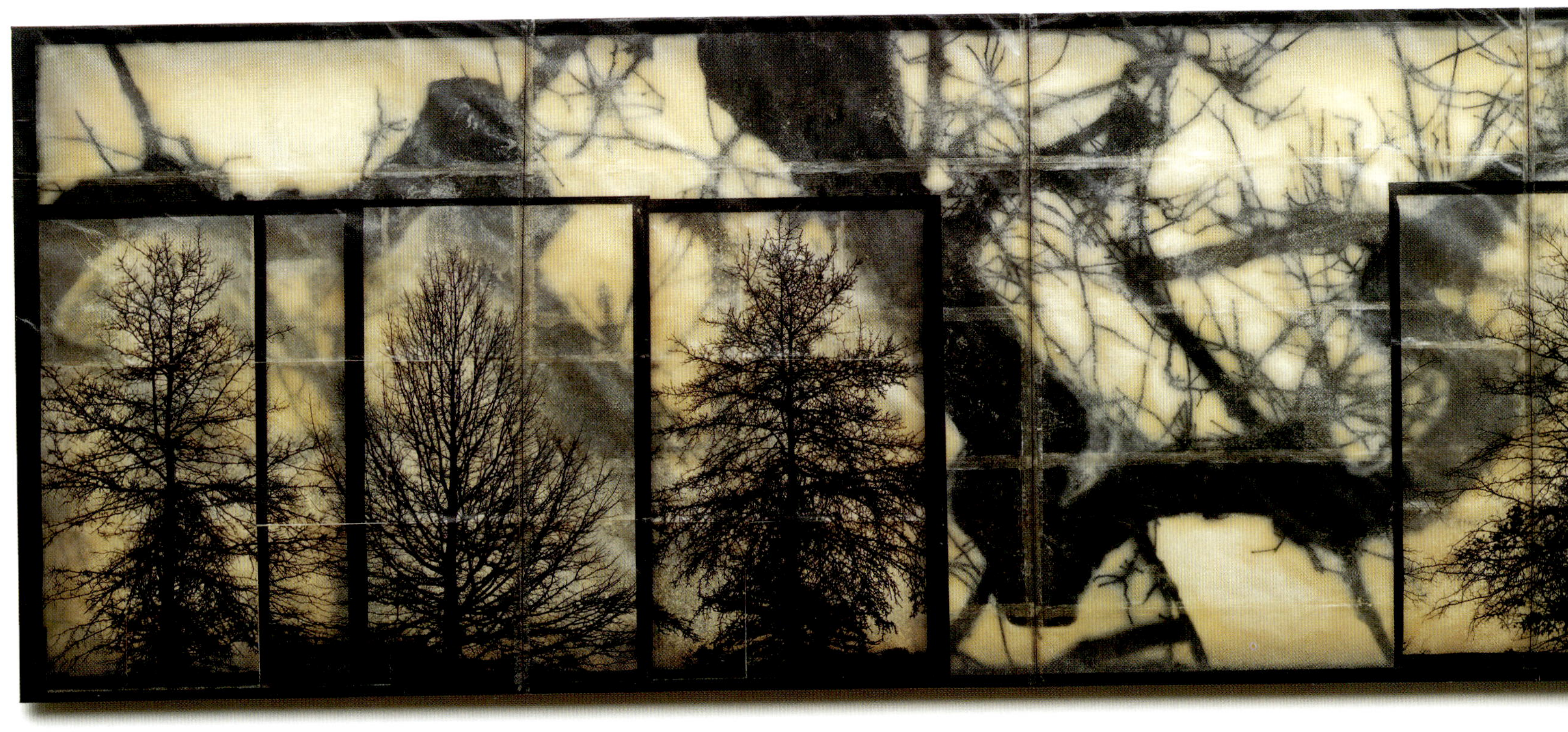

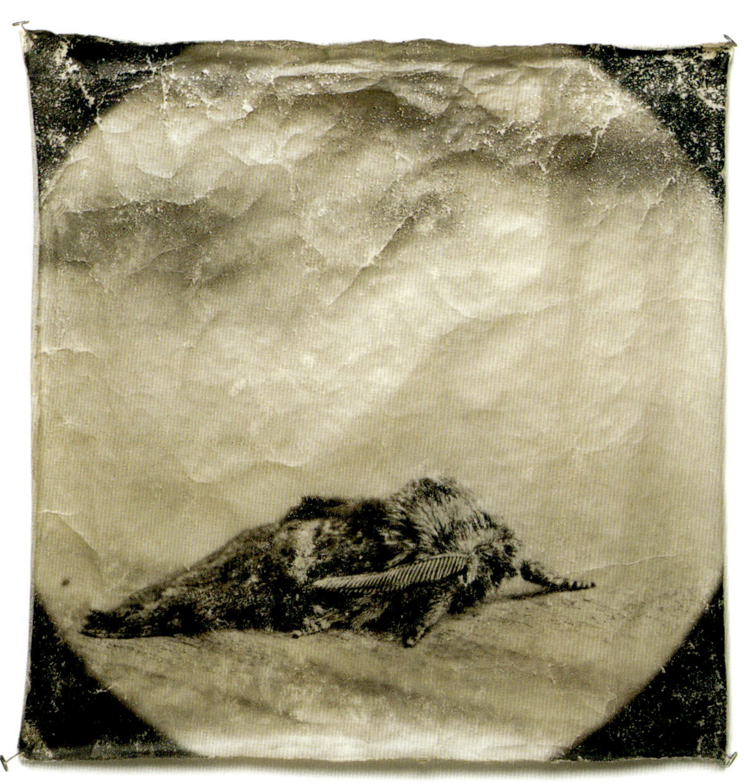

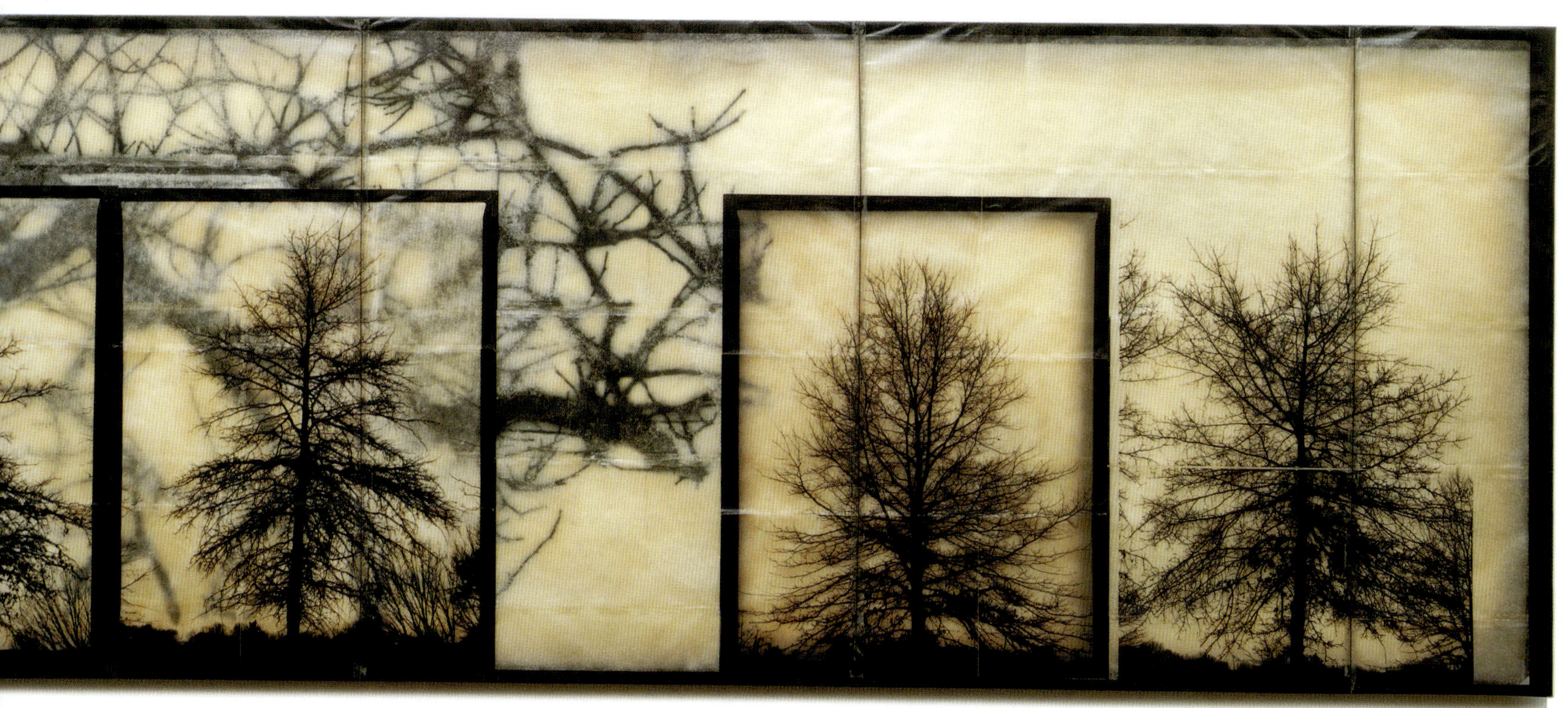

THESE PAGES: photographs by Mike and Doug Starn. **OPPOSITE TOP:** *Attracted to Light #D*, 1996–2001. **THIS PAGE TOP:** *Attracted to Light #G*, 1996–2001. **BOTTOM:** *Structure of Thought #7*, 2001.

Warning: If experiencing a photograph can not be done with some of the abandon of a boy riding a bicycle, or children wading in the gutters after a rain, there is no reason to experience photographs.

—**Minor White and Walter Chappell, from "Some Methods for Experiencing Photographs," *Aperture* vol. 5, no. 4, 1957**

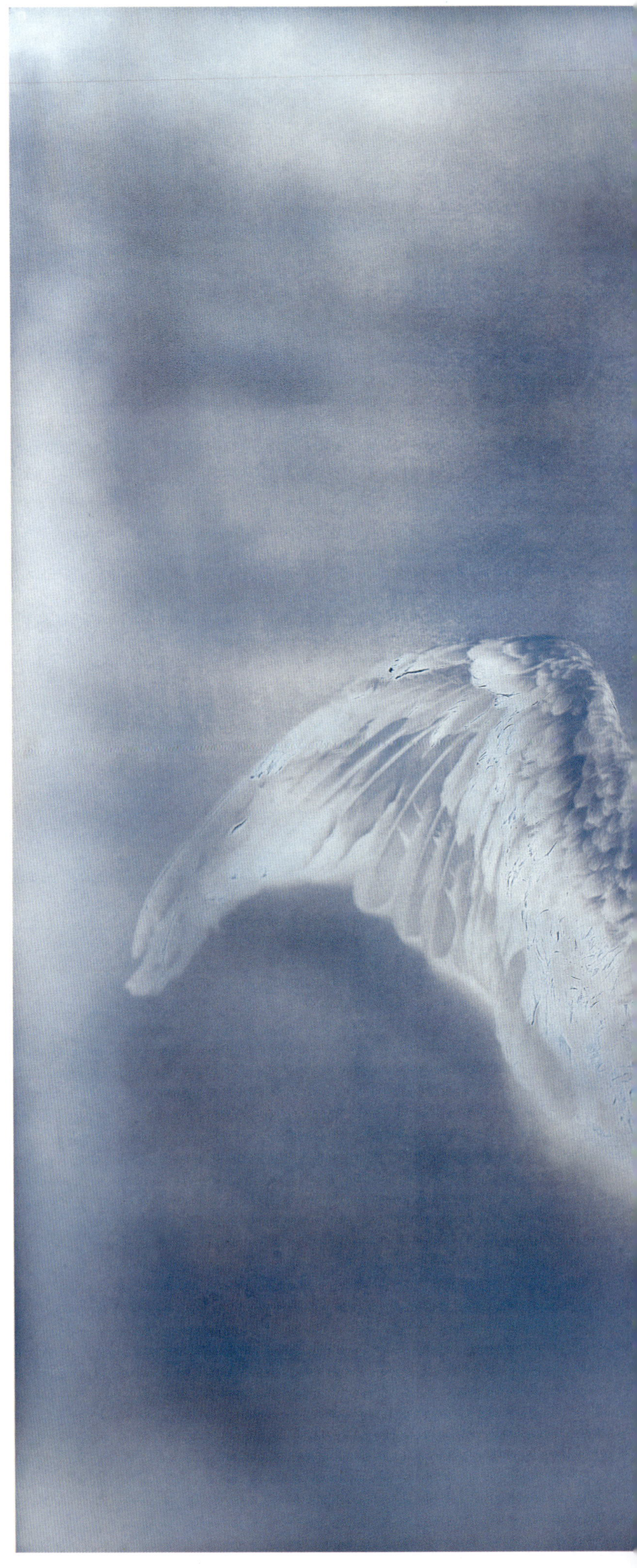

Adam Fuss, daguerreotype, from the series "My Ghost," 1999.

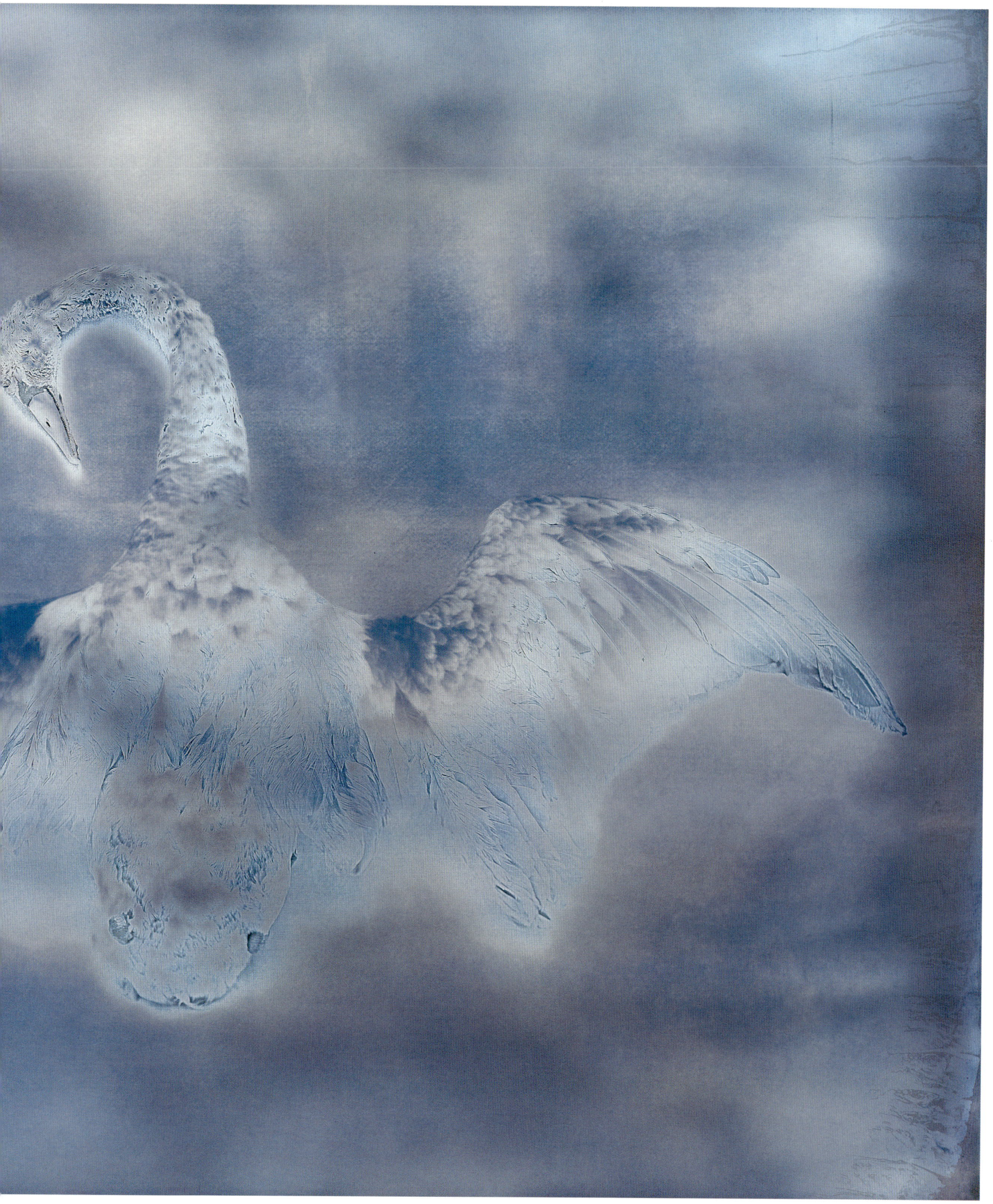

A MAJOR TRAVELING EXHIBITION, "PHOTOGRAPHY PAST*FORWARD*: APERTURE AT 50" WILL BE LAUNCHED IN NEW YORK AT SOTHEBY'S IN JANUARY 2003.

BIOGRAPHY: R. H. Cravens, a contributing editor to Aperture for a quarter-century, has provided the texts of more than a dozen Aperture monographs, various articles for the magazine, and most recently co-authored, with T.K.V. Desikachar, *Health Healing & Beyond: Yoga and the Living Tradition of Krishnamacharya*.

ACKNOWLEDGMENTS: R. H. Cravens is grateful to Peter Bunnell, Robert Haiko, Carole Kismaric, Susan Pakulis, Charles Simic, Jill and Lanny Shore, John Szarkowski, Jonathan Williams, and the staff of Aperture, especially Diana Stoll, for their help in compiling this book's essay. In particular, throughout this project, Assistant Editor Michael Famighetti has rendered invaluable support and research assistance. With the exceptions of the chapter epigraphs and the passage from Sinclair Lewis's *Babbitt*, all citations in the text were culled from personal interviews or from Aperture publications. Research for the essay was also aided by Penelope Niven's *Steichen: A Biography* (New York: Clarkson Potter, 1997); and Beaumont Newhall's *History of Photography* (New York: Museum of Modern Art, 1964) and *Focus: Memoirs of a Life in Photography* (Boston: Bulfinch, 1993).

Aperture: #169, Winter 2002 **TO SUBSCRIBE**: *Aperture* (ISSN 0003-6420) is published quarterly, in spring, summer, fall, and winter, at 20 East 23rd Street, New York, NY 10010. A one-year subscription (four issues) is $40 and a two-year subscription (eight issues) is $66. A subscription for four issues outside the United States is $60. Single copies may be purchased at $18.50 for most issues. Periodicals postage is paid at New York and additional offices. Postmaster: Send address changes to *Aperture*, P.O. Box 3000, Denville, NJ 07834. Address queries regarding subscriptions, renewals, or gifts to: *Aperture* Subscription Service, 1-866-457-4603. For U.K. subscriptions, contact Falsten Partnership at subscriptions@falsten.com or call (020) 88062301.

Library of Congress Catalog Card No.: 58-30845. Printed by Sing Cheong Printing Co. Ltd., Hong Kong. Duotone separations by Martin Senn. Color separations by Bright Arts (H.K.), Ltd., China.

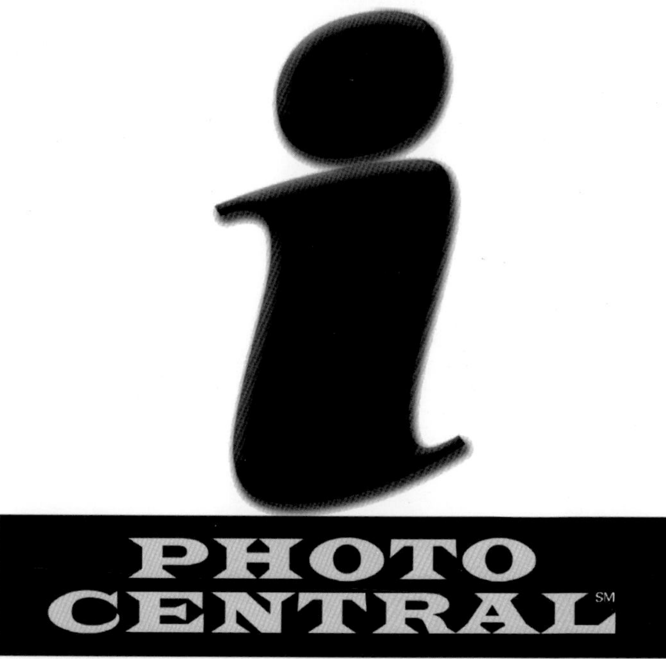
PHOTO
CENTRAL SM